GRASSROOTS

CHIEFS IN AFRICA AND THE AFRO-CARIBBEAN

GOVERNANCE?

AFRICA
Missing
Voices
series

GENERAL EDITORS
DONALD I. RAY AND PETER SHINNIE

University of Calgary Press has a long history of publishing academic works on Africa. We are again taking up African themes in our new series *Africa: Missing Voices,* which illuminates issues and topics concerning Africa that have been ignored or are missing from current global debates. This series fills a gap in African scholarship by addressing authentic concerns that have been overlooked in political, social, and historical discussions about this continent. We invite authors to submit book proposals and manuscripts to us for consideration.

INTERNATIONAL ASSOCIATION OF SCHOOLS
AND INSTITUTES OF ADMINISTRATION

The International Association of Schools and Institutes of Administration (IASIA) is an association of organizations and individuals whose activities and interests focus on public administration and management. Its main emphasis is on the development and use of human resources. From a concept first articulated in Vienna in 1962, the Association, which is a constituent organ of the International Institute of Administrative Sciences (IIAS), was formally incorporated in Rome during the IIAS Congress of 1971. IASIA now has a worldwide membership of over 170 institutions in sixty-one countries as well as several international organizations. Members are grouped in seven geographical regions. The activities of its members include education and training of administrators and managers and related research, consulting, and publications. Its offices are at the headquarters of the IIAS in Brussels, Belgium.

The worldwide membership of IASIA provides individuals/organizations from various parts of the world having the same concerns with the opportunity to consider and advance their interests from a global perspective. This capacity at once makes mutual support and assistance more possible and helps serve the needs arising from the increasingly international nature of the environment in which governments and their public services are called upon to operate. It also facilitates initiatives that may enhance the institutional and operational effectiveness of member organizations and of the public sector internationally.

IASIA is a not-for-profit association supported by membership fees, income from services, the voluntary services of its members, and contributions from funding organizations.

IASIA Secretariat
Rue Defacqz 1, Bte 11
B-1000 Brussels, Belgium
Tel.: 32/2-536.08.89 Fax: 32/2-537.97.02
E-mail: iasia@iiasiisa.be, www.iiasiisa.be

GRASSROOTS
CHIEFS IN AFRICA AND THE AFRO-CARIBBEAN
GOVERNANCE?

Edited by

DONALD I. RAY

University of Calgary and International Co-ordinator,
Traditional Authority Applied Research Network (TAARN)

and

P. S. REDDY

University of Durban–Westville and Project Director,
Working Group on Local Government Management and Development,
International Association of Schools and Institutes of Administration (IASIA)

International Association of Schools and Institutes of Administration (IASIA)

UNIVERSITY OF
CALGARY
PRESS

University of Calgary Press
2500 University Drive NW
Calgary, Alberta
Canada T2N 1N4
www.uofcpress.com

National Library of Canada Cataloguing in Publication Data

Main entry under title:

Grassroots governance? : chiefs in Africa and the Afro-Caribbean /
Donald I. Ray, P.S. Reddy, eds.

(Africa : missing voices, ISSN 1703-1826 ; 1)
Copublished by: International Association of Schools and Institutes of Administration.
Includes bibliographical references and index.
ISBN 1-55238-080-7

1. Local government—Africa, Sub-Saharan. 2. Local
government—Caribbean Area. I. Ray, Donald Iain, 1949– II. Reddy, P.
S. (Purshottama Sivanarian), 1957– III. International Association of
Schools and Institutes of Administration. IV. Series.
JS7525.G72 2002   352.14'0967   C2002-911251-6

 We acknowledge the financial support of the Government of Canada through the
Book Publishing Industry Development Program (BPIDP) for our publishing
activities.

 The Canada Council for the Arts
Le Conseil des Arts du Canada

Printed and bound in Canada by Transcontinental Printing
♾ This book is printed on acid-free paper.

Page, cover design, and typesetting by Mieka West.

CONTENTS

SUMMARY

Traditional leadership is a factor that has been significantly overlooked in evaluations of rural local government in much of contemporary Sub-Saharan Africa and in many parts of the Afro-Caribbean. This oversight continues to result in lost opportunities for rural local government. This interdisciplinary and intercontinental volume responds to this perception and seeks to establish a base line for best practice in rural local government and traditional leadership (also called chiefs) in Africa and elsewhere that policy practitioners, political leaders, traditional leaders, researchers, and other citizens can use.

Case studies from Ghana, South Africa, Botswana, Lesotho, other Commonwealth countries in West, East and Southern Africa, as well as Jamaica (with its heritage links to West Africa) are the bases of the analyses of traditional leadership and rural local government. Case studies are analyzed within country and regional contexts. The question of how to integrate, or indeed reconcile, traditional leadership into democratic systems of local government is addressed. The prevalence, importance, and contribution of traditional leadership to the culture of local governance are examined. The importance of traditional leadership's involvement in the administration of land at the local government level is scrutinized. The development and management implications of having traditional leadership participate in rural local government are explored. Drawing comparisons between the case studies, the book discovers lessons and trends. Some initial implications of this for Canadian chiefs are considered, especially in the realm of the use and creation of Houses of Chiefs as an instrument of governance.

PREFACE

The Working Group on Local Government Management and Development of the International Association of Schools and Institutes of Administration (IASIA) was officially established in 1997 following the interest generated in the subject area in the breakaway sessions during three conferences. The objective of the group is to focus on key trends and developments in the local government sphere in both developed and developing countries. It is generally accepted that certain distinct thematic issues have to be addressed during the lifespan of any working group of IASIA. The themes, which directed the activities of the group for the past four years, were Democratization, Decentralization and Development, Intergovernmental Relations, Metropolitization/Unicity Development and Rural Local Government and Traditional Leadership. The thematic issues, which are generally addressed through country reports, comparative studies, and theoretical appraisal, are presented at the annual conferences of IASIA. This publication has developed out of the activities and deliberations focusing on the theme, "Rural Local Government and Traditional Leadership."

Local government is the second or third sphere of government, which has been established to develop closer linkages between the government and the local citizenry. It also seeks to ensure that the local citizenry have a sense of involvement in the political process that regulate their daily lives and ultimately improve their quality of life.

The weak economic and political position of the rural populace and their institutions highlight the difficulties of sustaining a viable local government system, particularly in the developing countries. The central, state (provincial) government, and the non-governmental sector have a pivotal role to play in providing the required assistance and support to capacitate rural local government institutions. Intergovernmental relations are one of the issues that have to be taken cognizance of in any consideration of how strong structures of representation and, furthermore, accountability could be established and sustained within the rural areas. Another aspect that has to be addressed is financial considerations and, more importantly, the capacity to generate revenue. The importance of assistance from the central, state (provincial) government, and the non-governmental sector is also critical in this process. The key questions that have to be addressed include, *inter alia*, how to establish and sustain local structures of representation and accountability; the impact on development service, intergovernmental relationships (with central/provincial and civic and community-based organizations); and what strategies are in place to facilitate rural development and poverty alleviation. The majority of the developing countries have acknowledged that the rural areas have been neglected, and consequently have embarked on the required political, administrative and fiscal measures to address these issues. Some of the measures that have been taken to date include, the ushering in of policies and concomitant legislation to strengthen rural structures, increased sources of funding, human resources capacity development, and the incorporation of traditional leadership in rural governance.

On a global level, traditional leadership is generally hereditary and not subject to the universal adult suffrage electoral process. Traditional leaders broadly exercise governmental functions ranging from the provision of services to the preservation of law and order, and to the allocation of tribal land generally held in trust. Subject to their relationship with the national government, they do tend to have some form of local government in place to address the needs of rural communities. In this context, the policy issues that have to be addressed include, inter alia, the extent to which the institution of traditional leadership retains popular legitimacy and how it should be accommodated in a formal local government system; what their role is in municipal service delivery and development initiatives; and how their capacity can be developed to facilitate efficient and effective local governance in the rural areas. The issue of formal recognition and protection of the institution of traditional leadership has to be given serious consideration. Despite the fact that traditional authorities are responsible for a large number of functions, there has not been much capacity-development or even allocation of the required human, financial, and technical resources to ensure efficiency and effectiveness. Consequently, much has to be done to ensure that traditional leaders and structures are empowered to actually function as local government and, furthermore, as facilitators of development at the local level. A complementary relationship has to exist between traditional leadership and local democracy, thereby ensuring maximum development of the rural areas.

This publication addresses some of the policy issues highlighted above in seventeen Sub-Saharan and Afro-Caribbean countries, with particular reference to recent trends and developments. It is hoped that this publication would prove to be relevant, insightful and a valuable source of information to practitioners, academics, researchers, and students alike. The Working Group would like to record its sincere appreciation to Prof. D. Ray, attached to the University of Calgary in Canada for his leadership, positive enthusiasm and commitment in the completion of this study and the publication of this book. The Working Group would also like to gratefully acknowledge the leadership and vision of Dr. Mohan Kaul, the President of IASIA,

Prof. Ian Thynne of the Publications Committee and Dr. E. H. Valsan, Chairperson of the Group who facilitated the publication of this book.

Prof. P. S. Reddy
Project Director
Working Group: Local Government
Management And Development
IASIA

RURAL LOCAL GOVERNANCE AND TRADITIONAL LEADERSHIP IN AFRICA AND THE AFRO-CARIBBEAN: POLICY AND RESEARCH IMPLICATIONS FROM AFRICA TO THE AMERICAS AND AUSTRALASIA

CHAPTER 1

DONALD I. RAY

PURPOSE OF THIS BOOK

Traditional leadership is a factor that has been significantly overlooked in the evaluations of rural local government and governance in much of contemporary Sub-Saharan Africa and in parts of the Afro-Caribbean. This oversight continues to result in lost opportunities for rural local government and governance, in terms of both development and understanding. This interdisciplinary and intercontinental volume responds to this perception by using a series of innovative studies to establish a baseline for best practice and research in rural local government and governance to which traditional leaders (also called "chiefs") can contribute in co-operation with other policy practitioners, political leaders, researchers, citizens, and other members of civil society in Africa, as well as in other areas of the world where indigenous peoples and/or political structures exist, whether this be Fiji or Canada.[1] Of course such efforts are not without their problems and these are frankly addressed in a number of the case studies.

POLICY IMPLICATIONS OF THE MAJOR CONCEPTS AND THEMES

Traditional leaders are also known in English as chiefs, traditional authorities, traditional rulers, monarchs, kings, nobles, aristocrats, and natural rulers in a variety of African and other countries. While the literature has little problem with the use of this variety of names, in some countries the use of one name or another may invoke political problems. Thus, in South Africa, the term "traditional leader" is the desired official usage by government bodies such as the National House of Traditional Leaders and the six provincial Houses of Traditional Leaders, or a non-governmental body such as the Congress of Traditional Leaders of South Africa (Contralesa), because some see the term "chief" as being associated with the racist apartheid regime that was ended only in 1994. By contrast, in countries such as Ghana and Botswana, no such stigma or sensitivity is usually attached to the term "chief": Botswana has a House of Chiefs, and Ghana has a National House of Chiefs and ten Regional Houses of Chiefs. In this volume, the various terms for *traditional authority* are used interchangeably in a neutral sense. Traditional leadership is meant to include those political, socio-political and politico-religious structures that are rooted in the pre-colonial period rather than in the creations of the colonial and post-colonial states. By this key consideration, traditional leaders can include kings, other aristocrats holding offices, heads of extended families, and office holders in decentralized polities, as long as their offices are rooted in pre-colonial states and other political entities. If the office is purely a creation of the colonial or post-colonial states but still involves indigenous peoples, then perhaps the office should be called "neo-traditional." Furthermore authors in this volume may or may not be using the terms *traditional authority* and *tradition* in the Weberian sense.

The division of the chronology of African political organization into three periods (pre-colonial, colonial, and post-colonial) is well-accepted, but should not be seen as being applicable only to Africa. As well, the special significance of this terminological genealogy needs to be noted briefly here.[2] The trilogy of pre-colonial state, colonial state, and post-colonial state applies to any contemporary state in Africa, Asia, the Americas or elsewhere that was the product of the imposition of European imperialism and colonialism since the expansion of capitalism out of Europe from the 1400s onwards. However, one might characterize the pre-colonial states and other political entities as being rooted in political legitimacies that were particular to their special histories which existed before these pre-colonial states and other polities were *absorbed* one way or another by European empires.

Such absorption involved the creation of colonial states by which the European ruled their newly subjugated and/or subordinated colonies into which the various pre-colonial states and polities were drawn. These pre-colonial states and other polities were then processed into various components of the colonial states. In many cases, the indigenous peoples had their political leadership turned into instruments of colonial rule for the benefit of the empires, but the empires were not strong enough to eliminate completely all elements or traces of this pre-colonial heritage: "kings" became "chiefs" in the lexicon of imperialism and colonialism. While the colonial state intended to indicate the subordinated status of the former pre-colonial leader by this linguistic trick, ironically the real pre-colonial terms of the "chiefs" survived in their own languages. Even more ironically for colonialism, often these "chiefs" or "traditional leaders" became rallying points of resistance to colonialism and sources of cultural pride to those indigenous peoples who had been colonised. Where traditional leaders/chiefs thus survived into the periods of the colonial state and the post-colonial state, they retained sources of political legitimacy rooted in the pre-colonial period,

Kgosi* Mosadi Sebotto, Paramount Chief, Bamalete Tribal Administration, Ramotswa, Botswana, is the first woman to be paramount chief in Botswana (June 14, 2002).

Paramount Chief Chamba of Malawi. She is paramount chief over more than two hundred villages. Photo taken at the Commonwealth Local Government Forum's Symposium on Traditional Leadership, Gaberone, Botswana (September 1997).

Kgosi* Seepapitso II, Paramount Chief, Kanye, Botswana and then President of the House of Chiefs. Taken at the Commonwealth Local Government Forum's Symposium on Traditional Leadership, Gabarone, Botswana (September 1997).

(*traditional leadership title)
(above photos by D. Ray).

and which were unavailable to the colonial state because it had been forced on the indigenous people.

Traditional leaders/chiefs can claim special legitimacy in the eyes of their people because these institutions can be seen to embody their people's history, culture, laws and values, religion, and even remnants of pre-colonial sovereignty. The colonial states and the post-colonial states draw upon different roots of legitimacy and sovereignty than those of the pre-colonial states. Looked at in the brilliant light of democracy, the colonial state would have to admit that its claims to sovereignty were based in the main on violence, racism, and diplomatic trickery, and that its claims to legitimacy as to why the indigenous people should obey its dictates were usually based on (1) rights of the conqueror rather than the consent of the people, (2) assertions of culture or racial superiority of the colonizers over the indigenous people, and (3) the use of a constitutional and legal order based on or rooted in the imperial power. For these and other reasons, the colonial state was unable to take over the legitimacy base of the pre-colonial period: to do so would be to call into question its own legitimacy.

The post-colonial state is in a more ambiguous position with regard to the pre-colonial period and to traditional leaders than is the colonial state. Although the post-colonial state has often had its constitutional and legal legitimacy rooted in the colonial state, especially when there was a peaceful handover of power from the colonial state to the post-colonial state, the post-colonial state can claim its legitimacy from the additional roots of (1) the nationalist struggle for independence by the people, and (2) the expression of the democratic will of the people through elections and other political processes and, eventually, a legal-constitutional system that has been processed, re-validated and created by the institutions created by the post-colonial state which express the democratic will of the people.

However, the legitimacy of traditional leadership/chieftaincy institutions remains, in nearly all cases beyond the grasp of the post-colonial state precisely because chieftaincy legitimacy is rooted in the pre-colonial period and there has been a fundamental rupture in the political fabric that the imposition of colonialism brings. Thus a people may choose to express themselves politically for many policy areas through the legislative, executive, and judicial institutions of the post-colonial state, but also decide that certain policy matters, e.g., custom, land, other local matters, are best expressed by their traditional leaders. Thus, because the people of a post-colonial state recognize that the roots of political legitimacy are divided between the post-colonial state and the traditional (i.e., pre-colonially rooted) leadership, these

The elephant tusk trumpet band announces the arrival of the Asante king, Osei Tutu II at the Manhyia Palace reception court in Kumasi Ghana. The umbrellas are symbols of legitimacy and authority of the Asante paramount chiefs who serve the king. Some of the elephant tusk trumpets have been bound with "elephant tape" (also known as "duct tape") (photo by D. Ray).

peoples may well decide that their democratic practice includes aspects of both the post-colonial state and traditional leadership.

How the traditional leadership is practiced within the post-colonial state should determine our evaluation of whether or not traditional leadership is compatible with democratic practice at the local government and state levels. These points seem to have been lost or overlooked by much of the literature on democratization and democratic transitions.[3]

Some might raise the related question: is chieftaincy compatible with democratic local governance or even transitions to democracy? This is a very complex question that may produce surprises for those who raise this question if we think outside the hegemonic ideas box. While this question deserves a much fuller examination that must be given elsewhere because of the constraints of space, several points do need to be advanced. First, those who suggest that traditional leadership is not compatible with democracy may do so, inter alia, because they are steeped in the republicanism[4] of the United States which was itself a breakaway from the monarchical British state. U.S. republicanism could thus be viewed as being rather self-justifying in the legitimation of the separatist post-colonial state called the United States. By so doing, the U.S. could reject the institutions of the monarchy and then promptly substitute a rotating indirectly-elected kingship called a president for the office of a hereditary monarchy.[5] Republicans (not necessarily of the U.S. political party) might argue further that presidents are democratically elected by all the citizens and are thus accountable to every citizen, but that hereditary monarchs or traditional leaders are not. While there appears to be much validity to the argument, it is not unchallengeable. American presidents are not directly elected by every citizen, rather the president is chosen by a small elite. They are elected but by a very imperfect system that may well not have followed the wishes of the majority of U.S. voters in at least one case: George W. Bush's legitimacy as president may well be challenged by the confusion of the Florida vote in 2000. When the democratic legitimacy of the president of a republic can be questioned, how democratic is the republic?

Britain is known as the mother of democracy which evolved into a democratic parliamentary system with a constitutional monarchy. Canada shares its monarch with Britain. Can it be seriously argued that Canada and Britain are not democracies, but the United States is democratic because it rather has a president – one whose office is increasingly called the "imperial presidency"?

The mere presence of traditional leaders otherwise called monarchs, does not automatically render them anti-democratic. What republicans often seem to forget

Nana* Fredua Agyeman is the Chief-of-Staff for the Office of the Okyenhene or the king of Akyem Abuakwa. He spends part of the year in New Jersey and the other part serving the king in Ghana. He assists the kingdom in local government development projects on the environment, education, health (especially HIV/AIDS) and income generation such as the snail farms (*traditional leadership title) (photo by D. Ray).

is that traditional leaders/monarchs can have their own legitimacy in the eyes of the citizens based on history and political culture preferences. Countries such as Canada and Britain have so far chosen to retain their monarchies.[6] In short, the principle of monarchy has been intertwined with the Canadian and British political cultures for quite some time. Even the attempts by British Prime Minister Tony Blair to abolish the House of Lords has run into unexpected opposition from the citizens of Britain: such attempts to reform further this British *House of Chiefs* have been bogged down for some time.

Traditional leadership, it seems, continues to exist in Britain, Canada, and many African countries because the citizens want this, but they want this only under conditions that ensure that the traditional leaders are not seen to abuse their offices or the citizens. In a sense, to be a traditional leader is to be subject to informal referendums that are held on a daily basis forever: When the people decide not to honour the traditional leader, when the citizens decide to withdraw their legitimation of the chiefs, then these offices will no longer function. What republicans and their ilk seem to forget is that in many African countries traditional leaders continue to enjoy popular support because of their particular bases of legitimacy (see the chapters by Ray and Crothers). Chiefs, in these circumstances, remain important political actors, especially at the level of local government and local governance.

A few words on the use of the terms *government* and *governance* are important to clarify a key argument of this volume. While *government* deals with the formal activities and political culture (including legitimacy) as designated by such formal state mechanisms as constitutions and legislation, *governance* refers to government plus unofficial political activities and culture (including legitimacy) not originally endorsed or rooted in the post-colonial state. Thus the term *rural local governance* includes not only the rural local government structures, processes, and political activities and culture (including legitimacy) that are rooted in the colonial state and the post-colonial state, but also those rooted in the pre-colonial states and other pre-colonial political organizations. By so conceptualizing rural local governance, it is possible to include chieftaincy in our discussions even when chiefs are not formally included in such local government state structures. We need to consider what role in rural local government that traditional leaders might play, as well as the ways in which traditional leadership might enhance development at the level of rural local government on which so many demands are placed by those who are citizens of the post-colonial state and subjects of the traditional leaders.

Four main themes serve as the main focuses of this volume. The first focus is to analyze how to integrate, or indeed reconcile traditional leadership with democratic systems of local government in the post-colonial state. The second focus is to scrutinize what traditional leadership brings to the culture of local governance in terms of political values, prevalence, importance, and contributions. The third focus is to examine the importance and performance of traditional leadership in the key local government function of the administration of land. The fourth focus is evaluating the development and management implications of having traditional leaders participate in rural local government and governance. Drawing comparisons between the case studies, the book discovers lessons and trends for such involvement. Some initial implications of this for Canadian chiefs, both traditional and neo-traditional, are considered in light of the African cases. The case studies are drawn from Ghana, South Africa, Botswana, Lesotho, other Commonwealth countries in West, East and Southern Africa, as well as the South American Commonwealth country of Jamaica which has heritage links to West Africa. Case studies are examined within the country and regional contexts.

POLICY AND RESEARCH ROOTS OF THIS BOOK

After millennia of existence, the pre-colonial states and other political entities of Africa were nearly all subordinated by treaty or conquest to the European empires by the beginning of the twentieth century. These processes of colonial incorporation brought in their wake the subordination or elimination of the pre-colonial states, other political entities, and numbers of their political offices. Sovereign kings and other office-holders were converted by the European empires and their colonial and colonial-settler states into *chiefs*, also known as *traditional leaders*, and other similar terms. The European colonial states in Africa often attempted to use chiefs, both traditional and neo-traditional, as auxiliaries to colonial rule. A considerable literature on chiefs grew during this period for a variety of reasons, not least the desire of those who controlled and administered the colonial state to better understand their traditional authority subordinates.

Independence and the creation of the post-colonial states resulted in a shifting of interest and research to the post-colonial states in their search for democracy and development. From independence in the late 1950s and 1960s, until the late 1980s and early 1990s, there was a decline in interest in traditional leadership as a potential complement to the efforts of the post-colonial state to promote development and democracy at a variety of levels, including that of rural local government. This trend represents a certain change in the way that traditional leaders have been viewed in some quarters by some leaders of the newly independent states of Africa.[7] Within four years of Uganda's independence in 1963, Prime Minister Milton Obote used the Ugandan army in 1966 to capture the palace of the king of Buganda (who at that point was also president of Uganda), forced the Buganda king into exile, and abolished all the kingdoms by means of Uganda's 1967 Constitution.[8] Chiefs lost their formal constitutional recognition in less dramatic manners in Tanzania and Guinea. Ghana's future prime minister and president, Kwame Nkrumah, stated in 1950 that if Ghanaian chiefs did not support his nationalist movement – the Convention People's Party (CPP) – in the drive for independence from Britain, then the chiefs might eventually find themselves overthrown (Nkrumah 1957, 120; Arhin 1991, 31). In South Africa, there were doubts by some political leaders as to whether or not traditional leaders were to survive from the colonial, colonial-settler apartheid era into the new democracy (Bank and Southall 1996).

In part, these doubts and concerns reflected the perceptions of (at least) some nationalist leaders and other democrats that at least some traditional leaders were perceived by these people as having co-operated with the colonial or apartheid regimes, and that therefore those traditional leaders who had so co-operated were in effect the opponents of those who led the drive to independence. In other cases, democrats had raised the question of how could traditional leaders be incorporated into a democratic system when the principles of traditional leadership were interpreted to be not democratic; in as much as not every adult could be selected as a chief – only those who belonged to aristocratic families; and not every adult could *vote* for their candidate – only the electoral college *king-makers* (if they existed) could.[9] Given that the leaders of the post-colonial African state have had reasons and the ability to abolish traditional leadership as an institution, why have they not done so right across the continent? Indeed, why has there been a growing interest in a significant number of African states in involving traditional leaders in local government, governance, and development?

By the early 1990s, there was a revival of interest in traditional leaders amongst a growing number of African and Western governments,[10] researchers, foreign aid agencies, and civil society organizations and members. There has been a growing

Obaapanyin* Yaa Kronama, Queenmother of Anyinam, birthplace of the founder of the Asante kingdom, which now has some three hundred residents (2002, photo by D. Ray) (*traditional leadership title).

recognition, within and without Africa, of the need to incorporate somehow the traditional leaders of Africa into local governance, as one of a number of measures, if local government management and development are to be fully effective. At the initiative of the International Association of Schools and Institutes of Administration (IASIA), this volume brings together three networks of research into traditional leadership in Africa.

The Traditional Authority Applied Research Network (TAARN) is one such network that was founded in 1994. Following three years of planning in Ghana, Canada, and the Netherlands, researchers from seventeen countries in Africa, North America, Europe, and South America presented papers to their fellow researchers, chiefs, and other policy-makers on traditional authority in sixteen African countries and two South American countries (in which there are remnants of African-rooted traditional authority) to the September 1994 "Conference on the Contribution of Traditional Authority to Development, Democracy, Human Rights and Environmental Protection: Strategies for Africa."[11] This was held in Ghana at the Institute of African Studies, University of Ghana in Accra and at the National House of Chiefs in Kumasi. The conference resulted in two books (Arhin, Ray, and van Rouveroy 1995; van Rouveroy and Ray 1996), the mandate to create the Traditional Authority Applied Research Network (TAARN),[12] and a panel in Vienna which further generated another book (Zips and van Rouveroy 1998). The list of funding sources for the 1994 Ghana conference clearly indicates the widespread interest in reappraising African traditional leadership from a policy-based focus: the International Development Research Centre (IDRC),[13] the Netherlands government, the Ghana government, the government of Canada, the British Council, the University of Ghana, the University of Calgary, the African Studies Centre (Leiden, Netherlands), the University of Vienna (Austria), the University of Durban–Westville (South Africa), and Rhodes University (South Africa). Subsequent to this, TAARN received significant funding from the Research Development Initiative of the Social Sciences and Humanities Research Council of Canada (SSHRCC) for the electronic network component of TAARN. TAARN also received a major grant from the International Development Research Centre (IDRC), based in Ottawa, for the project "Traditional Leadership and Local Governance in Social Policy in West and Southern Africa." This project has country research teams in Ghana, Botswana, and South Africa as well as the co-ordination centre at the University of Calgary, Canada (Ray and Dalrymple 2000).

Another network exploring the possible contributions of traditional leadership to local government in African member states of the Commonwealth has been organized by the Commonwealth Local Government Forum (CLGF). Shortly after the founding of CLGF in 1994, it co-operated with the Federation of Canadian Municipalities (FCM) and officials and researchers from Botswana, Kenya, Sierra Leone, Zimbabwe, and South Africa to run two small workshops in 1994 and 1995 on traditional systems of administration which resulted in a report (Venson/CLGF 1995). The question of the potential and actual contributions of traditional leadership to democratization and decentralization in local government was raised at the June 1995 Commonwealth Roundtable on Democratization and Decentralization that was held in Harare, Zimbabwe, and which also resulted in a report (CLGF 1995).[14] The roundtable endorsed a program of action that included the following statement on the need for the legitimacy of traditional leaders to be mobilized somehow in order to benefit local government and development:

> Traditional leadership is afforded considerable credibility and functions in many local communities and that with the creation of appropriate mechanisms for their involvement, such leadership can assist in the realization of development goals. (CLGF 1995, 31)

These leaders called for a follow-up meeting.

The "Symposium on Traditional Leadership and Local Government" was held 23–26 September 1997 in Gaborone, Botswana. It was organized by the CLGF in association with the International Union of Local Authorities – Africa Section (IULA–AS), the Botswana Association of Local Authorities, and the Botswana Ministry of Local Government, Lands and Housing.[15] Over fifty traditional leaders, elected mayors and councillors, senior local and central government officials, and researchers attended from the Commonwealth member countries of Botswana, Canada, The Gambia, Ghana, Lesotho, Malawi, Mozambique, Namibia, Sierra Leone, South Africa, Swaziland, Uganda, the United Kingdom, Zambia, and Zimbabwe, as well as Austria.[16] C. Wright, the CLGF Director, noted that this widespread participation demonstrated "the growing interest throughout Africa in the role that traditional leaders could play in the modern, pluralistic state." The symposium participants made four pages of recommendations in the report (Ray, Sharma, and May-Parker/CLGF 1997, 4–7) that needed to be recognized or have further follow-up work carried out. This symposium also brought together participants from the CLGF, TAARN (IDRC-funded), and the International Association of Schools and Institutes of Administration (IASIA).

The third research network, which is more fully analyzed in this volume's *preface*, has focused entirely on traditional leadership and rural local governance.

The Local Government Management and Development Group of IASIA, chaired by Prof. E. H. Valsan (Egypt) and with Prof. P. S. Reddy (South Africa) as Project Director, has developed four major themes, including "Rural Local Governance and Traditional Leadership." This last IASIA project has been developed at a series of conferences, especially those in Paris (1998) and in Athens (2001). IASIA has led the way in promoting policy analysis of traditional leadership's contributions to rural local governance. This volume is the result of IASIA's vision and dedication to the importance of this theme. Most of Africa's people live in rural areas yet these are precisely the areas that are often underserved in terms of resources, development, and techniques of governance. IASIA conceived of this book as one way of addressing these concerns.

POLICY AND CONCEPTUAL TRENDS AND LESSONS OF THE CHAPTERS

Christiane Owusu-Sarpong introduces us to those traditional political values about traditional governance that may well set the context in the minds of many Ghanaians for part of their expectations towards the rural local governments of the post-colonial state. She identifies these values by cultural analyses of oral and written texts to establish what exists on the ground as the articulated political culture expectations for traditional leaders. Such values provide the context for "the institutionalized *local government* structure and the perennial *traditional authority* structure." Owusu-Sarpong thus weaves cultural and governmental factors, using such concepts as divided legitimacy and sovereignty, political and legal pluralism, and her concept of "resurgent heritage," into a fresh approach to rural local governance. She argues that if the rural local government structures of the Ghanaian post-colonial state want to reflect the true range of values of their citizens, then such structures need to recognize the reality that some of the attitudes that their citizens bring to the practice of democracy is rooted in the pre-colonial period, and that the offices of traditional leaders are the survivors from that period, even if they are much changed. Owusu-Sarpong argues that "a profound awareness of the importance of the revival of 'indigenous' African values is now widespread amongst the peoples of Africa." Africans need to embrace their "resurgent heritage" in order to free themselves from

Local police, Ramotswe, Botswana. These police serve the chief's courts. Taken at the Commonwealth Local Government Forum – Symposium on Traditional Leadership (CLGF), Gabarone, Botswana, September 1997 (photo by D. Ray).

the colonial and neo-colonial structures that have been imposed on them. To ignore African values may be to fall prey to a type of false independence and economic strategies that do not really enhance human development and welfare. For such true development to occur, African countries such as Ghana need to respect the "legal and political pluralism" that marks the co-existence of traditional authority and the rural local government structures of the post-colonial state. Chiefs in Ghana are influential with their subjects in terms of their abilities to mobilize their people for development, to articulate their sense of public morality, and to influence and shape public opinion. Traditional leaders are thus needed by the state to be involved in rural local government.

Charles Crothers uses survey data to explore the socio-economic characteristics of traditional leaders and the degree of support that they have in South Africa. Using quantitative techniques to analyze chiefs – a research strategy rarely if ever applied to chiefs before – he finds that in socio-economic terms traditional leaders are not a homogenous social category in South Africa.[17] While some traditional leaders are wealthy, others are poor. Similarly, chiefs in South Africa range from the well-educated to those who have little or no education. Crothers found that there was widespread support for the participation of traditional leaders in local governance. This support is expressed in very particular ways in South Africa based on age, education, geographic location, and "race-group." The responses to surveys suggest that in some cases, South Africans believe that traditional leaders wishing to take part in the local government structures of the state should be subject to election, not appointment to those bodies. Traditional leaders were not expected to take part in party politics nor to take public stances.[18]

Donald I. Ray uses the concepts of the pre-colonial, colonial, and post-colonial states, divided sovereignty, and divided legitimacy to argue that traditional leaders have long been recognized by the colonial and post-colonial states as being important to the processes of rural local government in what is now Ghana. While the actual powers granted to chiefs for the exercise of local government by the colonial state and the post-colonial state have varied considerably, chiefs continue to be seen by the state as being junior partners, but partners nevertheless. This may well be because chiefs draw upon different roots of legitimacy, such as pre-colonial religion and history to which the post-colonial state does not have direct access. The Houses of Chiefs system contributes to rural local governance in Ghana.

Robert Thornton argues that South African chiefs and government have different sources of power. While governments rely on statutes and the idea of the state, the source of chiefs' power runs parallel to such governments. Thornton argues that the source of chiefs' power, and, indeed, the nature of traditional leadership itself, needs to be reconceptualized. Such a reassessment will help to explain the attitudes of those South Africans who, for example, see chiefs as exercising "non-political" powers, yet also are not surprised to see chiefs lobbying governments and political parties. Traditional leaders, while not having a substantial formal role in rural local government, do carry out a number of important local governance functions that formal local government is not carrying out because it lacks the resources, capacity, or understanding. In South Africa, the formal local government structures of the post-colonial state operate, basically, on values and a system of dominance rooted in the European state (what others might link to the concepts of the colonial and post-colonial states). The traditional leader's power is rooted in the power that land gives. This is not simply the western-style instrumental relationship, but rather one that "derives from the concept of land and space that empowers the chief." Thus, the traditional leader has power and autonomy when he is on *his* land because this makes the traditional leader's office into an autochthonous (or pre-colonial) office with all of the attached legitimacy of independence. Thus, traditional leadership and rural local government can be seen as two overlapping "spatial orders" which are not at ease with each other. Development and democratic governance in South Africa will need to address these considerations that at present are being articulated as: "How can the local power of the chief be integrated into the overarching state system of political power?"

Tim Quinlan and Malcolm Wallis argue that traditional leaders have a central role in rural local governance in Lesotho. The historical experience of the people in Lesotho as Basotho has meant that their identity, rooted in the pre-colonial period, has continued into the period of the post-colonial state. Their identity has been and continues to be intertwined with that of the chiefs. Thus, chiefs have their own basis for legitimacy. Moreover, these traditional leaders perform many important local government functions at the grassroots in the relative absence of the national government and its bureaucracy. However, Quinlan and Wallis argue, this is not to say that chiefs and the state exist in a dual structure of government, nor in a "'traditional'–'modern' dichotomy," but rather that "chiefs and national governments are always enmeshed in each other's intentions such that neither party ever succeeds in supplanting the other." Lesotho is a case study of how chiefs have retained their legitimacy with the people while avoiding the efforts of the colonial and post-colonial states to change traditional leaders into "functionaries of the state." Lesotho chiefs remain a cornerstone of rural local governance.

Lungisile Ntsebeza examines the implications for the development and democratization of post-apartheid South Africa that the interaction of traditional leaders, rural local government, and rural land tenure reform have had. These latter three form an interactive triad that need to be examined not individually but as a whole in order to better understand the prospects for rural local government in South Africa. Moreover, in order to understand the present and the future, it is necessary to understand the past. Ntsebeza explores how British colonialism and its follow-on, apartheid South Africa, acted to try to capture the descendents of the pre-colonial African political structures (states, etc.) so as to create a system of colonized rural local government in which traditional leaders worked within a framework increasingly controlled by the colonial and apartheid states. During this time, much of the accountability of traditional leaders was thus switched from their people and pre-colonial principles of governance to the authoritarian colonial and apartheid states. At the same time, the colonial and apartheid states took the vast majority of the land away from the traditional leaders and their peoples. These processes have had a profound effect on rural local government, even after the end of formal apartheid and the holding of the first truly democratic elections in 1994 as the post-colonial state was established. Ntsebeza argues that "current initiatives to implement policy and legislation on land tenure and local government are frustrated" by conflicting constitutional principles in post-apartheid South Africa: elected representative government and unelected traditional authorities. Since 1994 rural local government in the Eastern Cape Province was often ineffective because it lacked the resources and skills as well as having to cover too large a territory for the number of elected representatives. While elected rural government was too thin on the ground, traditional leaders were numerous and formed their own system of governance which was able to block or channel the land tenure reform efforts of the government when chiefs' interests in controlling land were threatened. Accordingly, Ntsebeza recommends that traditional leaders have a much less decisive role in rural local government, but that they should not be abolished. The role of the Eastern Cape traditional leaders in rural local governance needs to be reconsidered and reoperationalized in order to overcome the heritage of colonialism and apartheid.

Werner Zips examines the transformed survival of Ghanaian traditional authority values and structures in the Maroons in Jamaica, and examines its implications for rural local governance in Jamaica. Present-day Maroons are descendents of Africans who had been enslaved and transported to the Americas (e.g., Jamaica, Surinam,

This 1996 photo shows the former Asante King's police station in Kumasi which is now a Ghana Police station. Chiefs in Ghana had their own police forces up to the early 1950s (photo by D. Ray).

Colombia, Brazil) to work in the slavelabour plantations of these then European colonies, but who had successfully escaped. The Maroons of Jamaica carved out their own territory in the 1600s and 1700s by fighting off British colonial forces until the peace treaties of 1738 and 1739 were signed between the Maroon state and the British empire. Maroons had thus successfully created a society and a state, albeit a small one, using their interpretation of what was remembered from their cultural and political roots in the pre-colonial states and other polities of Ghana. As Zips demonstrates, the British colonial state and its successor, the Jamaican post-colonial state, have been uneasy with the presence of a potential rival state in the midst of their state. This certainly is a case of divided sovereignty. Since independence, Jamaica has not fully recognized the traditional authority structures of the Maroons. Zips argues that this is a matter of regret for several reasons. First, the downgrading of Maroon traditional authority structures lessens the cultural heritage for Jamaicans and others of Jamaica's first freedom fighters against slavery and colonialism: the Maroons. Second, the Maroons with their African-rooted institutions add to Jamaica's cultural, legal, and political richness. Third, the Maroons themselves as Jamaicans would like to see their governance institutions legitimized by the Jamaican post-colonial state. Finally Zips calls for these points to be recognized by implementing a type of complementary sovereignty in which independent Jamaica incorporates in some way Maroon institutions into Jamaican rural local government.

Keshav Sharma examines the history and changes of the involvement of traditional leadership in rural local government in Botswana from pre-colonial times through the colonial period and now into the independence period. Having shown the resilience of traditional authority as it was subordinated and changed under British colonial rule until independence in 1966, Sharma argues that in Botswana the principles of democratic elected representative government have been reconciled and articulated with the political-cultural indigenous heritage of governance manifested in chieftaincy. Chiefs in Botswana have had their powers limited by the post-colonial state over such aspects of rural local government as control of land tenure and the withdrawal of chiefs' former automatic membership in the Land Boards or in the elected District Councils. Chiefs can even be deposed for not implementing the instructions of the Minister of Local Government. Yet chiefs continue to play key roles in Tribal Administration and the local level chiefs' courts, albeit under the supervision of the state. Moreover, the participation of chiefs in Botswana's House of Chiefs gives them access to the lawmakers and executive of Botswana at the highest levels. While chiefs may be dissatisfied with the fact that the House of Chiefs is not a U.S. or Canadian

Senate, nevertheless the Botswana House of Chiefs remains important to the chiefs and people of Botswana.[19]

P. S. Reddy and B. B. Biyela's analysis of the relationship between traditional leadership and rural local government in the KwaZulu-Natal province of South Africa during the post-apartheid era reveals a strikingly different situation in certain ways to those in the areas elsewhere in South Africa that Ntsebeza and Thornton examine. In the province of KwaZulu-Natal, traditional leaders extended their authority, or claimed to do so, over virtually all of the rural areas. The Zulu king is recognized by the constitution to be the king of all people in the entire province, although what this means exactly in practice is still being worked out. Under apartheid, the Zulu chiefs' authority was exercised in the so-called "homelands;" i.e., those rural areas of the then Natal province not taken by the settler regime. Since the ending of apartheid in 1994, major reforms of the local government system in South Africa have been having or might have significant effects on the powers of traditional leaders in rural local government. These involve the replacement of previous rural local government structures with elected District Councils. Chiefs will play a much less powerful role in rural local government, including land allocation, as the District Councils grow in strength. However, at this time, the new District Councils greatly lack resources and the capacity to carry out their assigned tasks in KwaZulu-Natal. Given this, traditional leaders continue to fulfill some local government functions in some cases. In other cases there is friction between the traditional leaders and the elected councillors. Furthermore, this friction is complicated by the bitter partisan rivalries between the African National Congress (ANC) and the Inkatha Freedom Party (IFP). Such is the legitimacy and influence, not to say power, of traditional leaders in the KwaZulu-Natal province of South Africa, that the question of how to incorporate them into the new South African system of local government has continued into the present.

As an active policy practitioner at the interface of policy implementation and research, Carl Wright brings a unique perspective to this debate. Wright discusses what the elected leaders and the officials of local government as well as the traditional leaders from twelve Commonwealth African countries in East, West and Southern Africa agreed should be done with regard to involving traditional leaders in local government. At this 1997 conference held in Botswana, they agreed that in many African countries traditional leaders continue to be seen as legitimate political actors by their people. Local government structures, policies and other development may well be enhanced by the participation of traditional leaders. Chiefs may be able to mobilize the support of their people for various development policies and projects as well as enhancing "social and cultural stability" within the context of promoting the health and self-worth of all within the community. The symposium ended in the issuing of a detailed list of policy recommendations and a call for more networking between African and other countries with regard to the participation of traditional leaders in rural local governance.

A NEW STRUCTURE OF GOVERNANCE FOR CANADA, THE UNITED STATES, SOUTH AMERICA AND AUSTRALASIA? – LESSONS FROM AFRICA'S HOUSES OF CHIEFS

Canada, the United States, many of the countries of South America, Australia, New Zealand, and others are post-colonial states controlled by the settler population, but in which there are continuing, unresolved questions with regard to the indigenous peoples. One of the lessons that Canadians and others in the United States, South America, and Australasia might learn from examining the role of African chieftaincy in rural local government may well come from one of Africa's structures of governance: the House of Chiefs. While there are important differences[20] between the institutions of chieftaincy (both traditional and neo-traditional leadership) in Canada and other similar countries as compared to various African countries, Canadians and others should at least examine the contributions that a House of Chiefs or House of First Peoples as, for example, Canada's Third House of Parliament might make to the self-governance of Canada's indigenous peoples.[21] Such a House of Chiefs would create a forum for the recognition and implementation of traditional methods of governance as well as creating a forum for raising the public awareness on aboriginal issues and rights and then acting on those questions.

The principle underlying the Houses of Chiefs is simple. All democracies have at least one House of Parliament that represents all citizens on questions of national (i.e., state-wide) importance. Some countries, like Canada, the U.K., and the U.S., also have a second House of Parliament – a Senate or House of Lords – based on situations or interests related to geography, regional equality, or history. In Ghana, Botswana, and South Africa, there are also Houses of Chiefs or Houses of Traditional Leaders.[22] These *houses* are not second or upper houses *per se* but are designed to address special

Daily life in the commercial area of Nkawkaw, Ghana (2000, photo by D. Ray).

aspects of their country's political culture. These Houses of Chiefs exist because they represent different roots of political legitimacy than commanded by the main House of Parliament: Houses of Chiefs are meant to express the political legitimacy of those institutions rooted in the pre-colonial period and to which the post-colonial state has great difficulty accessing for reasons of political history.[23] These bodies are concerned with how the post-colonial state – the government – should respond to the problems of indigenous people (rooted in the pre-colonial period) who have been colonized, but whose political, social, cultural, and economic (including land) values, relationships, and structures have survived to a greater or lesser degree.[24]

The Ghanaian, South African, and Botswana Houses of Chiefs have the authority to advise their government on all sorts of issues. Depending upon the country, these issues can range from landownership or governance questions to the evaluation of "traditional customs and usages" that the House of Chiefs believes are in need of change. In Ghana, for instance, at the request of the government, the Houses of Chiefs have participated in the delicate questions of landownership and concluded that traditional forms of communal landownership, under which virtually every Ghanaian has or had rights to some land, should be maintained despite pressures from foreign and domestic investors to allow private ownership. Also, numbers of male and female traditional leaders and state leaders are collaborating in the national strategy against HIV-AIDS.

Unlike the situation in Canada and other settler-dominated post-colonial states, indigenous peoples in Ghana, South Africa, and Botswana now control the post-colonial states. They have decided that matters that concern all citizens will be dealt with by their parliaments, and that special *traditional* or indigenous questions will be handled by their Houses of Chiefs, which have the power to debate and arrive at decisions.

The Houses of Chiefs often invite presidents or other heads of state, cabinet ministers, civil servants, judges, and other officials to address and debate issues. Chiefs often play a key role as local community advocates, articulating local needs in the Houses of Chiefs. In Botswana, the House of Chiefs can summon a cabinet minister to answer questions about her or his government portfolio. In these ways, the Houses of Chiefs have the power to raise issues with the government and to push for more accountability than if they did not exist.

The Houses of Chiefs act as a conflict resolution mechanism when disputes arise between ethnic groups over traditional matters. In Ghana, such disputes may be taken first to the Regional House of Chiefs and then, if need be, to the National House of Chiefs. At each stage, careful and thorough, informal and formal discussions and committee work ensure that many traditional ethnic questions are resolved. When they fail, the results may be disastrous. Such *houses* are not infallible, but they do offer another tool with which political conflicts may be settled.

The role of women in traditional local governance is also important. In southern Ghana, women are included in nearly all paramount chieftaincies as *queenmothers*. These women, who are not necessarily the mothers of the chiefs, have the right to nominate – even impeach – chiefs. Queenmothers advise chiefs and also act as moral leaders of the community. But while these women traditional leaders are represented at the grassroots level of the Houses of Chiefs (i.e., the Traditional Councils), they are not yet in the Regional and National Houses of Chiefs. In Botswana, the first woman was selected as a paramount chief and now sits in the House of Chiefs as a full member. As Canada has a number of elected women chiefs, the question of gender could be usefully discussed by both Canadians and Africans.

There may be merit in investigating the usefulness of adapting Africa's Houses of Chiefs to the needs of Canada's First Peoples. Of course it is for Canada's First Peoples to examine this possibility. This evaluation could start with information exchanges between Canadian and African chiefs, researchers, officials, and others. Other similar countries in North America, South America, Australasia and elsewhere might well wish to join this process.

Ultimately, the creation of a House of First Peoples could give indigenous leaders an ongoing institutional capacity to deal with their issues, as well as opportunities to raise these issues – as colleagues – with members of the Canadian House of Commons and Senate, as well as with civil servants and the national media. A House of First Peoples could also be delegated responsibility and funding to deal with aboriginal issues. This would seem to be in keeping with recent statements by both Indian Affairs and Northern Development Minister Robert Nault and Deputy Minister Shirley Serafini that the Canadian government "must rethink our role and shift to being facilitative while Aboriginal communities build up the government side of the equation to develop more independence and autonomy." A House of First Peoples might also be of interest to the Assembly of First Nations and others, given the desire for self-government and development as articulated by National Chief Matthew Coon Come, who launched the First Nations Governance Institute on 7 May 2001.[25] Good governance is essential to sustained social and economic development: Africa's Houses of Chiefs could provide a governance model built on the principles of inclusion, equality, cultural heritage and responsibility.

ACKNOWLEDGMENTS

Donald I. Ray would like to thank the Calgary Institute for the Humanities, University of Calgary, for awarding him a 2000–01 Annual Fellowship that provided the space and time to finish this book. His research was carried out with the aid of a grant from the International Development Research Centre (IDRC), Ottawa, Canada as well as a grant from the Social Sciences and Humanities Research Council of Canada (SSHRCC). Grants from the University of Calgary's University Research Grants Committee contributed to the awarding of the IDRC and SSHRCC grants. I would like to thank my family for their support over the years; my mother, Honey Ray; my late father, Don Ray; my wife, Rosemary Brown; and our children, Michael Ray, Matthew Ray and Jenevieve Ray. We would like to acknowledge gratefully the contributions of Meghan Dalrymple (Canada) and Morgan Nyendu (Ghana) who were research assistants and graduate students of D. Ray at the University of Calgary. Their sterling work was funded by IDRC and SSHRCC.

The editors, Prof. P. S. Reddy and Prof. D. I. Ray, would like to thank the staff and the editorial board of the University of Calgary Press for their excellent work in the production of this book. Special appreciation goes to Walter Hildebrandt (Director), John King (Production), Mieka West (Graphic Design), Sharon Boyle (Promotions/Marketing), Joan Barton (Editorial Secretary), Irene Kmet (Acquisitions), and Joan Eadie (Indexing). They clearly demonstrate the importance for an internationally ranked university of having a university press. We would also like to thank the anonymous referees for their comments.

REFERENCES

Anderson, Lisa, ed. 1999. *Transitions to Democracy*. New York: Columbia University Press.
Arhin, K. 1991. "The Search for 'Constitutional Chieftaincy'," in K. Arhin, ed., *The Life and Work of Kwame Nkrumah*. Accra: Sedco: 27–54.
Arhin, Kwame, Donald I. Ray, and E. A. B. van Rouveroy, eds. 1995. *Proceedings of the Conference on the Contribution of Traditional Authority to Development, Human Rights and Environmental Protection: Strategies for Africa*. Leiden, Netherlands: African Studies Centre.
Bank, Leslie, and Roger Southall. 1996. "Traditional Leaders in South Africa's New Democracy," *Journal of Legal Pluralism* 37/38: 407–30.
Commonwealth Local Government Forum (CLGF). 1995. *Commonwealth Roundtable on Democratisation and Decentralisation*. Harare, 27–29 June 1995, London: Commonwealth Local Government Forum.
Di Palma, Giuseppe. 1990. *To Craft Democracies: An Essay on Democratic Transitions*. Berkeley, Calif.: University of California Press.

Joseph, Richard. 1994. "Imperfect Transitions," in Richard Joseph, ed., *The Democratic Challenge in Africa.* Atlanta, Ga.: The Carter Center, pp. 52–57.

Nkrumah, K. 1957. *The Autobiography of Kwame Nkrumah.* London: Thomas Nelson and Sons.

Oloka-Onyango, J. 1997. "The Question of Buganda in Contemporary Ugandan Politics," *Journal of Contemporary African Studies* 15, no. 2: 173–89.

Ray, Donald I. 1992. "Contemporary Asante Chieftaincy: Characteristics and Development," in J. Sterner and N. David, eds. *An African Commitment.* Calgary: University of Calgary Press, pp. 105–21.

Ray, Donald I., and E. A. B. van Rouveroy van Niewaal. 1996. "The New Relevance of Traditional Authorities in Africa: An Introduction," *Journal of Legal Pluralism* 37/38: 1–38 [*The New Relevance of Traditional Authorities to Africa's Future,* special double issue edited by E. A. B. van Rouveroy and Donald I. Ray.].

Ray, Donald I., and T. Quinlan. 1997. "Chieftaincy Studies – The Traditional Authority Applied Research Network (TAARN): CHIEFS NET." Paper presented to the Human Sciences Research Council of South Africa (Centre for Science Development), Pretoria, 22 August.

Ray, Donald I., K. Sharma, and I. I. May-Parker, eds. 1997. *Symposium on Traditional Leadership and Local Government: Gaborone, Botswana, 23–26 September, 1997.* London: Commonwealth Local Government Forum.

Ray, Donald I., and M. Dalrymple. 2000. "Non-Traditional Communications and Traditional Leadership in Africa: The Case of TAARN (the Traditional Authority Applied Research Network)." Paper presented to the Third Conference of the Africa Society, University of Alberta, Edmonton, 25 February.

Tettey, Wisdom. 2001. "Human Factor Analysis and Democratic Transitions in Africa," in Senyo B-S. K. Adjibolosoo, ed., *Portraits of Human Behavior and Performance: The Human Factor in Action.* Lanham, N.Y., and Oxford: University Press of America, pp. 111–38.

van Rouveroy van Nieuwaal, E. A. B., and Donald I. Ray, eds. 1996. *The New Relevance of Traditional Authorities to Africa's Future* [Special double issue of *Journal of Legal Pluralism* 37/38].

Venson, Pelonomi, ed. 1995. *Traditional Leadership in Africa: A Research Report on Traditional Systems of Administration and their Role in the Promotion of Good Governance.* London and Cape Town: Commonwealth Local Government Forum and the Institute for Local Governance and Development.

Zips, Werner, and E. A. B. van Rouveroy van Niewaal, eds. 1998. *Sovereignty, Legitimacy, and Power in West African Societies: Perspectives from Legal Anthropology*, Hamburg: LIT (African Studies Series, Vol. 10).

NOTES

1. The federal government in Canada has initiated a process involving changes in what amounts, inter alia, to a level of rural local government for Canada's treaty status First Nations.

2. For a fuller discussion of the key concepts of pre-colonial, colonial, and post-colonial states, with their attendant significance for the concepts of traditional leaders existing in the post-colonial state, but being rooted in the pre-colonial states and other polities, as well as divided legitimacy and divided sovereignty, see the section entitled "The Effects of Traditional Leadership on the Concepts of the State, Sovereignty and Legitimacy" in Ray's Ghana chapter.

3. There are massive literatures in these fields and approaches to democracy, but which often seem to overlook this point. See, for example, Di Palma (1992), Anderson (1999) or Joseph (1994) for interesting examinations of democratization and democratic transitions. See also Tettey (2000) who clearly warns us against the uncritical romanticism and revivalism prevalent in some quarters that uncritically equates all aspects of pre-colonial culture and politics as being inherently democratic. As Tettey notes, contextualisation is key to any analysis.

4. I do not mean necessarily to attack the idea of republicanism, but rather to show that there are other ways of conceiving the concept of democracy without automatically adopting the assumption that democracy cannot exist without republicanism.

5. Is it not interesting to note that there have been more female British/Canadian monarchs as heads of state than there have been female U.S. presidents?

6. Indeed, Canada was in part settled by British North Americans who remained loyal to their monarch during the U.S. republican breakaway. Significant numbers of English-speaking loyalists and francophone Canadians joined British troops to fight off the republican invasions during the war of 1812.

7. Of course, in countries such as Ghana and Botswana there had been an on-going interest in traditional leaders during this period.

8. The kingdom of Buganda was one of the powerful pre-colonial kingdoms that Britain incorporated into their Uganda colony. The post-colonial state of Uganda incorporated the Buganda kingdom at independence.

9. The parallels to such bodies as the presidential electoral college in the United States need to be further explored, especially in light of the major problems in the U.S. voting system that emerged in the 2000 presidential election in the state of Florida that cast doubt over the legitimacy of the 2000 presidential election of the U.S. democracy.

10. For example, the Buganda monarchy was restored to a certain extent in 1993 by President Yoweri Museveni of Uganda. For one interpretation of these events, see Oloka-Onyango 1997.

11. For more information on the conference, see Ray's section in Ray and van Rouveroy 1996, 1–22.

12. For more information on TAARN, see Ray's section in Ray and van Rouveroy 1996; Ray and Quinlan 1997, as well as pp. 7, 9, and 58 in Ray, Sharma, and May-Parker 1997 and especially Ray and Dalrymple 2000. TAARN's website address is www.ucalgary.ca/uofc/faculties/SS/POLI/RUPP/taarn

13. IDRC's funding was key to the success of the conference. IDRC, especially Dr. J. M. Labatut, has continued to play a very significant role in the development of TAARN.

14. The roundtable was organized by the CLGF with the co-operation of the International Union of Local Government Authorities – Africa Section (IULA–AS) and the support of the Federation of Canadian Municipalities (FCM). The attending local government ministers, deputy ministers, and other senior local government officials and leaders were from Zimbabwe, Zambia, Uganda, Tanzania, Swaziland, South Africa, Sierra Leone, Seychelles, Nigeria, Namibia, Mozambique (observer), Mauritius, Malawi, Lesotho, Kenya, Ghana, the Gambia, Cameroon (observer), and Botswana.

15. Additional assistance was also provided by the Botswana House of Chiefs and Gaborone City Council. The symposium was sponsored by the Commonwealth Secretariat, the Municipal Development Programme and the Federation of Canadian Municipalities (FCM).

16. Since Sierra Leone was suspended from the Commonwealth at the time because of the military coup, the paper on Sierra Leone was presented by the Sierra Leonean researcher Mr. I. May-Parker. Dr. W. Zips attended on behalf of the Institute for Cultural and Social Anthropology, University of Vienna. Prof. P. S. Reddy attended on behalf of the University of Durban–Westville in South Africa and on behalf of the Rural Local Governance Project of the International Association of Schools and Institutes of Administration (IASIA).

17. See also Ray (1992) for a discussion of the socio-demographic characteristics of chiefs in the Ashanti region of Ghana.

18. Interestingly, in Ghana and Botswana, chiefs are constitutionally banned from taking part in party politics, while this is not yet the case in South Africa. The 1995 South Africa survey results have to be considered within the context of (a) the 1994 ending of formal apartheid with the first democratic elections in which some chiefs did act on behalf of certain parties and also the bloody civil war that pre-dated this and in which some chiefs in certain areas

who were aligned with political parties did take part. The point here is that the 1995 survey did not take place in a vacuum but within the context of a very immediate contentious history of which nearly all South Africans would be aware. Seen in this way Carrouthers' results seem to suggest a remarkable survival of popular support for traditional leadership. How would Ghana's chiefs fared if such a survey had been conducted in the aftermath of the 1950's struggle between Nkrumah's nationalists and those chiefs opposed to them?

19. Further evidence of this can be seen from the major dispute over which people were entitled to have their traditional leaders as members of the House of Chiefs. In late 2000 and 2001, a presidential commission of inquiry investigated the issue amidst much delicacy, but the issue still had not been finally resolved as this book went to press.

20. These differences are beyond the scope of this book, but in both sets of cases the underlying context of indigenous peoples having to deal with the consequences of colonialism in the form of the post-colonial state, etc., is shared.

21. The governance modalities would vary from country to country.

22. Ghana has a National House of Chiefs and ten Regional Houses of Chiefs. Botswana has a House of Chiefs. South Africa has a National House of Traditional Leaders and six Provincial Houses of Traditional Leaders. I refer to them all as being a generic category entitled "House of Chiefs."

23. This dynamic is discussed above in this chapter and also in Ray's chapter.

24. My research, supported by the International Development Research Centre of Canada as well as the Social Sciences and Humanities Research Council of Canada, is looking at ways in which state and traditional leaders can work together to foster development in these countries.

25. *Windspeaker*, June 2001, 19, no. 2, p. 1.

SETTING THE GHANAIAN CONTEXT OF RURAL LOCAL GOVERNMENT: TRADITIONAL AUTHORITY VALUES

CHAPTER 2

CHRISTIANE OWUSU-SARPONG

CHRISTIANE OWUSU-SARPONG holds a BA in modern languages (Strasbourg), an MA in ethnolinguistics (Sorbonne), and an MPhil and a PhD in literary semiotics (Besançon). From 1979 to 2001, she lectured at the University of Kumasi (KNUST) in Ghana, where she rose to the rank of associate professor. In August 2001, the Calgary Institute for the Humanities awarded her a research fellowship. She has been participating in two international research projects (Women Writing Africa and the Traditional Authority Applied Research Network [TAARN]); has published numerous articles and books, applying theories in ethnolinguistics and semiotics to Akan oral literature, including *La mort Akan – Etude ethno-sémiotique des textes funéraires akan* (L'Harmattan); she also edited a yearly journal (*Le Griot*) for nine years and two trilingual anthologies of Akan folktales. She is presently living in Paris, where her husband was recently appointed Ghana's ambassador to France.

Otumfuo* Osei Tutu II (Asante King or Asantehene) having an Adae reception at his palace in Kumasi, Ghana (2000, photo by D. Ray). (*traditional leadership title)

INTRODUCTION

Whilst the UN millennium summit was in process, the *Financial Times* published an interview of Kofi Annan, in which the famous Ghanaian Secretary-General summarized his vision in the following manner:

> I have made clear that the UN should put the human being at the centre of everything it does, and, indeed, the whole discussion – whether it is on issues of human right, issues of lifting people out of poverty, the issue of development – all focuses and centres on the people. (Annan 2000)

The topics mentioned by Kofi Annan are central to all African governments and, in particular, to the government of Ghana; and the Secretary-General's persistent concern for the people – their wishes, their needs, their most intimate thoughts, and the representations of their minds – does encourage us to try and understand how a political system like the rural local government of Ghana can help solve the nation's problems with the support of the traditional authorities still in place, only by concerning itself directly with the rural folks and their expectations.

If *culture*, on the other hand, is, in Mathew Arnold's words; "the pursuit of our total perfection by getting to know, on all matters which concern us, the best which has been thought and said in the world" (quoted in Briggs 1992, 4), then the study of the evolving process of the political culture of Ghanaians – acquired, refined, modified over time, by choice or imposition – is central to the understanding of the contemporary history of this West African composite group of people.

Kwame Arhin has, in a number of studies, outlined the changes that have occurred over the past centuries in the traditional political culture(s) of Ghana: He mainly discusses the internal changes in the system of chieftaincy, the Asante political structure remaining a model soon imitated and adopted by other ethnic groups of Ghana, and the external forces which tried, in vain, to suppress it (under and after colonial rule).

The present chapter will revisit the topic of traditional authority values, in order to set the context of the contemporary Ghanaian Rural Local Government. This seems to be a necessary intellectual step which could promote a better understanding of how and why the central government of Ghana, still an abstract entity for the majority of rural folks, can safely carry out its development projects only by relying on a strong co-operation between the two complementary local political entities: the institutionalized local government structure and the perennial traditional authority structure; for the latter remains close to the heart of the people.

We will first locate the argument within the context of the African Cultural Renaissance movement. Thereafter, we will briefly present the system of political and legal pluralism in Ghana, as it has apparently come to stay, focusing the analysis mainly on Donald Ray's studies. We will then proceed to demonstrate the viability of this system through a survey of its positive representations in the Ghanaian press over the recent months. Finally, an overview of the various images of the traditional leader in a variety of discourses and genres will attempt to unravel the conundrum of the surviving popularity of traditional authorities in a country whose people are just as much attracted by all the facets of modernity.

THE HIDDEN DANGERS OF GLOBALIZATION

> La culture clonée est une culture avortée, parce que lorsqu'elle cesse d'être une relation, elle cesse d'être une culture. La relation est sa marque principale, au point de l'identifier. Or, cette relation est métissage, donc tout le contraire du clonage. Avec le clonage, l'autre est le décalque de l'un; avec le métissage, l'un et l'autre donnent naissance à un nouvel être différent mais qui conserve aussi, naturellement, l'identité de ses origines. (Portella[1] 2000, 9)

Politicians and economists are carrying on with the accelerated process of globalization, which aims at transforming the whole wide world into one big village, by attempting to unify all judicial, economic, and political systems under the umbrella of the human rights culture which brought about the Western model of the liberal welfare state, now to be generalized.

Yet the hidden dangers of globalization are being exposed both by Western intellectuals and artists who strongly support the necessity of a dialogue of cultures and by the partisans of a cultural renaissance, in particular in the endangered Sub-Saharan regions of Africa, who lament the near-death situation of their original languages, (oral) literatures, and entire cultures. In the words of a writer in a popular Ghanaian newspaper:

> Globalization is re-colonising the world, particularly Africa whose
> political independence is becoming increasingly meaningless.
> The IMF-World Bank prescriptions for economic recovery do
> no more than emasculate Africa's political will to take effective
> decisions in its own interest, or develop its economies in the
> interest of its people. (Krafona 2000)

The entry into the Third Millennium seems to be characterized by a tremendous meltingpot of ideas, by a deconstructionist reconceptualization of *one's own world* in the light of the discovery and acceptance of the *other self* (that is of people of *other* cultures and places, and of one's own ancestors of *other* times).

THE RESURGENT HERITAGE

> Se wo were fi na wo sankofa a yenkyiri.

> "Should you have forgotten something / to do something / or to say
> something…, you may go back because it is never too late to get it
> / to do it / or to say it…" (Akan proverb)

The word "tradition" has often been misconstrued and perceived as referring to an ancient body of rules, of habits, of beliefs, of knowledge, only worthy of preservation in the ethnographic *Museum of Mankind*, notwithstanding the Latin origin of the noun *tradition*, itself derived from two Latin verbs (*tradere* + *transmittere*). As a matter of fact, Quintilian, the rhetorician, did use *traditio* with the meaning of *teaching* in his *De institutione oratorio* (Alleau n.d.); and this usage implies that, right from its creation, the noun *traditio* did suppose not only the mere passing on from one generation to another of the same cultural contents (*tradere*), but also and more so the continuous reactivating of values (*transmittere*) a specific society considers as *traditional* – that is, as inherited from its founding fathers.

This etymological clarification is further exemplified by the paradoxical answer recently given by Alain Finkielkraut, the contemporary French philosopher, when he was asked to identify the value(s) which is (were) to be absolutely preserved in this new millennium:

> Avant même de s'interroger sur les valeurs, l'essentiel serait
> pour moi que nous puissions transmettre une certaine idée de
> la transmission. Je dois avouer que je suis assez inquiet devant
> la fascination que ce changement de millésime provoque un peu
> partout, car j'y vois une bizarre impatience et l'idée que ce qui
> importe avant tout, c'est de s'adapter à des mutations ... si l'on
> s'abandonne complètement à cet enthousiasme, on risque d'en
> arriver au paradoxe selon lequel la seule chose à transmettre
> serait le futur! Or justement l'idée de la transmission repose
> sur le fait que le présent ne connaît pas toutes ses réponses. S'il
> est livré à lui-même ou s'il ne se conçoit qu'ouvert sur le futur,
> le présent est une prison. Nous devons savoir nous distancer de
> nous-mêmes, et les œuvres du passé peuvent nous y aider....
> Ainsi je dirai qu'il faudrait léguer *une exigence de transmission*
> et une valeur essentielle, qui est la passion de comprendre.
> (Finkielkraut 2000, 2)

But, unfortunately, this passion for a real transmission is receding. This is all the more disastrous in societies that have only recently adopted writing as a mode of transmission and whose most authentic and original values used to be handed down and, at the same time, constantly re-evaluated through very structured forms of their oral tradition.

African societies, so claims Amadou Hampâté Ba, are suffering nowadays from a "rupture in transmission," as their last living *traditionalists* are about to die without successors and, with them, the vast treasures of their knowledge and understanding of African traditions. The Bambaras called these traditionalists *Doma* or *Soma*, that is the "knowledgeable"; the Peuls, in their various regional languages, called them *Silatigi, Gando* or *Tchiorinké,* with the same meaning; some African societies of the Savanna, like those of Mali, had schools of thought, such as the *Komo*, the *Koré*, the *Nama*, the *Dô* ..., where the great Masters of the Word were trained; some of these *knowledgeable* people were also members of corporations (weavers, blacksmiths, herdsmen, healers, hunters ...), and additional duties of transmission related to their art and craft had been assigned to them (Ba 1995, 191–230).

These traditionalists were the living memory of their communities, their oral poets, their historians; they were the counsellors of the political and religious leaders, the mouthpiece of the commoners, the link in the unbroken chain between the living and the dead. In their words rested the most precious seeds of wisdom; their soothing and rejuvenating texts were able to achieve wonders whenever they were orally performed during a traditional ceremonial event, or in the daily resolution of conflicts: they fostered in each individual member of the society a sense of pride, of belonging, of togetherness, and they instilled in each of them the desire to continue to build on the common heritage.

But the successive historical tempests of the past two centuries – colonialism and post-colonial modernism – have attempted to erase all traces of the pre-colonial African past, and this long and subtle process of acculturation and of socio-political change could well result in the complete vaporization of the last monuments of Africa's oral tradition in the heat of the rush for technological advancement.

Providentially though, the strong belief in the need for a cultural renaissance of Africa, launched in the 1930s by the *Négritude* poets of francophone West Africa (Léopold Sédhar Senghor, David Diop, Bernard Dadié) and of the Black diaspora (Langston Hughes, Richard Wright, Léon G. Damas, Aimé Césaire), has gradually permeated all levels of contemporary African societies (A. Owusu-Sarpong 1998). Beyond this fundamental literary and political movement of the pre-independence era, a profound awareness of the importance of the revival of indigenous African values is now widespread amongst the people of Africa: amongst the young and the old; the rural folks and the urban-dwellers; the literate and the non-literate; the rich and the poor. It has become evident to all that political independence did not lead to a return to the African grassroots, but to what many times has been tagged as neo-colonialism, and that economic growth, wherever it had been achieved through the instrumentality of foreign agencies, was achieved to the detriment of human development and welfare.

A quick listing of media titles sampled randomly from recent editions of Ghanaian dailies may suffice to indicate the vivid interest shown by Ghanaian readers and writers of today in *traditional* matters:

- "Chieftaincy forever" (*The Ghanaian Chronicle*, 12–13 May 1999)

- "Traditional arbitration, a model for communal responsibility" (*The Ghanaian Chronicle*, 28–30 August 1999)

- "Don't condemn African Traditional Religion" (*The Daily Graphic*, 12 January 2000)

- "Respect our traditional values" (*The Mirror*, 15 January 2000)

- "Herbalists urged to pass knowledge to others" (*The Pioneer*, 2 February 2000)

- "We have lost our identity" (*The Statesman*, 27 February 2000)

- "Culture does not mean only drumming and dancing" (*The Pioneer*, 2 March 2000)

- "A need to re-organize our social values" (*The Ghanaian Chronicle*, 8–9 March 2000)

- "Christianity and traditional practices" (*The Weekend Statesman*, week ending 26 March 2000)

- "We cannot become what we need to be by remaining what we are" (*The Pioneer*, 29 March 2000)

- "Cultural values under threat" (*The Ghanaian Chronicle*, 29–30 March 2000)

- "The great prophet Okomfo Anokye" (*The Ghanaian Chronicle*, 5–6 April 2000)

- "Adhere to traditional norms" (*The Mirror*, 15 April 2000)

- "Sustain Traditional Values" (*The Pioneer*, 18 April 2000)

- "Nana Yaa Asantewaa is back in my dream" (*The Pioneer*, 27 July 2000)

- "Let's honour Yaa Asantewaa" (*The Daily Graphic*, 29 July 2000)

The African youth, which is the most vulnerable component of the population and the most likely to be disturbed by the exercise in cultural ambiguity Africa has embarked upon over the last fifty years, is participating in its own creative way in this intense claim for the recovery of an already fading heritage. So did Allavi Solomon, in January 2000, when he sent in the following poem for publication in *The Daily Graphic*'s "Children World" – thus voicing his protest against the cultural no-man's-land created by the adults around him, as well as his request for a cultural identity:

Our fading heritage

Tell me stories, Nana,
Blood-and-thunder tales of your days,
Of those memorable heroic days

That now belongs to the past.
My spirit yearns for accounts, Nana,
For the stories of the unforgettable,
Who shed their rich royal blood,
To redeem our beloved land.
Nana, wise Nana,
Let me hear of your potent kings,
Of Osei Tutu, the unbeatable,
And the architects of your boundless domains.
Let me hear of your women too, of Yaa Asantewaa and Dwaben Seewa.
They were gentle yet unyielding spirits, who nursed and forstered our warriors.
Feed me from your wisdom pot, Nana,
Sweet Nana of the grey hairs,
Nourish me with our rich heritage,
Lest it fade away.

POLITICAL AND LEGAL PLURALISM IN GHANA

In its awareness of its continent's triple heritage (indigenous, Islamic and Western),[2] Africa's intelligentsia is craving for a total understanding of the continent's complex experience of what Georges Balandier described as its dynamic, sometimes turbulent, and incredibly creative re-invention of the present, over the centuries and in the light of its constant memory of its past. When inaugurating the yearly Marcel Mauss Conference of the Société des Africanistes, in Paris, on 26 March 1999, Georges Balandier emphasized the enormous task that is confronting the makers of the newly-born African nation-states of today, especially in the arena of political power, that determines the relationship between those who govern and those who are governed:

> L'unité qui donne à celui-ci [à l'État moderne naissant] son assise est d'abord bureaucratique, les forces économiques et les intérêts particuliers y prévalent rapidement, le pouvoir n'est plus contenu dans des limites définies par une "charte" mystique, originelle, mais dans des rapports de forces instables, et sa légitimation, encore mal assurée, contient insuffisamment les tendances à l'autocratie et aux confrontations. L'Afrique est engagée dans

Main street, Kokofu town in the Ashanti Region, Ghana. Mourners gathering at a funeral (photo by D. Ray).

une période de refaçonnage des espaces politiques et de mutation
dont l'État moderne est l'instrument, et le tragique peut surgir.
(Balandier 1999, 267)

In several West African countries, various forms of traditional authority still do coexist with the new rules of governance set (with or without a constitution) within the modern (republican or military) nation-states, and this situation has often led to internal struggles over sovereignty, legitimacy, and power.

The topic of political and legal pluralism in West Africa has already been the sole focus of two recent symposia. The first one, held in September 1994 in Kumasi and Accra (Ghana), and co-organized by Nana Kwame Brempong Arhin, Professor Donald I. Ray, and Professor E. A. B. van Rouveroy van Nieuwaal[3] addressed the theme of "The Contribution of Traditional Authority to Development, Human Rights and Environmental Protection: Strategies for Africa." One year later, a symposium on Legal Anthropology was held at the University of Vienna and resulted in the publication of a book on *Sovereignty, Legitimacy and Power in West African Societies* in 1998. The topic remains central to an international research project launched in Durban (South Africa) in December 1999, the Traditional Authority Applied Research Network (TAARN),[4] which is presently embarking upon a comparative study of the relationship between traditional leaders and the modern states in South Africa, Botswana, and Ghana.

These new avenues of research, and the integrated and/or multidisciplinary approach followed by researchers in this field, could certainly facilitate the dialogue between the representatives of the modern African states in question and their traditional authorities. The success of such a dialogue, nevertheless, may depend, as Zips and van Rouveroy van Nieuwaal point out, "on the humility with which the power holders of modern African states are willing to acknowledge the authority of original African institutions and learn from the democratic principles on which these institutions rest" (1998, xv).

Ghana has been noted, in this respect, by the same scholars, as having taken an interesting "stance towards chieftaincy that strives towards co-operation, transparency, and internal peaceful relation" (van Rouveroy van Nieuwaal and Zips, 1998): Even though the June 1999 blunder, committed by the then president of Ghana, Fl. Lt. J. J. Rawlings, when he (insultingly) waved his left finger at the newly installed Asantehene, Otumfuo Osei Tutu II, in front of television cameras, nearly provoked an ethnic confrontation and points to the fact that "all is not entirely well in this best of all political worlds of West Africa" – to paraphrase Voltaire.[5]

The 1992 constitutional provisions on chieftaincy certainly indicate that traditional rulers were still relevant in Ghana at the end of the twentieth century, and that chieftaincy may well become one of the traditional values to regain new strength and importance for the building of an authentically African *and* modern nation-state in the Third Millennium.

In his article on "Chief-State Relations in Ghana," Donald Ray seems, to us, to have rightly concluded his analysis of the positions towards chieftaincy adopted by the successive governing and legislative bodies under and after the colonial rule in Ghana, by stating that "the 1992 Constitution of the Fourth Republic contained a shift back to the Third Republic's policy of constitutionally-limiting the sovereignty of the state over chiefs" (Ray, 1998, 62–63).

He was referring, in particular, to ART. 270, which deals with the power to control the recognition of chiefs – that is, to control their selection, the process of enstoolment and/or enskinning, and that of destoolment and/or deskinning – and has now taken that power from Parliament and given it to the National House of Chiefs, the Regional Houses of Chiefs, and the local Traditional Councils.

Donald Ray's argument is that there was constitutional evidence that "chiefs should not be considered to be 'inferior agents'"; that, in Ghana, "an entity (i.e., the state) which is sovereign in most respects coexists with an entity (i.e., traditional authority) that seems to be sovereign in this respect"; and that "history and religion combine to provide the distinctive basis of legitimacy for chiefs" in Ghana. Donald Ray thus restates an earlier claim: "In Ghana the relation between the state and chiefs has been characterized by divided sovereignty and legitimacy" (Ray, 1998, 64–65).

Although the 1992 constitution establishes clearly that "A chief shall not take part in party politics" (ART. 276), it does assign new and important tasks to the National and Regional Houses of Chiefs – in particular that of a re-evaluation and a transcoding (or systematizing and putting in writing) of traditional rule and of all socio-cultural practices classified as "tradition" under *Customary Law* (ART. 272).

In practice, this constitutional recognition of "the honour and dignity of chieftaincy" (ART. 270 2b), which sounds more like an official acceptance of traditional authority, did certainly derive, first and foremost, from the actual influence traditional rulers of Ghana still have over their people; 70 per cent of Ghana's population lives in rural areas and tends to recognize its traditional rulers as its legitimate moral and social leaders (not to talk about the political influence some partisan and corrupt chiefs could and do have during and even outside electoral periods).

The current policy of decentralization and local government in Ghana is, in this set-up, a major factor contributing to the conducive atmosphere of co-operation which seems to prevail between locally elected representatives of the District Assemblies and the traditional rulers of the same regions.

RURAL LOCAL GOVERNMENT AND CHIEFTAINCY IN GHANA TODAY

In the media, decentralization has been perceived favourably in most cases, and is often described as an important aspect of Ghana's current democratic dispensation:

> The decentralization policy has brought about a lot of improve-
> ment in the management of affairs, in particular in the rural
> areas. The policy has enhanced the participation of the people
> in the decision-making process. District municipal and district
> assemblies have executive, deliberative and administrative powers.
> The assemblies can now enact by-laws to regulate the activities of
> the people and organizations operating in their areas of jurisdiction.
> (Onoma-Barnes 2000)

Local government representatives and traditional rulers in the same traditional areas/ regions of Ghana, appear as working hand-in-hand for the benefit of the people; the Ghanaian newspapers have been reporting frequently on this positive development and chiefs are now perceived more and more as valuable intermediaries between the State, NGOs and the people, as development agents. and as mediators in conflicts. The following story is an interesting point in case:

> The Cape-Coast Municipal Assembly has appealed to the Oguaa
> Traditional Council to help resolve the differences between the
> assembly and the Member of Parliament (MP) for the area, Ms.
> Christine Churcher. The Municipal Chief Executive, Mr. Percy
> Ashun … said the Assembly has appealed to the Omanhene,
> Osabarima Kwasi Atta, and his elders to settle the matter to enable
> the Assembly and the MP to work together for the development of
> the municipality. (Owusu-Sekyere 2000)

Osagyefuo* Ofori Atta is the Okyenhene or King of Akyem Abuakwa in the Eastern Region of Ghana. In order to promote income generation possibilities in his kingdom, he has established a pilot scheme for local people to grow large snails for sale as a protein source (2002, photo by D. Ray). (*traditional leader title)

In this case, the traditional ruler and his elders were called upon to use their good offices to arbitrate on a very *modern* moneypalaver that had led to a serious disagreement between agents of central and local government.

The chiefs of contemporary Ghana are active opinion leaders whose words and actions are often quoted in the papers; their presence alone, reproduced in numerous pictures taken at official – and not necessarily traditional – gatherings, serves as a guarantee of the regional and national importance and significance of the event:

- "Okyenhene wants Akwatia mines turned into mining college," in *The Ghanaian Chronicle* (29–30 November 1999).

- "The Omanhene of Banda Traditional Area … has expressed great concern over the high rate at which some timber species and savannah trees are being destroyed in the area through illegal felling of trees…." in *The Free Press* (7–13 January 2000).

- "Queenmother advocates women empowerment," in *The Mirror* (26 February 2000): "I believe [declared the queenmother] women can contribute significantly if they are given the chance. Women are better managers and if they are economically empowered, they can help their husbands to raise up happy families."

- "Chiefs are urged to promote census" by Odeefo Boa Amponsem III, Denkyirahene, who is also the President of the National House of Chiefs and a member of the Council of State, as reported in *The Daily Graphic* (25 March 2000).

- Under the title "Romeo village teacher sent to another village after impregnating thirteen-year-old," *The Ghanaian Chronicle* (28–30 March 2000) reported on a local scandal which provoked the ire of the people and their chief, Barima Asiedu Boafo II; in this instance, the moral condemnation of an irresponsible adult by a village community was channelled through a petition by the chief to the Regional Director of Education.

- "Establish camps for AIDS patients," so said the Asantehene's Nsumankwahene Baffour Domfe Gyeabour III addressing newsmen; he, according to *The Pioneer* (6 July 2000), "advised the public to refrain from indiscriminate sex and to stick to one partner, adding 'the disease is real and no cure has been found for it'."

Most of the time though, it is at official functions where chiefs play significant roles (such as the opening of a school and/or of a health centre in their area, and of course on the occasion of their enstoolment and/or enskinning, or at royal funerals) that the traditional leaders do express their concerns.

Traditional festivals have now become a forum for the renewed celebration of indigenous Ghanaian cultures, led by traditional rulers, and for the discussion of matters of public concern in the presence of representatives of the local and central government, as well as of foreign agencies. As a result of this reshaping of traditional gatherings, festivals that had been consigned to the dustbin of history are being revived. An interesting report on this contemporary interface was given on the Upper East Region by the regional editor of *The Daily Graphic:*

> Festivals are occasions during which chiefs and their people show appreciation to their gods and ancestors for the protection, guidance, and blessings bestowed on them in the course of the year. They equally provide the appropriate forum for the chiefs and the people to showcase the beauty and glamour of their traditional values and potentials to the outside world. While some also use the occasion to launch appeals for funds to undertake development projects to augment the efforts of both the district assemblies and the central government, others choose to enjoy the occasions through mere merrymaking. As a result, festivals that were not even being celebrated in the northern parts of the country have now been revived. Such festivals include the Tenglebigre of the Nabdams in the Sakoti Traditional Area, the Kuure (Hoe) Festival of the people of Zaare, and the Adakoya Festival of the Bolgatanga Traditional Area. While one fully supports the celebration of such festivals in the three northern regions, it is the belief of many concerned citizens that such celebrations could have more positive dividends if they were used more seriously to take stock of the people's activities during the year considering the numerous problems facing the three regions. (Seini 2000, 16)

Amongst all present-day traditional rulers of Ghana, the Asantehene, Otumfuo Osei Tutu II, who was enstooled on the prestigious Golden Stool of Asante a year ago, has started emerging as a main figure to be reckoned with in all domains of interest, not only within his region but within the country at large.

In December 1999, officials from the World Bank paid a courtesy visit to Manhyia and, as *The Pioneer* reported, Otumfuo gave them "food for thought" by stressing "the need for officials of the World Bank to have constant interactions with the people at the grassroots and stop dealing with government [alone]." (Editorial, 21 December 2000).

A few days later, at the end of year meeting of the Ashanti Regional House of Chiefs, Otumfuo, already acclaimed as "the Millennium King," touched on the necessary re-evaluation of Asante culture and, in particular, of chieftaincy itself, given the constraints of modern life:

> Touching on cultural practices, Otumfuo called on the chiefs to examine Asante culture in the light of the harsh economic realities, to rid them of unnecessary and burdensome aspects such as expensive funerals. As chieftaincy enters the new millennium, and as a traditional authority within a secular state, Otumfuo said there was the need for chiefs to ensure that the vision they created for the institution will be more relevant just as their predecessors were able to preserve its relevance over the years by adapting to changes. (*The Pioneer,* 22 December 1999)

During the watch-night service at the Wesley Methodist Church in Kumasi,

> .... he advised Ghanaians to make truth, honesty, integrity and uprightness their guiding principle. "We can only succeed as a nation if we abide by these principles," so said He. (*The Pioneer,* "Otumfuo's Millennium Message," 3 January 2000)

Otumfuo, the Asante people's King Solomon, has, in the short period between January and February 2000:

- launched an immunization campaign at Manhyia

- urged the Public Health Department of Kumasi to "eschew filtering, laxity, backbiting and indiscipline"

- urged members of the Neighbourhood Watch to "help the police flush out the bad nuts in society so as to sustain peace and stability"

- called on chiefs "not to sell off large portions of peri-urban land as individual plots for residential development to deny indigenous food-crop farmers the traditional right to cultivate their family lands"

- urged "academics and researchers to intensify their efforts at documenting the heroic deeds of Ghanaians," when receiving members of the Yaa Asantewaa Festival planning committee

- announced that the "Asanteman Council was to institute a health endowment fund to train doctors in and outside the country to improve on health care delivery."

Otumfuo Osei Tutu II's magnificent efforts as a *modern traditional leader*, and in particular his contribution to the development of education, through the launching of an Education Fund destined to provide financial assistance to bright and needy children and students of Asante descent and to renovate schools, has earned him the Millennium SYMONS Award. This award was conferred on him by a forty-two-member delegation of the Association of Commonwealth Universities (ACU) on 22 April 2000. This particular achievement has also warmed the heart of his people so much so that a singular Valentine poem, written by a social worker of Kumasi, appeared in *The Pioneer* on 14 February 2000:

Great King Osei Tutu
Nana Osei Tutu Ababio

The symbol and touch bearer of the great Ashanti Nation
The soul and embodiment of the good People of Ashanti
The progressive and dynamic leader of whom we are very proud
Nana, we don't only love you
We adore you and cherish you
We praise you and worship you, 'cause
You deserve praise and worship.
Many are those who would look back
At the year 2000 with delightful memories
Memories of glee and happiness
With the intent of stretching similar helping hands to those who might need it
This is the result of your love for education
The result of your good foresight and generosity
Many are those who would miss their right to education but for your goodwill and
initiative
Allow us then to sing your praises whilst alive
Mother Ghana is grateful to the Creator of Mankind for a great King
Nana Osei Tutu II

. . . .
Amen!

Darling Ode (A Social Worker) – Kumasi

Otumfuo's fiftieth birthday, which coincided with the first anniversary of his accession to the Golden Stool, was celebrated in grand style on 6 May. In the morning, Nana Osei Tutu II was acclaimed in the streets of Kumasi by five thousand school children, for whom he held a party at Manhyia later that same morning: And in the evening, during a banquet attended by ministers of state, members of Parliament, members of the diplomatic corps, senior academics, and important citizens (three hundred invited guests in all), and amidst many goodwill messages, Otumfuo, dressed in an impeccable tuxedo suit, expressed joy and hope for the future:

> Indeed, the past year has come to pass with some good and pleasant memories for me personally. The tremendous support I received from the government and people of Ghana towards the burial and funeral of my late brother, and the overwhelming response by corporate bodies and well meaning individuals like your good selves to my Educational Fund launch, have not only warmed my heart but have also given me strength and encouragement to pursue my quest to help find lasting solutions to some of the socio-economical problems facing my people. Tonight, as I enter my second year on the Golden Stool, I am more than determined to work towards the attainment of the objectives I have set for myself: to continue with the crusade of promoting education and health care for my people and to harness our resources, strength, and unity to develop Asanteman as my contribution towards Government efforts to develop the entire nation.[6]

As he began the second year of reign, Otumfuo Osei Tutu II prepared for his first trip abroad, to the U.K., at the invitation of Queen Elizabeth II who, owing to the official program drawn up by the Ghana government when she visited in November 1999, could not go to Kumasi as she had wished. This historic meeting, during which the Asante king was received in a private audience by the queen at Buckingham Palace on 18 May, continued to symbolically demarcate the future from the past turbulent relationship between the British Crown and the Asante Confederacy. During his stay in the U.K., Otumfuo also held discussions with British companies (including the Cocoa Association of London Limited); he met directors of the British Council and it was agreed that an Information and Technology Centre would be built in Kumasi; he visited the House of Commons and House of Lords, and travelled to Cambridge where he discussed the issue of drugs and delinquents with educationists (Agyeman-Dua 2000, 40–41).

Commenting on Otumfuo Osei Tutu's first year on the Golden Stool, the Ghanaian novelist Kwaku Akuoko developed the theme of the rebirth of Asanteman (the Asante state) under the new king, as against what he described as "the 29-year vacuum of Otumfuo Opoku Ware II." In this incisive article, the author started with a historical account of the first 180 years of the Asante nation's history under the able leadership of competent chiefs with a vision and foresight. The last 120 years, in contrast, had been, according to him "rather dim and demure," due to the fact that some Asantehenes became totally alienated and powerless because of their conversion to Christianity (like Prempeh I or Opoku Ware II) or to Islam (Osei Kwame):

> "In spite of our arrival in the twenty-first century," asserts the writer, "the Asante nation of the 1870s was a much more sophisticated society than the Asante nation of today. Its government, civil and public servants, its diplomats were far more skilled than anything that can probably be pitted against them today.... Asantehene Osei Tutu Ababio will quickly need to bridge the gap between 1880 and 2000 if the nation is to make any progress.... For the next generation to do better means we must educate Asante children of today. That must be done independently of the government of Ghana ... we need to teach our history, culture and language in order to reinforce our heritage, values, conservatism and pride. It would be a most appalling tragedy if we should end up, in spite of their relative affluence, like African Americans or worse still West Indians. Both being people with no history or culture in search of a dream.... If Asantehene Osei Tutu Ababio," concludes the writer, "does nothing at all, other than be remembered as the one who re-laid the foundation for the education of Asantes, then the bridge between 1880 and 2000 would have been bridged and with it the nation would have been reborn." (Kwaku-Akuoko 2000)

The young and dynamic Asantehene of today has, unmistakably, already become the model of what an African nation-state like Ghana (modern but, at the same time, very much aware of the importance of its cultural heritage) expects of a contemporary traditional leader, in particular in the context of (rural) local government: A national expectation which was summarized by the Brong-Ahafo Regional Minister, Mr. Donald Adabre, in his address to the chiefs at the Brong-Ahafo Regional House of Chiefs, on 27 April 2000 when:

... [he] reminded the chiefs that as custodians of the country's heritage and values, they have a great responsibility to lead their traditional areas in the effort to preserve their cultural values, which have been weakened or abandoned in the name of so-called modernization. He noted that it is this "modernization" which has brought a breakdown in moral values in the society. He said the focus of chieftaincy now is socio-economic development and not wars of expansion as it used to be in the past. (*The Daily Graphic*, 29 April 2000)

SETTING THE GHANAIAN CONTEXT OF RURAL LOCAL GOVERNMENT: TRADITIONAL AUTHORITY VALUES

The active role traditional leaders of Ghana are expected to play nowadays, both as moral boosters of their people and as agents of development of their regions, rests on the fact that these traditional authorities are still perceived – especially by the rural folk and despite the fact that all political power has been taken from them – as the legitimate *rulers*.

In fact, no decision taken at the level of central government, and directly concerning the people in matters such as communal health, education, use and distribution of land, gender issues, etc., can easily be implemented without the active involvement of the traditional authorities in the various regions. This explains the multiplicity of workshops recently organized to educate chiefs on new policies and trends to enable them to play their role as intermediaries between the distant ministries, Parliament, and the people most effectively.[7]

This is so because, despite the fast process of modernization and the moral degradation of the youth of today, traditional authorities are still held in high esteem. They are considered as the sacred embodiment of the traditional values that strengthened their communities in the past, and can still (if reviewed) help both the rural and town folks in their daily struggles for survival as individuals, as family members, and as citizens.

Although the perceptions of these traditional authorities have slightly changed over the years, there remains a striking resemblance between the oftentimes positive images of chiefs presented in various forms, and the contemporary social discourse on chieftancy. We shall verify this through a brief survey of oral literature texts still performed today:

- a sample of recently published books, and

- a series of interviews.[8]

IMAGES OF THE TRADITIONAL LEADER IN AKAN ORATURE

Although Asante oral texts have naturally been altered and continuously re-created over the centuries, some poetic texts performed during royal funerals or during *adaes* (periodic festivals in commemoration of the spirits of dead Asantehenes and chiefs) are very reminiscent of, if not totally similar to their original form. These fixed panegyric texts mainly belong to the royal funeral genre, whose classification we have attempted elsewhere (C. Owusu-Sarpong 1995, 2001). Particular attention may be given to drum histories (*ayan*) played on the *fontomfrom* and *atumpan* talking drums, to dirges and laments (*ayinan, abodinsu*) for royals played on *atenteben* and *odurogya* horns and flutes, to libation prayers (*nsaguokasa/mpaebo*) addressed to dead kings, and to royal oaths (*ntam*) – all of which have in common their historic and religious attributes.

Through the regular and ritual performance of these sacred texts, the link between the living and the dead remains unbroken: The community gathered on the ritual scene of performance draws a sense of pride from the epic stories of their ancestral heroes (the first settlers, the seventeenth- and eighteenth-century empire builders and conquerors, and the nineteenthcentury ferocious opponents of the British invaders). These themes, retold by the masters of *dwamu kasa* or *public speech* (*akyeame*, the spokesmen; *akyerema*, the drummers; *kwadwomfoo*, the ministrels; *abrafoo*, the executioners, etc.,) are being remembered in the poetic praise-genre of the olden days (*tetesem*) mentioned above, such as the following drumstanza:

> Onoborobo Osei Tutu e,
> Bonsu who fought and seized Kings,
> Osei Tutu Birempon,
> Thou art a warrior,
> Thou art ever a man,

[You whose motto is] "Were I alone, I should go and fight,"
Onoborobo Osei Tutu,
The hero who holds a gun and a sword when he goes to battle,
Bonsu who fought and seized Kings,
Osei Tutu Birempon.[9]

But it would be a misconception to imagine that the ideal chief of the past was solely praised and feared as a cold-blooded warrior, exercising a kind of feudal autocracy over his people. As A. L. Adu rightly pointed out, appellations given to chiefs in panegyrics rested, as they do today, on special virtues expected of them, and which brought them close to the heart of their people:

> The ideal Akan chief is the head of a great big family of which
> his subjects are members. He is their ruler and their judge, their
> counsellor and their moral guide, a tower of strength in time
> of trouble and their captain in time of war. He is all-powerful
> (Otumfuo), a conqueror (Osagyefuo), courageous (Katakyie), a
> benefactor (Daasebre), a kind master (Odeefuo), and wise (Nana).
> (Adu 1949, 6)

K. A. Busia, in the same fashion, emphasized the fact that if a chief had power and authority, he was only "wealthy in terms of services which he received, not in transferable wealth":

> The tribute of firstfruits which he received at the Odwira ceremony
> was redistributed as presents to the elders and their subjects.
> The palmwine sent him was used to entertain all and sundry.
> The food and meat went to feed the large number of attendants
> in the royal household, and anyone who cared to go to the chief's
> house for a meal. One of the strict injunctions given to a chief on his
> enstoolment was that he should be generous. (Busia 1951, 51)[10]

The chief's powers, as well as his duties were conceptualized (like all socio-cultural norms of the Akan) in proverbial sayings (ebe), some of which are still in use today. Rev. J. G. Christaller, the Basel missionary mentioned quite a few (nineteen) in his 1881 collection of *Akwapem* proverbs, amongst which the following may be extracted (Christaller 1933):

POWERS

Ohene bekum wo a, ennim ahmantwe. (1305)

When a chief is going to kill you, it is useless consulting the lots.

Ohene na oyi dansefo. (1306)

The chief reveals the false witness. (The chief selects the witness)

Ohene aso te se osono aso. (1312)

The ears of a chief are as the ears of an elephant.

Ohene ntam te se bayere amoa, obi nto mu mfa neho totroto mfi adi da. (1314)

A chief's oath is like the hole a yam is planted in, no one falls into it and gets out again unhurt.

Ohene aso te se odum, onni anim onni akyiri. (1317)

A chief's ear is like an odum tree, he has no front and no back.

DUTIES

Ohene nufuo dooso a, amansan na enum. (1309)

When a chief has plenty of milk (large breasts), then all people drink of him.

Ohene bedi wo kasa, efiri manfo. (1304)

When a chief is going to fine you/ to compel you to do something, he does so by the authority of his people.

Ohene nya ahotrafo pa a, na ne bere so dwo. (1310)

When a chief has good councillors, then his reign is peaceful.

The two last maxims give us a hint of the democratic processes which sanctioned the authority of the chiefs in the past, and at the complex and subtle system of checks and balances all traditional Akan societies had put in place. There again, A. L. Adu magnificently summarized how "all power and authority of Chiefs derived from the people" and how "they [the people] set the manner in which they (power and authority) can be exercised":

> Within the limits imposed by custom and tradition ... the chief has a very wide measure of power. But the chief can, by issuing arbitrary and unreasonable orders, soon lose the active support of his people, and thereafter, his actions will be closely watched, and he will be

deposed on the slightest excuse. This right of impeachment by people, that sooner or later caught up with the tyrannical chief, was, and still is, the most powerful and democratic check the people had on arbitrary invocation of customary sanctions. There is of course the day-to-day check which the councillors, who represent the people as family heads or sub-chiefs, have in advising the chief, reminding him of his duties, and in assisting him to regulate the life of the community through legislation and enforcement of laws. In some Akan states, the presence of the "Asafo," that active company of "young men," always serves as a quick reminder to the autocratic chief that he has to watch his steps. In the past, an unpopular chief ran the risk of desertion from his people in a battle. Even now, in some places, a most potent way of dealing with an unpopular chief is to refuse to render him such customary services as calling at the "ahenfie" to greet him and going out of one's way to render him homage. He can enforce customary observance and duties, but no one will give voluntary service. A chief can, normally, not go too far, particularly if his position is not as lofty as that of a paramount ruler. The Akan system provides for a democratic climate of opinion in which democracy must prevail. (Adu 1949, 12–13)[11]

It is therefore quite amazing that, amongst the five proverbs mentioned in a contemporary collection by a living traditional ruler of the Brong-Ahafo Region, Agyewodin Nana Adu Gyamfi Ampem II,[12] one notes four proverbs on a chief's powers and only one on his duty to remain open to advice. This choice of proverbs, old and new, amidst a very recently published anthology, tends to indicate that some present-day chiefs have a false and over bloated image of their *traditional* power and authority in a society which is, paradoxically, swiftly moving towards social levelling, through the abolition of privileges and the introduction of free education for all:

Ohene a onku wo na obo wo boo. (1186)
The King who does not want to kill you gives you the option of a fine.

Ohene akondwa nye bamma na nnipa mmienu anaa dodoo atena so preko. (1187)

A throne is not a bench to be occupied by two or more people at the same time.

Ohene akokorawa na yesisi no, na enye ohene ababunu. (1188)
It is the aged king who can be bluffed but not the young king.

Ohene kyiniie; ebi da bi akyi. (1189)
The order of the king's umbrella: some precede others.

Ohene tufuantee na odi ntakraboa a, onni tire. (1190)
A chief who is impervious to advice eats a headless bird.
(Ampem 1999)

All too soon do the chiefs of today (and, sometimes, so did those of the past) forget that a chief is only the provisional occupant of a sacred stool, that he comes and goes whilst the stool lives on, and that he can be destooled the moment he disregards the traditional warning speech he was given on the day of his enstoolment:

> Kuronti, Akwamu, Bokoro, Konton, Asere, Kyidom, Benkum, Twafo, Adonten, Nifa – all the elders say that I shall give you the Stool. Do not go after women. Do not become a drunkard. When we give you advice, listen to it. Do not gamble. We do not want you to disclose the origins of your subjects. We do not want you to abuse us. We do not want you to be miserly; we do not want one who disregards advice; we do not want you to regard us as fools; we do not want autocratic ways; we do not want bullying; we do not want beating. Take the Stool. We bless the Stool and give it to you. The Elders say that they give the Stool to you. (trans. in Busia 1951, 12)

Folktales are also, as Jean Cauvin rightly points out (Cauvin 1980), constantly and more perhaps than any other oral genre, at the crossroads of the past and the present, at the junction of two worlds (the ideal traditional world built by the ancestors, and the real world perverted by their descendants over the years). The harmonious village set-up into which everyone fits with total submissiveness to the religious and political order is, during each tale's performance, presented as threatened. The narration of folktales (*anansesem*, lit. "*Ananse* stories," in Akan), sometimes in the midst of similar social upheavals, is supposed to have a cathartic effect on the audience: that is, generally, on members of the society that is being described by analogy. Each one of these texts exemplifies (at the moment of its performance) particular movements of the "texture" as defined by Simon Battestini.[13] The tales, when performed, represent *points* of views of individuals on the dynamics of their society.

Amidst the twenty Akan folktales we have so far edited and published in trilingual versions (A. Owusu-Sarpong 1998) – all of which were recorded in the rural areas of Asante and Brong-Ahafo over the past ten years – fifteen main *dramatis personae* are traditional authorities. Amongst those fifteen chiefs and queenmothers, two can be considered as anti-heroes, or as unpopular chiefs:

- the helpless chief of tale thirteen, who was unable to protect his townsfolk against the danger of a murderous monster and who had to, in the end, bequeath half of his wealth to this godforsaken kingdom's redeemers, and

- the haughty, preposterous and unfair chief of tale seventeen, who endangered the life of his village youth by overpricing his daughter's beauty and who did as a result, lose her to prostitution.

All the other thirteen traditional authorities, represented in this corpus of Akan tales, are representative of the virtues and qualities expected of *good* chiefs:

- they are moral leaders, problem solvers, intermediaries, intercessors, and peacemakers, capable of reconciling individuals aggrieved against one another (tales two, four, and nineteen)

- they are achievers, builders, hardworking and enterprising, worthy of their title (Nana), kind, welcoming, willing to share their wealth with their people and foreigners, and therefore respected and feared by all (tales four and sixteen)

- in their own, personal lives, they are model fathers (tales nine and twelve), husbands and sons (tale four), always dignified, understanding, merciful and just, rewarding those deserving reward and punishing those who, amongst their closest relatives, called their wrath upon themselves; they are able to accept their faults and to make amends, in particular when they have meted out unfair treatment to one of their wives in a polygamous marriage (tales six and sixteen)

- they are the central figures of all public affairs, where and when problems of communal importance are to be solved at the royal courts or during festivals, on the durbar grounds; in the courts, they appear surrounded by their advisers, the elders and they administer justice without fear (tales nine, thirteen, sixteen, eighteen, and nineteen); they defend the truth in all its glory amidst the pageantry surrounding them in public gatherings and during ritual ceremonies (tales four, six, twelve, and sixteen).

Although they are, here and there, portrayed as morally frail and human, the final image one gets from this short overview is that of a sacred office belonging to a community: That of a temporary occupant of an ancestral stool, of a spiritual leader of the people, who no more belongs to him/herself (tale eighteen).

IMAGES OF TRADITIONAL AUTHORITIES IN RECENTLY PUBLISHED BOOKS

It may be of interest, at this point, to refer to one of the Right Reverend Dr. Peter K. Sarpong's most recent publications (Sarpong 1998), in which the Catholic archbishop of Kumasi symbolically makes an invocation to his ancestor to explain, in an epistolary format, the theme of inculturation. He deals, in particular, with the topic of chieftaincy and confirms the recognition still given the traditional authorities by Akan storytellers in this book of contemporary Christian theology.

In letter thirty-one, the Right Reverend Dr. Sarpong dwells on ancestral epithets, on appellations now given to Jesus, the founder of the Church, and borrowed from Akan royalty; Jesus' praise-names, now frequently in use during sermons, or in hymns and prayers, are traditional panegyrics, until then attributed to acclaimed chiefs:

- *Osagyefoo* (the conqueror)

- *Odayefoo* (doctor of medicine, healer)

- *Kantamanto* (the one who does not deceive you for he keeps his oath / he who has the power to do anything he wants)

- *Kurotwiamansa* (the leopard, cf., the *Asantehene*: the commander of the forest, fierce and beautiful / a majestic and dignified king)

- *Daasebre* (lit. "the one who wants to thank him will get tired" or "to thank him enough is a herculean effort" = the provider)

- *Nyaamanehose* (a refuge for those in trouble)

- *Paapa* (a father to all)

- *Ahummobro* (a softhearted, merciful king).

The Akan Christian therefore identifies Christ with the perfect leader, who combines – without any human foibles – all the traditional leadership qualities the author had previously summarized in letter twenty-eight:

> A traditional Asante leader, who later becomes the ancestor, is a man for others. He is chosen not for himself but for his people, and he is chosen to lead to a successful end. A traditional Asante leader, … has, as his first task, to play a religious role. He is the intermediary between the living and the ancestors. He it is who has to lead the veneration of the ancestors. There are certain days during the year when he has to offer prayers to the ancestors; he has to see to it that the rules and regulations of the ancestors are kept; he has to keep the ancestors in the constant memory of his people…. This religious role is so important that if a chief fails to play it, he can easily be dismissed or destooled. The chief too is a legislator. Together with his counsellors, he makes laws for his people, regulations that stand the people in good stead. At the same time, he plays a judicial role, looking to it that the laws of his predecessors are kept and applied. He is the chief executive who sees to the smooth running of the society. He has a social role that he plays as father, brother and friend of those who belong to his society. His should not be a role of terror, of lording it over his subjects, but a role of love, paternal love. He must see to it that the customs and traditions of the society are kept; this is his cultural role. He must see to the aesthetic side of his society so that what is beautiful in the general connotation of the word, remains undisrupted, intact. A major role of the chief in the past was that of the military leader. He was a person that saw to it that his people were rid of the menace of internal and external aggression; and a chief who failed to play this role of courage and of protection of his people also stood in danger of being rejected. (Sarpong 1998, 141–42)

In *The Just King – The Story of Osei Tutu Kwame Asibe Bonsu*, two female writers of the Kwame Nkrumah University of Science and Technology, Kumasi, Dr. Frederika Dadson and Dr. Wilhelmina Donkoh,[14] put their historical knowledge and their literary skills together to retell, for a young readership, and through the mouth of Opanin Owusu, a schoolboy's grandfather, the vivid story of one of the greatest amongst all Asante kings:

> The story of Osei Tutu Kwamina is a good one. Long, but good.
> It is a good place to start. It was during his reign that the Asante
> people engaged both the British people and the Fante in a more
> direct confrontation than any Asantehene before him.... A great
> man, a great warrior, Osei Tutu Kwame Asibe Bonsu.... Brave and
> strong, a great father of the Asante nation and a great leader of
> the Asante army.... Osei Tutu Kwamina was never one to act in a
> hurry. This is one of the secrets of his success. He always seemed
> to reflect on the consequences of war and peaceful settlement...
> Osei Tutu was ... his old self, an understanding leader. (Dadson
> and Donkoh 2000)

These are some of the messages passed on by a fictional grandfather to his enthusiastic grandson, full of expectations about his history classes; messages passed on by two academics, desirous to transmit not only knowledge about historical facts, but a certain representation of a *good* traditional (and, why not contemporary) leader: that of a true peacemaker.

Finally, a third book worth mentioning here, is the collection of lifestories of *Ten Women Achievers from the Ashanti Region of Ghana* (Dolphyne 2000), amongst whom figures Nana Boatema-Afrakoma II, the queenmother of Juansua. She was chosen because, as indicated by the editor;

> In Asante culture, the position of the queenmother is a very
> important one. She is the chief's major councillor. In the
> selection of a new chief her word is final. She also has traditional
> responsibilities relating to the role of women in society and the
> moral education of the young girls in the society.
> Nana has been able to use her position to make meaningful
> contribution to her community and to the role of queenmothers ...
> she has organized workshops for queenmothers on various issues
> affecting their people. This is because she believes they need to
> reflect on the conditions prevailing in their communities and find

> ways of introducing changes that will promote development.
> For example, … she has advocated a reduction in the cost of
> funerals, and has organized workshops on environmental issues
> and the proper use of markets.

Nana Boatema-Afrakoma II thus appears as *the* progressive female rolemodel in this new area of traditional Asante (dual) authority described by scholars such as Beverly Stoeltje and Takyiwaa Manuh.

IMAGES OF TRADITIONAL AUTHORITIES DRAWN FROM A SURVEY CONDUCTED IN THE ASANTE REGION

The positive appraisal of chieftaincy by contemporary court minstrels or by rural story-tellers, by a recognized Church leader, and by female academicians, was further echoed in many answers given by a cross-section of the Asante population during a series of interviews conducted as part of our TAARN Research Project (TAARN 2000).

We shall have to limit ourselves, for the purpose of this chapter, to three significant answers only, which all touch on the cherished memories of the past as well as on the hopes for the future. These three answers also illustrate the awareness and objective rationalization of the Ghanaian of today as far as the process of alteration of his culture is concerned.

> "There are so many traditional values; some of them are truth and
> honesty, love and respect for the fellow man, respect for authority
> and long suffering," said a seventy-year-old queenmother,
> Nana Serwaah Kwarteng, of Asante. "To me," she added, "the
> most important is the respect for authority and for chieftaincy
> in particular. In the past, the chieftaincy institution wielded
> considerable influence because citizens could be banished from
> their hometowns when they constantly erred. With the introduction
> of the White man's rule of law, who talks of banishment?
> The people are even in a hurry to leave the town already."

Two other interviewees did propose a very balanced and critical view of the institution of chieftaincy (past and present); the first one was Akwasi Emmanuel, a thirty-five-year-old Asante headmaster who declared:

Daasebre* Osei Bonsu II, Mamponghene. He is the second in command of the Asante kingdom in Ghana. He is the Hon. Ghana Country Team Leader for the Traditional Authority Applied Research Network. He was also the registrar of the Kwame Nkrumah University of Science and Technology, Kumasi, Ghana. (*traditional leader title)

"Each society needs a leader to direct its affairs. This is the reason why we enstool chiefs. A chief brings peace, he is a legislator. He solves conflicts, as soon as they surge forward. In the past he led his people to war; today problems are solved more amicably. A chief is now considered as an intermediary between his people and central government. This is how our contemporary society can develop effectively.... Unfortunately, the installation of a chief sometimes brings forth misunderstandings, disputes amongst royal families. A chief can also become an autocrat – which is dangerous; it can lead to dictatorship. Anyway, before the arrival of the Europeans, this was the system of government in our territory; it presented more advantages than disadvantages." (TAARN 2000, no. 167)

A fifty-five-year-old banker, Richard Adusei, had this to say:

"Chieftaincy is an ideal leadership. A chief is the spiritual leader of his people. He is the leader of an army. In times of war, he goes ahead of the army, he faces the battle, as the Akan proverb says: "If the royal retreats from the battle front, the servant will be nowhere." A chief is the father of his people. He is the link between the people and the gods. He is the supreme judge. A chief helps to improve his people's living conditions. As their spiritual leader, he is the intermediary between his people and the gods in times of natural disasters.... A chief brings peace and creates harmony in his society. One unfortunate thing is that chiefs are only eligible amongst royals. And it happens that when a chief is a bad ruler/leader there is nobody to replace him meaningfully. Someone else might be competent to be a chief, but because he is not of royal blood he is not eligible. This state of affairs can lead to dictatorship and to corruption on the part of kingmakers. It is at the origin of chieftaincy disputes. But on the whole I believe that chieftaincy is a good system of traditional governance." (TAARN 2000, no. 172)

CONCLUSION

To describe *all* traditional values which serve as a context for rural local government in Ghana (such as the communal way of life), would require several chapters. For the purpose of this book, and in relationship with its other chapters, it was imperative that we limited ourselves to the sole domain of chieftaincy as a traditional form of government: Who were the *ideal* chiefs in the past? Who were they supposed to be? Who are the chiefs of today? What role does the Ghana Constitution of today devolve on them and what, from the point of view of their people especially, is expected of them? Chieftaincy for the people, of the people, and by the people.

The result of this varied survey of discourses is amazing: A wonderful consensus, both in tone and accent, transpires from all those voices that we have questioned from past oral sources, or from contemporary scholars, researchers, and interviews. Chieftaincy as an institution has come to stay in a country whose modern leaders have understood that the traditional authorities remain a vital source of inspiration for the Ghanaian population. Chieftaincy can survive in glory if regenerated according to the wishes of the people over whom the chiefs rule. But chieftaincy is also likely to degenerate and, thereby, lose its moral legitimacy if the chiefs of today give in to corruption and graft, self-seeking aggrandizement, when they should be looking for the vested and time-tested interests of the people that they are supposed to represent.

In this respect, Louise Bourgeois' artistic mural statement[15] of 1999 on "The Marriage of Reason and Squalor," in the Museum of Modern Art (New York), is, it seems to us, instructive:

"HAS THE DAY INVADED THE NIGHT

OR

HAS THE NIGHT INVADED THE DAY?"

ACKNOWLEDGMENTS

This work was carried out with the aid of a grant from the International Development Research Centre (IDRC), Ottawa, Canada.

REFERENCES

Adu, A. L. (Assistant District Commissioner). 1949. *The Role of Chiefs in the Akan Social Structure: An Essay,* Accra: Government Printing Department.

Agyeman-Dua, Ivor. 2000. "Asantehene gets busy in London," *West Africa*, 29 May – 4 June.

Alleau, R. n.d. Article on "Tradition," in *Encyclopoedia Universalis*.

Ampem, Agyewodin Adu Gyamfi. 1999. *Akan Mmebusem bi*. Kumasi: University Press.

Annan, Kofi. 2000. Interview in Carola Hoyos and David Buchan, "World's lonely moral compass," *Financial Times* (London), 6 September, 7.

Arhin, Nana Kwame Brempong, D. I. Ray, and E. A. B. van Rouveroy van Niewaal, eds. 1995. *Proceedings of the Conference on the Contributions of Traditional Authority to Development, Human Rights and Environmental Protection*, Leiden, Netherlands: African Studies Centre.

Ba, Amadou Hampâté. 1995. « La tradition vivante. » In *Histoire Générale de l'Afrique*, Vol. 1, Unesco/N.E.A. (1st ed. 1980).

Balandier, Georges. 1999. « Ce que j'ai appris de l'Afrique, » Conférence Marcel Mauss, 1999, *Journal des Africanistes*, 69, no. 1.

Battestini, Simon. 1997. *Ecriture et texte – Contribution africaine*, Les Presses de l'Université de Laval / Présence africaine.

Briggs, Asa. 1992. "Culture." In Richard Baumann, ed., *Folklore, Cultural Performances, and Popular Entertainments*, Oxford: Oxford University Press.

Busia, K. A. 1951. *The Position of the Chief in the Modern Political System of Ashanti: A Study of the Influence of Contemporary Social Changes on Ashanti Political Institutions,* London: Oxford University Press.

Cauvin, Jean. 1980. *Les contes*, Issy-les-Moulineaux: Editions St. Paul.

Christaller, J. G. 1933. *Dictionnary of the Asante and the Fante Language called Tshi (Twi)* Basel Evangelical Missionary Society (1st ed., 1881).

Dadson, Frederika, and Wilhelmina Donkoh. 2000. *The Just King: The Story of Osei Tutu Kwame Asibe Bonsu,* Accra: Woeli Publishing Services.

Dolphyne, Florence, ed. 2000. *Ten Women Achievers from the Ashanti Region of Ghana*, CEDEP Women Forum. Kumasi: CEDEP.

Finkielkraut, Alain. 2000. « Le sens de l'héritage. » In *Label France*, N°38, *Ensemble vers le XXIe siècle*, Paris,January.

Krafona, Kwasi. 2000. "Globalization – The hidden dangers," *The Daily Graphic,* 21 March.

Kwaku-Akuoko. 2000. "Asanteman reborn: Otumfuo Osei Tutu's First Year on Golden Stool," *The Free Press*, 12–18 May (Part 1) and 17–23 May (Part 2).

Mazrui, Ali A., and Toby Kleban Levine, eds. 1986.*The Africans: A Reader*, New York: Praeger

Onoma-Barnes, Emmanuel. 2000. "This is disgraceful," *The Daily Graphic*, 3 April.

Owusu-Sarpong, Albert. 1998. "Literature and Political Development: Ideological Dimensions in Francophone Black/African Poetics," Professorial Inaugural Lecture, 29 May, Great Hall, KNUST, Kumasi.

Owusu-Sarpong, Christiane. 1995. "Akan Funeral Texts – Classification, interrelation and alteration of genres," paper read at the *2nd International Conference on Oral Litarature in Africa*, at the University of Ghana, Legon, 24–30 October.

Owusu-Sarpong, Christiane. 2001. *La mort akan – Etude ethnosémiotique des textes funéraires akan,* Paris: L'Harmattan.

Owusu-Sarpong, Christiane, ed. 1998 and 2001. *Trilingual Anthology of Akan Folktales*, Vol. I,Department of Book Industry, KNUST. Vol. II, Accra: Woeli Publishing Services.

Owusu-Sekyere, Ben. 2000. "Resolve Assembly, MP differences – Ashun," *The Daily Graphic*, 28 March.

Perrot, Claude-Hélène. 1999. « Un nouveau souverain à Kumasi: Royaume ashanti et pouvoir central au Ghana », *Afrique contemporaine*, 191 (July-September).

Portella, Eduardo. 2000. « Culture clonée et métissage, » *Le Courrier de l'Unesco*, April.

Rattray, R. S. 1969. *Ashanti*. Oxford: Clarendon Press (1st ed. 1923).

Ray, Donald I. 1998. "Chief-State Relations in Ghana – Divided Sovereignty and Legitimacy." In E. A. B. van Rouveroy van Nieuwaal, and Werner Zips, eds., *Sovereignty, Legitimacy, and Power in West African Societies: Perspectives from Legal Anthropology*, Hamburg: LIT.

Ray, Donald I., and E. A. B. van Rouveroy van Niewaal. 1996. "The New Relevance of Traditional Authorities in Africa: The Conference; Major Themes; Reflections on Chieftaincy in Africa; Future Directions," *Journal of Legal Pluralism,* 37–38: 1–22.

Rouveroy van Nieuwaal, van E. Adriaan B., and Werner Zips. 1998. "Political and Legal Pluralism in West Africa: Introduction and Overview." In E. A. B. van Rouveroy van Nieuwaal and Werner Zips, eds., *Sovereignty, Legitimacy, and Power in West African Societies: Perspectives from Legal Anthropology,* Hamburg: LIT.

Sarpong, Peter K. 1998. *Dear Nana: Letters to My Ancestor,* Takoradi: Franciscan Publications.

Seini, Iddrisu. 2000. "Environment holds key to survival," *The Daily Graphic,* 16 March.

TAARN. 2000. "Traditions and Traditional Values in Ghana." Two hundred interviews conducted in January 2000 for Christiane Owusu-Sarpong by a group of students of the Faculty of Social Sciences in relation to the international TAARN Project. Kumasi: KNUST.

NOTES

1. Eduardo Portella, a Brazilian philosopher and writer, was the director of Unesco from 1988 to 1993 and minister of Education in Brazil from 1979 to 1980.

2. Cf. Ali A. Mazrui's films and Mazrui and Levine 1986.

3. For an account of the conference, see Ray and van Rouveroy van Niewaal 1996. See also the edited complete collection of papers from the conference: Arhin, Ray and van Rouveroy 1995.

4. Project financed by the IDRC, Canada and coordinated by Donald I. Ray of the University of Calgary, Albert Owusu-Sarpong of the University of Kumasi, Tim Quinlan of the University of Durban–Westville, and Keshaw Sharma of the University of Botswana.

5. Cf. the multiple articles in the Ghanaian press, between 18 June and 13 July 1999, amongst which one may quote some vitriolic titles like "Mr. President, it is wrong to wave a finger at Nananom" (The *Pioneer,* 24 June 1999), "Rawlings must apologize to Asanteman" (The *Free Press,* 23–29 June 1999), "Is Ghana's unity under threat?" (The *Free Press,* 25 June – 1 July 1999), "Disrespect and contempt for Otumfuo" (The *Weekend Statesman,* 2–8 July 1999), "John, Ghanaians saw and heard it all" (The *Free Press,* 2–8 July 1999), or "Frankness or rudeness?" (The *Ghanaian Chronicle,* 12–13 July 1999). Cf. also Perrot 1999.

6. "Message from Otumfuo Osei Tutu II-Asantehene," as read and printed in the Official Programme distributed during the Banquet held at the Prempeh Assembly Hall, Kumasi, on Saturday, 6 May 2000.

7. For instance, the two-day seminar on HIV/AIDS organized jointly by the Manhyia Palace, the Ministry of Health, and the Ministry of Employment and Social Welfare; and the three-day Workshop on Land Management and Development organized by Otumfuo's Planning, Environment and Development Committee on "Chiefs: Custodians of Land, Inspiration for its sound use and Development," National House of Chiefs, both in Kumasi, in July 2000.

8. N.B. For the purpose of this chapter, we shall restrict ourselves to Akan texts, to books launched recently in Kumasi, and to a survey conducted in the Asante Region.

9. Extracts from the "History of *Mampon* in the Drum Language," in Rattray 1969.

10. K. A. Busia, *The Position of the Chief in the Modern Political System of Ashanti: A Study of the Influence of Contemporary Social Changes on Ashanti Political Institutions,* London: Oxford University Press, 1951, p. 51.

11. A. L. Adu, *The Role of Chiefs in the Akan Social Structure,* op. cit.

12. Alias Prof. Kessey, who was at the time of writing the Chairman of Council, Kwame Nkrumah University of Science and Technology, Kumasi.

13. Battestini 1997, 434: « Autour du mot, il y a les règles et le jeu de ses transformations, de ses associations dans le cadre général de la culture, de l'expérience, de l'histoire, de la psychologie de chacun et de chaque groupe humain. Cet ensemble de formes vivantes, imbriquées et dynamiques, paradoxalement libres, existe dans toutes les sociétés et pour tous les individus. Nous proposons de la nommer *texture*... ».

14. Dr. Donkoh is also a member of the IDRC-funded TAARN project.

15. Prof. Albert Owusu-Sarpong took pains to read through the text and offered a number of useful insights. For this we are grateful to him.

SOCIAL CHARACTERISTICS OF TRADITIONAL LEADERS AND PUBLIC VIEWS ON THEIR POLITICAL ROLE

CHAPTER 3

CHARLES CROTHERS

CHARLES CROTHERS is an associate professor in sociology in the School of Social Sciences, Auckland University of Technology. Earlier positions have included lecturing stints at Victoria University of Wellington and the University of Auckland and five years as professor and head of sociology at the University of Natal–Durban. Charles's academic work spans social research methods, social theory (especially the theory of social structure), history of the social sciences, social science-based policy, and the political economy and sociology of settler societies.

There is some descriptive literature on the institution of traditional leaders in South Africa, and rather more political debate about their role in society, particularly because of their critical perceived role in *delivering* the rural African vote. There is a particular link between the key role of traditional leaders in relation to the control of land and local authorities that are the level of government most concerned with land-use controls, and perhaps ownership. So it is particularly the role of traditional leaders in local government which is at issue. Indeed, much of the literature (see references) relates to the political role of traditional leaders. However, there is little information on what the social characteristics of traditional leaders are, or on how the public views them.

A CONCEPTUAL FRAMEWORK

A crucial ideological point is where traditional leaders might seem to best fit in with a modernizing *new* South Africa. To modernizing purists, traditional leaders clearly appear anachronistic: an affront to democracy and, as public administrators, producing little or nothing of economic value. Worse, since traditional leaders are securely installed without mechanisms of accountability, let alone mechanisms to encourage good performance, traditional leaders are seen as entirely beyond the pale. Even worse, since they are not supervised by any other authority, traditional leaders are open to exploit those under their control, through the charging of fees or demanding of services beyond market value for services which should be performed at cost or even free. This is especially so given the extent to which, by virtue of governmental interference in successions and appointments, the claims to legitimacy flowing from ancestry or from popular support are contestable.

However, the purist position may need to be offset by a closer examination of the full range of costs and benefits involved. By appointing traditional leaders the costs of elections are reduced, and there may be other services towards the achievement of community unity that traditional leaders perform either without recompense, or more efficiently and effectively than alternative mechanisms. The proper role of any social position cannot be determined by theoretical reflection alone, but deserves careful empirical study.

People are likely to vary in their views about the political role of traditional leaders. It is difficult to predict on theoretical grounds how respondents (and people in general) feel about the political role of traditional leaders. Presumably, as in many other areas of life, people's views are shaped by their interests and also by their ideologies. Traditional leaders are clearly barely salient for the vast range of South African citizens, except perhaps as traditional leaders impinge on people's views about how they see the new South Africa emerging.

But some variation in views will also clearly follow from the social position in which people are placed, especially in relation to traditional leaders. Those more closely linked to traditional leaders are certainly more likely to hold more intense views. Clearly, those occupying land in the dispensation of a traditional leader, and perhaps operating under the traditional leaders' surveillance, are presumably most intensely involved. If they have had bad experiences with traditional leaders or get on poorly with the present traditional leader incumbent, it is possible that they will generalize their concern into a broader negative attitude. However, it is also possible, whatever the exact content of the relationship between a particular follower and their traditional leader, that they will see their traditional leader as a representative of their broader interests as rural blacks.

Attitudes to the political role of traditional leaders may also be influenced by the class situation in which people live. If they see themselves as separated from the interests of their traditional leader, who instead represents the interests of traditional leaders in general, there will be more negative views. It is likely that many traditional leaders portray themselves as representing the interests of their constituents. It is likely, though, at least on some issues, that in practice they also (or instead) represent views which reflect their own particular interest as traditional leaders.

There is a methodological problem with the data collection. The views of most respondents may be influenced by the characteristics of interviewers, but some of those most closely tied in with traditional leaders might also feel that they are not entirely free to express their views in an interview situation, since any critical opinions might come to the notice of their traditional leader, and so they might have hedged their opinions accordingly. This point follows from the more general view that correctly tapping politically-orientated opinions in rural areas through interviews can be difficult.

With the information at hand it is not possible to adjudicate between these various considerations. However, the reader may find them useful in endeavouring to understand the broader patterns that are reported here.

THE SOCIAL CHARACTERISTICS
OF TRADITIONAL LEADERS

In the October Household Surveys (OHS) carried out annually by Statistics South Africa since 1993, some 30,000 households are visited annually. The occupations of respondents (and more generally those in responding households) are coded and in each survey some traditional leaders have been covered. Although the sample is small, I have only used results from the 1995 survey. (Further work pooling the results for several surveys would hopefully validate the findings given here.) The data allows the depiction of traditional leaders in terms of the socio-biological characteristics and also their household structures, dwelling characteristics, education, income etc. In this part of the study, I also make some general comparisons between traditional leaders and other black African households (see tables 1–3 at end of chapter).

Only thirty-two respondents who reported their occupation as a traditional leader were included in the 1995 OHS. The sample is inadequate for generalizing to the whole population of traditional leaders with any degree of accuracy, but should be of a sufficient size to indicate some of their main characteristics. Of these, two considered themselves self-employed and the remainder had their answers recorded as employees. Interestingly, there were two quite separate groupings in terms of industry. Just under one-third of respondents were involved in industry, specifically the mining industry. Others appeared to retain the more traditional involvement in agriculture. This is reflected in their locations: with the rural traditional leaders to be found in Eastern Cape, Northern Province, or KwaZulu-Natal, while the industrial traditional leaders are concentrated in Gauteng. One-sixth of traditional leaders are women: all rural. Two-thirds of the industrial traditional leaders were union members, but nearly half of the rural ones too (it is possible that the latter are involved with associations of traditional leaders). Educational qualifications were spread across a wide range, with a higher proportion of rural traditional leaders having higher qualifications. Industrial traditional leaders are slightly younger on average (forty-six compared to fifty for rural traditional leaders). Rural traditional leaders reported better incomes: some 50 per cent higher overall than industrial traditional leaders. Also, rural traditional leaders report other income sources other than wages, which helps boost their overall remuneration.

Whereas rural traditional leaders are split between those living in formal dwellings and those living in traditional dwellings, industrial traditional leaders live in hostels. Not surprisingly, most rural traditional leaders own their dwelling, although there is clearly a minority in more complex situations. Rural traditional leaders feel safer than industrial traditional leaders, although there are some rural traditional leaders who do not feel so safe. They do not seem to have been much at risk in terms of crime. While all the industrial traditional leaders are unconcerned with air pollution, some rural traditional leaders clearly see difficulties. A large proportion of rural traditional leaders report that at times during the year they have insufficient income to adequately feed their children. On the whole, traditional leaders are moderately satisfied with their lives. Rural traditional leaders are evenly divided by those who feel that their living situation is better than a year before, whereas the industrial traditional leaders tend to be considerably more optimistic.

There are several interesting points in this portrait:

- not all traditional leaders are rural/agricultural

- not all are elderly, in fact they are only slightly older than most occupational groupings

- while their pay levels are quite high compared to other black Africans, a substantial proportion receive low incomes and (at least in terms of the hunger measure) live in poverty.

PUBLIC ATTITUDES:

In the Idasa post-election survey carried out in 1995, respondents were asked their views about several aspects of the local political role of traditional leaders (see tables 4–6 at end of chapter). The six questions cover:

- the political role of traditional leaders

- whether there is a perceived conflict between tradition and democratic authority

- whether traditional leaders should be in local government

- whether traditional leaders should be awarded a seat or be required to be elected

- whether traditional leaders should be aligned to party views or not
- whether traditional leaders should take public stances or not.

The survey from which this data is garnered is of high quality (for example, its measurement of voting distribution mirrors that of the general election). The questions on traditional leaders are asked within the broad context of many questions of a political complexion. There is quite a large proportion of "don't knows" on several of the questions, which is an indication that some respondents are not familiar with the topic.

Over the whole sample, the majority (just under three-fourths) saw traditional leaders as playing a political role and one-fifth saw them as playing an important role. On whether there is a conflict between traditional and democratic authority, the sample was fairly evenly spread amongst the five response categories; except that there is a distinct bias towards emphasizing conflict, with over one-quarter perceiving serious conflict and just under 10 per cent perceiving that the two types of authority can easily go together. Some 60 per cent of the sample were supportive of traditional leaders being in local government, with similar proportions arguing that traditional leaders should run for election, and that they should not take public stances. A somewhat higher proportion (75 per cent) opposed the political alignment of traditional leaders. The broad consensus is, on the one hand, to accord traditional leaders a role in public life including in local government, but on the other hand to prescribe that role to "non-political politics" and requiring them to be elected. On the other hand, a substantial minority are prepared to accord traditional leaders a more active politically political role, and to allow them *de jure* political status.

In order to examine the pattern of views within the set of attitude items, a factor analysis was carried out. Two factors were extracted and rotated: The first four items are moderately correlated, and the last pair is strongly correlated. What do the two factors mean? The first factor contrasts those who see traditional leaders as having an important role which does not conflict with democratic authority, i.e., who should be in local government and who would be awarded a seat with those who do not see traditional leaders as having an important role; who see conflicts between traditional and democratic authorities; and who think that either traditional leaders should keep out of local government or should be made to run for their seat. The second factor tends not to be correlated with the first. It, unsurprisingly, links political alignment and taking a stance.

However, the overall public of South Africa is likely comprised of a multitude of more specific viewpoints. Presumably, it is black Africans living in rural areas for whom the issue is most salient. But before examining the views of these respondents let us compare them to those of other groupings. Respondents from each of the racegroups do not differ greatly in terms of their support of the role of traditional leaders. Black respondents are slightly more supportive and Indian respondents somewhat less supportive (coloured respondents have the highest proportion suggesting no role at all.) Rural compared to urban respondents are not dissimilar. Similarly there are few differences in views on the conflict (or lack of conflict) between the two forms of political authority, although rural dwellers are a less inclined to see a difficulty. Blacks are much more supportive of a representation of traditional leaders in local government, while coloureds and Indians are less supportive. Rural dwellers give a slight edge of approval to traditional leaders. There is a major difference in terms of the electing of traditional leaders: whereas backs are split half-and-half on this question, the other race groups are overwhelmingly in support of requiring the traditional leaders to run for office. Rural dwellers are more inclined to support awarding of seats, although over half want to see elections being required. Black Africans are least supportive of traditional leaders being aligned or taking public stances, whereas other race groups and especially whites are more relaxed about this aspect. Similarly, it is rural dwellers rather than urban dwellers who are more keen to see the wings of traditional leaders clipped. In terms of the two broad factors then, blacks (and also rural dwellers) are more supportive of the political involvement of traditional leaders, although they do not particularly stress the importance of this role or see it as less conflictual. Both blacks and rural dwellers are slightly more concerned that traditional leaders play their political role in a "non-party" political way.

In the next section I examine internal differentiation in the views of black Africans living in rural areas. There clearly are some important age differences. The youngest age-group (under twenty-five) is least supportive of an important role for traditional leaders, whereas the oldest age-group (seventy plus) is substantially more supportive. There is a slight tilt, as respondents are older, towards seeing the relationship as non-conflictual. Similarly, support for representation, for awarding rather than requiring an election, allowing alignment, and taking public stances all increase with age (although the pattern is not sharp on several of these).

It might be expected that the age-pattern of views are considerably reflected in terms of education. While this is true, with less educated people more supportive of traditional leaders whereas more educated respondents are less responsive, the differences are often not especially marked. Where more educated respondents differ most is in their emphasis on democratic criteria (running for elections) and in taking stances.

The housing and employment situations of respondents may be particularly crucial in shaping people's views. Especially in relation to housing, rural black African households may particularly be under the fairly direct control of traditional leaders.

OVERALL CONCLUSION

There is a considerable level of support for the political role of traditional leaders. This support is highest amongst sectors of the population that are clearly most likely to be more generally traditional, older, rural uneducated respondents. But even amongst these core constituencies, respondents are careful. Almost one half suggest that traditional leaders should be elected not awarded a seat, and overwhelming majorities oppose political alignment and the taking of public stances.

Table 1: Personal Characteristics of Traditional Leaders

Industry in which Employed

	Traditional	Manufacturing/ Mining
	Col %	Col %
Province		
Eastern Cape	52.7%	
KwaZulu-Natal	16.2%	
Gauteng		92.3%
Mpumalanga	4.0%	
Northern Province	27.0%	7.7%
Gender		
Male	83.6%	100.0%
Female	16.4%	
Highest Level of Education		
None	8.0%	27.6%
Std 2	3.3%	
Std 3	8.0%	
Std 4	8.0%	
Std 5	4.3%	42.4%
Std 6	16.6%	
Std 7	16.1%	30.0%
Std 8 / NTC I	4.0%	
Std 10 / NTC III	28.0%	
Std 10 and Certificate or Diploma	3.6%	
Member of Trade Union		
Yes	40.0%	62.3%
No	60.0%	37.7%

Table 2: Age and Incomes
Industry in which Employed

	Traditional	Manufacturing/Mining
	Mean	Mean
Age	50.4	46.5
Total Monthly Salary (Rand)	1,879	1,307
Monthly Income of Employee (Rand)	1,670	1,307

Table 3: Household/Dwelling Characteristics
Industry in which Employed

	Traditional	Manufacturing/Mining
	Col%	Col%
Main Type of Dwelling		
Formal dwelling/separate house	44.3%	7.7%
Traditional dwelling/hut	45.6%	
Formal dwelling in backyard of another house	10.1%	
Room in hostel or compound		92.3%
Ownership		
Single dwelling owned by household/fully paid	83.8%	7.7%
Single dwelling owned by household /partly paid	2.6%	
Dwelling owned by househol/fully paid	9.5%	
Free (co benefit)		92.3%
Free (other)	4.1%	
Physical Safety in Neighbourhood		
Very safe	41.8%	7.7%
Rather safe	42.4%	92.3%
Rather unsafe	8.4%	
Very unsafe	7.4%	
Victim of Crime		
Yes	3.3%	
No	96.7%	100.0%
Smoke and Pollution		
Very difficult	5.3%	
Difficult	15.7%	
Slightly difficult	15.1%	
Not difficult	63.9%	100.0%
Money to Feed the Children		
Yes	42.7%	
No	57.3%	100.0%
Satisfied with Life These Days		
Very satisfied	8.3%	
Satisfied	38.9%	42.4%
Neither satisfied nor dissatisfied	20.3%	57.6%
Dissatisfied	19.5%	
Very dissatisfied	13.0%	
Compared to One Year Ago		
Things better	15.6%	42.4%
Things about same	68.0%	57.6%
Things worse	16.3%	

Table 4: Questions About the Political Role of Traditional Leaders.

	Count	Col %
Q74: Role of Traditional Leaders		
No role	590	28.5%
Some role	1064	51.3%
Important role	419	20.2%
Q75: Conflict Between Traditional and Democratic Authority		
A serious conflict	559	27.3%
A minor conflict	427	20.8%
Unsure	414	20.2%
Can go together	463	22.6%
Can easily go together	189	9.2%
Q76: Preferred Role of Traditional Leaders in Local Government		
Should be in local government	1207	61.1%
Should not be in local government	768	38.9%
Q77: Should Traditional Leaders be Elected?		
Awarded a seat	716	38.5%
Run for election	1145	61.5%
Q78: Should Traditional Leaders be Aligned?		
Yes, should be aligned	507	26.4%
No, shouldn't be aligned	1413	73.6%
Q79: Traditional Leaders take Public Stances?		
Yes, should take stances	766	39.7%
No, should not take stances	1161	60.3%

Table 5: Factor Analysis

Analysis number 1

Pairwise deletion of cases with missing values

	Mean	Std Dev	Cases	Label
VAR 1540	1.91720	.69299	2073	Q74 Role of Traditional Leaders
VAR 1550	2.65687	1.33256	2052	Q75: Conflict Between Traditional and Democratic Authority
VAR 1560	1.38864	.48757	1975	Q76: Preferred of Traditional Leaders in Local Government
VAR 1570	1.61519	.48668	1861	Q77: Should Traditional Leaders be Elected?
VAR 1580	1.73576	.44104	1920	Q78: Should Traditional Leaders be Aligned?
VAR 1590	1.60265	.48948	1927	Q79: Should Traditional Leaders take Public Stances?

Correlation Matrix

	VAR 1540	VAR 1550	VAR 1560	VAR 1570	VAR 1580	VAR 1590
VAR 1540	1.00000					
VAR 1550	.32030	1.00000				
VAR 1560	−.46645	−.31284	1.00000			
VAR 1570	−.32061	−.19503	.37482	1.00000		
VAR 1580	−.04613	−.11446	.20594	.01759	1.00000	
VAR 1590	−.19567	−.09527	.29836	.02572	.55867	1.00000

Initial Statistics

Variable	Communality	Factor	Eigenvalue	% of Variance	Cumulative %
VAR 1540	1.00000	1	2.22621	37.1	37.1
VAR 1550	1.00000	2	1.39485	23.2	60.4
VAR 1560	1.00000	3	.80654	13.4	73.8
VAR 1570	1.00000	4	.67066	11.2	85.0
VAR 1580	1.00000	5	.49800	8.3	93.3
VAR 1590	1.00000	6	.40374	6.7	100.0

Factor Matrix

	Factor 1	Factor 2
VAR 1560	.78341	−.14962
VAR 1540	−.68922	.33815
VAR 1550	−.55262	.24823
VAR 1570	.52641	−.46313
VAR 1580	.47725	.73317
VAR 1590	.57201	.66669

Final Statistics

Variable	Communality	Factor	Eigen value	% of Variance	Cumulative %
VAR 1540	.58938	1	2.22621	37.1	37.1
VAR 1550	.36701	2	1.39485	23.2	60.4
VAR 1560	.63611				
VAR 1570	.49160				
VAR 1580	.76530				
VAR 1590	.77166				

Rotated Factor Matrix

	Factor 1	Factor 2
VAR 1540	−.76377	−.07766
VAR 1550	.74396	.28747
VAR 1560	.69172	−.11453
VAR 1570	−.60028	−.08170
VAR 1580	.01713	.87465
VAR 1590	.13272	.86836

Factor Transformation Matrix

	Factor 1	Factor 2
Factor 1	.84861	.52903
Factor 2	−.52903	.84861

Table 6: Political Role by Population – Group/Settlement Type

Q74 Role of Traditional Leaders

		No Role	Some Role	Important Role
		Row %	Row %	Row %
Q96 Race				
Asian	VAR1840A			
	Urban	35.6%	55.4%	9.0%
	Rural		100.0%	
Black	VAR1840A			
	Urban	33.7%	45.3%	21.0%
	Rural	23.2%	55.0%	21.8%
Coloured	VAR1840A			
	Urban	33.5%	50.2%	16.4%
	Rural	47.2%	38.5%	14.3%
White	VAR1840A			
	Urban	25.4%	54.3%	20.3%
	Rural	38.6%	47.5%	13.9%

Q75 Conflict Between Traditional and Democratic Authority

		A Serious Conflict	Minor	Unsure	Can Go Together	Can Easily Go Together
		Row %	Row %	Row %	Row %	Row %
Q96Race						
Asian	VAR1840A					
	Urban	13.9%	28.7%	38.1%	16.8%	2.4%
	Rural	100.0%				
Black	VAR1840A					
	Urban	28.3%	21.8%	20.3%	22.0%	7.6%
	Rural	24.0%	19.0%	18.1%	26.4%	12.4%
Coloured	VAR1840A					
	Urban	37.5%	18.4%	17.3%	9.9%	16.9%
	Rural	29.8%	23.1%	24.3%	9.7%	13.2%
White	VAR1840A					
	Urban	28.0%	21.7%	23.9%	22.5%	3.9%
	Rural	44.2%	25.0%	15.9%	13.5%	1.5%

Q76 Preferred Role of Traditional Leaders in Local Government

		Should be in Local Government	Should not be in Local Government
		Row %	Row %
Q96 Race			
Asian	VAR1840A		
	Urban	50.0%	50.0%
	Rural	100.0%	
Black	VAR1840A		
	Urban	59.1%	40.9%
	Rural	67.0%	33.0%
Coloured	VAR1840A		
	Urban	54.6%	45.4%
	Rural	36.5%	63.5%
White	VAR1840A		
	Urban	61.8%	38.2%
	Rural	42.3%	57.7%

Q77 Should Traditional Leaders be Elected?

		Awarded a Seat	Run for Election
		Row %	Row %
Q96 Race			
Asian	VAR1840A		
	Urban	2.7%	97.3%
	Rural	100.0%	
Black	VAR1840A		
	Urban	44.7%	55.3%
	Rural	51.4%	48.6%
Coloured	VAR1840A		
	Urban	19.5%	80.5%
	Rural	8.7%	91.3%
White	VAR1840A		
	Urban	15.9%	84.1%
	Rural	12.6%	87.4%

Q78 Should Traditional Leaders be Aligned?

		Yes, Should be Aligned	No, Should not be Aligned
		Row%	Row%
Q96 Race			
Asian	VAR1840A		
	Urban	25.6%	74.4%
	Rural		100.0%
Black	VAR1840A		
	Urban	24.6%	75.4%
	Rural	23.2%	76.8%
Coloured	VAR1840A		
	Urban	37.4%	62.6%
	Rural	26.5%	73.5%
White	VAR1840A		
	Urban	37.9%	62.1%
	Rural	27.7%	72.3%

Q79 Traditional Leaders Take Public Stances?

		Yes, Should Take Stances	No, Should not Take Stances
		Row %	Row %
Q96 Race			
Asian	VAR1840A		
	Urban	35.7%	64.3%
	Rural	100.0%	
Black	VAR1840A		
	Urban	35.9%	64.1%
	Rural	33.0%	67.0%
Coloured	VAR1840A		
	Urban	50.5%	49.5%
	Rural	40.8%	59.2%
White	VAR1840A		
	Urban	61.3%	38.7%
	Rural	51.6%	48.4%

REFERENCES

Balatseng, D.; Du Plessis, W. 1996. "Succession of Chieftaincy: Hereditary, by Appointment or by Common Consent?" *Tydskrif vir hedendaagse Romeins-Hollandse reg.* 59, no. 2: 349–55.

Barnes, J.R.; Morris, M. 1997. "KwaZulu-Natal's Rural Institutional Environment: Its Impact on Local Service Delivery." *Development Southern Africa* 14, no. 2: 185–209.

Butler, M. 1998. "Participative Democracy and Rural Local Government in KwaZulu-Natal." *Indicator South Africa* 15, no. 3: 74–77.

Cross, C. 1997. "Rural Land Tenure Reform: Surrounded by Hungry Allocators." *Indicator South Africa* 14, no. 2:72–78.

Dzingirai, V. 1994. "Politics and Ideology in Human Settlement: Getting Settled in the Sikomena Area of Chief Dobola." *Zambezia* 21, no. 2: 167–76.

Galvin, M. 1996. "Rural Local Government in KwaZulu Natal: Development Dilemma or Disaster?" *Indicator South Africa* 13, no. 4: 44–48.

Keulder, Christian. 1998. *Traditional Leaders and Local Government in Africa: Lessons for South Africa.* Pretoria: HSRC. Includes bibliographies.

Konrad-Adenauer-Stiftung. 1994. The role of traditional leaders in local government. Johannesburg: Konrad-Adenauer-Stiftung. Seminar report.

Kunene, P. 1995. "Exploring Traditional Leadership." *Agenda* 26: 35–41.

Malan, J.S. 1994. "Debat oor etnisiteit, tradisionele leierskap en grondregte in Namibie." *South African Journal of Ethnology* 17, no. 3: 91–97.

Maritz, C.J. 1994. "KODESA en die tradisionele leiers: 'n oorsig." *South African Journal of Ethnology* 17, no. 1: 1–7.

McIntosh, A. 1996. "Traditional Authorities and Land Reform in South Africa: Lessons from KwaZulu Natal." *Development Southern Africa* 13, no. 3: 339–57.

Mtimkulu, P. 1996. "Traditional Leaders and the Constitution." *Politeia* 15, no. 2: 88–91.

Munro, W.; Barnes, J. 1997. "Dilemmas of Rural Local Government in KwaZulu-Natal." *Indicator South Africa* 14, no. 3: 75–80.

Pillay, N.; Prinsloo, C. 1995. "Tradition in Transition?: Exploring the Role of Traditional Authorities." *Information Update* 5, no. 3: 7–14.

Rakate, P.K. 1997. "The Status of Traditional Courts under the Final Constitution." *Comparative and International Law Journal of Southern Africa* 30, no. 2: 175–89.

South Africa. Laws, statutes, etc.. Council of Traditional Leaders Act.

Vijfhuizen, C. 1997. "Rain-making, Political Conflicts and Gender Images: A Case from Mutema Chieftaincy in Zimbabwe." *Zambezia* 24, no. 1: 31–49.

Vink, N. 1997. "Taxing Farm Land: Local Authority Options." *Indicator South Africa* 14, no. 2: 79–83.

Vorster, L.P. 1996. "Tradisionele leierskap in Suid-Afrika." *South African Journal of Ethnology* 19, no. 2: 76–82.

GHANA: TRADITIONAL LEADERSHIP
AND RURAL LOCAL GOVERNANCE

CHAPTER 4

DONALD I. RAY

DONALD I. RAY, BA (Calgary), MA (London), PhD (Toronto), is a professor in the Department of Political Science at the University of Calgary, Calgary, Canada. Author: *Ghana: Politics, Economics and Society* and *The Dictionary of the African Left*. Co-author: *São Tomé and Principe: Politics, Economics and Society* and co-author of *The Western Canada and Papua Secessionist Movements*. Co-editor: *The New Relevance of Traditional Authorities to Africa's Future; Proceedings of the Conference on the Contribution of Traditional Authority to Development, Human Rights and Environmental Protection: Strategies for Africa; Into the 80's..African Studies (2 volumes).* He has also written chapters and articles on African politics, African studies and western Canadian separatism. His current research focuses on chief–state relations in Africa, especially Ghana. He is the international co-ordinator, Traditional Authority Applied Research Network (TAARN) and the project leader of the IDRC-funded four-country TAARN research project. In 1997, he was awarded an Overseas Research Fellowship by the South African Human Sciences Research Council. He has twice been a Guest Professor at the University of Vienna's Institute of Cultural and Social Anthropology. He was a 2000–01 Annual Fellow of the Calgary Institute for the Humanities, University of Calgary. He has been working on this IASIA project since 1998.

To understand rural local government and the place and potential of traditional leadership within it in Ghana, first one must understand the transformation of state forms from the pre-colonial period to the colonial period, and thence to the post-colonial period. The presence of what is now called traditional leadership or chieftaincy has important consequences for the concepts of the state, sovereignty, and legitimacy. In turn, these have important consequences for the involvement of traditional leaders in rural local governance in the colonial and post-colonial states.

Having addressed this set of questions, there is a need to examine certain aspects of the attempts by the post-colonial state, and the colonial state before that, to incorporate traditional leaders into certain aspects of rural (and even at times, urban) local government and governance. The most notable aspect has been the creation of the House of Chiefs system. The potential of traditional leadership for enhancing rural local government and governance can be more fully appreciated only after carrying out this analysis.

The term *traditional leader* is used to include those who are classified by their subjects as being kings and other aristocrats holding offices in polities as well as in extended families, and those in decentralized polities holding politico-religious offices. The key point here for their classification as *traditional leaders* in today's parlance, is that their office in Ghana has to date back to the pre-colonial period, so that their claims to legitimacy, and sovereignty where appropriate, pre-date the existence of the colonial state and its successor, the post-colonial state, whose claims to legitimacy and sovereignty post-date those of the pre-colonial political entities. In Ghana today, traditional leaders are termed in English as being chiefs, kings, queenmothers, paramount chiefs, divisional chiefs, etc. There are appropriate terms for traditional leaders in all of Ghana's indigenous languages. Virtually all of rural and urban inhabited Ghana falls under the jurisdiction of one traditional leader or another. The degree of authority, power, influence, or legitimacy that any one traditional leader exercises, varies according to a number of factors. Every Ghanaian is a citizen of the Republic of Ghana. Many, if not the vast majority of Ghanaians, would see themselves as being subjects of their particular chief within the context of that and associated political structures rooted in the pre-colonial polities, but they would usually feel little loyalty to chiefs belonging to another pre-colonial-rooted political entity. Support for the institutions of chieftaincy, if not always for a particular office-holder, remains strongest in Ghana's rural areas. The institution of traditional leadership is thus placed to play a unique role in rural local government and governance in Ghana.

THE EFFECTS OF TRADITIONAL LEADERSHIP ON THE CONCEPTS OF THE STATE, SOVEREIGNTY, AND LEGITIMACY

The Ghanaian case suggests that the continuing presence of traditional authority or leadership during the colonial and post-colonial eras has arguably introduced new aspects for the operation of the concepts of the state, legitimacy, and sovereignty in Ghana and possibly other states of Africa. This has implications for rural (and even urban) local government in Ghana.

A canon is a set of expectations that a certain concept or theory is accepted by most people as being *true*, that it is part of the dominant world view and, therefore, is not to be challenged.[1] There is a canon that has come to be accepted, implicitly and/or explicitly, on what a *state* is amongst many researchers and policy practitioners. This canon of the *state* is commonly used to denote a set of political structures and processes directed ultimately by one political authority (be that an individual such as a king/sovereign or a body such as Parliament) that exercises control over all the people within its territorial boundaries. For example, Watkins defines the state in one of the voices of the canon, the *International Encyclopedia of the Social Sciences* (1968, 150), as being "a geographically delimited segment of human society united by common obedience to a sovereign." A key point for the argument of this paper is that Watkins highlights the Western notion that an undivided supreme political authority or sovereign is key to the whole understanding of the *state* or *government* (in its broadest sense). He notes: "The state is a territory in which a single authority exercises sovereign powers both *de jure* (in law) and *de facto* (in life)." Watkins' view of the state in this regard is not an isolated one. Indeed, it could be argued that virtually all the authors and approaches to the study of the state who are included in Chilcote's outstanding encyclopedic 1994 survey of comparative politics, share this assumption about the state, even if they disagree on other aspects of state analysis.[2] However, as this chapter argues, this assumption needs to be revised with regard to the state in Ghana because of the continued presence of traditional authority there. In turn, this suggests that local government management and development in Ghana, and especially rural areas,[3] needs to consist not only of state structures but also somehow include traditional leaders or chiefs. However, in order to better understand these aspects of the argument, it is useful to first consider the three main historic periods of the state in Ghana, i.e., pre-colonial, colonial and post-colonial, as well as briefly outline the main governments or regimes of the post-colonial state.

Now President John Kufuor of Ghana (right) at his family house in Kumasi with Prof. Don Ray. President Kufuor is a member of one of the royal families that run the court of the Asante king (2000, photo by D. Ray).

For the present purpose, the state in what is now Ghana can be seen being manifested in three different forms that accord with three different historical periods during the nineteenth, twentieth, and twenty-first centuries. While the Ghanaian state forms share many of the same characteristics as those of the canonical conceptualization of the state, they differ in several respects; most notably in terms of the effects of the imposition of colonialism on the factors of legitimacy and sovereignty. In turn, these effects have ramifications for the operation of both the colonial state and the post-colonial state. Of especial concern to this paper are the ramifications for local government.

At the beginning of the nineteenth century, a constellation of African states and other more decentralized political entities had long existed, and in some cases they could trace their existence and/or roots back several more centuries.[4] Until the 1830s or 1840s, these African states and other political entities in what is now Ghana existed virtually free from European colonial control. European states had little control beyond the cannonballs shot from their castles, forts, and trading posts on the coast. These pre-colonial states experienced growth, ascendancy, hegemony, decline, and incorporation into other states in rather similar ways to that experienced by the European states. These pre-colonial states had their own structures and processes for exercising authority and carrying out various functions, including that of local government.

Britain had begun the process of imposing its claim to control, administer, and exercise sovereignty by the early mid-1800s. This process was carried out tentatively at first as in the Bond of 1844 which extended limited British judicial jurisdiction to some of the coastal states. After Britain's defeat of the Asante state in 1874, Britain moved decisively by means of conquest or treaty to impose its colonial state over the political authorities who, in large measure, had run the pre-colonial states in what is now Ghana. In the main the British colonial state did not extinguish these political authorities, but rather transformed them from kings into *chiefs*, otherwise called traditional authorities or traditional leaders. The leaders of the former pre-colonial states and other political entities lost certain trappings of their states – such as their own armies and foreign policies – much of their control over their legislative, administrative, executive, and judicial powers, but they retained a significant if variable amount of their authority, legitimacy, influence, power, and even elements of sovereignty into the colonial and post-colonial periods.[5] These chiefs or traditional leaders may have lost power at the *national* or state-level, but in many cases they have remained influential at the local and regional levels, especially in the rural areas. Hence, one of the major questions of local government policy that the colonial state and its successor post-colonial state have faced has been how, if at all, chiefs or traditional leaders should be incorporated into the new structures and processes of local government.

The British colonial state in Ghana was fundamentally transformed after 1951 when nationalist forces led by Kwame Nkrumah's Convention Peoples' Party (CPP) shared power within the colonial state after the Nkrumah 1951 electoral victory. This sharing ended in 1957 when the British state handed over total colonial state control to Ghanaians who transformed this after independence into the Ghanaian post-colonial state. Despite the opposition of certain key traditional leaders to Nkrumah, he and subsequent regimes did not abolish chieftaincy.[6] Rather, the governments of the post-colonial state, following the predecessors of the colonial state, have sought to find the optimum relationship with traditional authority, often by adjusting formally the governmental powers and authority that the post-colonial state believed it was granting to the traditional leaders. These adjustments were formally manifested through a variety of legislative and constitutional instruments ranging from ordinances and laws to constitutions. Also, the post-colonial state in Ghana has attempted in part to incorporate traditional leaders by creating the Houses of Chiefs system which operates from the national or state level through to the regions and localities.

In order to understand the legislative and constitutional context of the various post-colonial governments, it is necessary to list these governments. These governments generated the legislative and constitutional instruments that the state used in its attempts to control traditional leaders, including their participation in rural and urban local government. Prime minister and later President Kwame Nkrumah's CPP rule included the dyarchy[7] of the colonial period (1951–57) as well as his post-colonial governments (including the First Republic, 1960–66). He was overthrown in 1966 by the military-based National Liberation Council (NLC) which handed over power in 1969 to the Second Republic, which in turn lasted until it was overthrown by the military in 1972. A series of military-led governments, including the National Redemption Council (NRC, 1972–75), the Supreme Military Council (SMC, 1975–79), and the Armed Forces Revolutionary Council (AFRC, June–September, 1979) then ruled Ghana before handing over to the Third Republic (1979–81). It was overthrown by the Provisional National Defence Council (PNDC, 1982–93) which in turn handed over to the Fourth Republic (1993–present).[8]

Political legitimacy deals with the reasons that people are expected to obey political authority, especially that of government. As Foucault (1980), Connolly (1987), Baynes (1993), and others have noted, political legitimacy is an important mechanism of the state to obtain the compliance of its citizens (or subjects) with the laws (or other wishes) of the state. Force can be used by a state (or government) to compel obedience or compliance from its people, be they citizens or subjects, but in the long run this is often an expensive and even ineffective strategy for the state. Drawing upon the European experience, Foucault (1980) argued that the modern state relies much more on hegemonic legitimacy strategies to convince its people that they should willingly obey its laws. Thus, certain lines of argument or knowledge are encouraged by the state and others may not only be discouraged but even be suppressed, so that a certain legitimacy of the state is created by the agreement of people to rule and be ruled in certain ways under certain conditions. One might go further and argue that when the state's canon of political legitimacy breaks down, riots, revolts, and revolutions begin. Thus, it would seem, at least in utilitarian terms, that the best interests of democratic government and people would be served if the political legitimacy of governments, including local government, could be expanded so as to create the conditions for democratic development. Such a political culture must be concerned with creating and enhancing the structures, processes, and values that promote both people and the various communities to which they see themselves belonging. Moreover, given the existence of political legitimacy roots going back to the pre-colonial, colonial, and post-colonial periods, people today may see themselves belonging simultaneously to a community rooted in the newly independent state as well as belonging to another type of community, one rooted in traditional authority.

A key point in the discussion of democratic political legitimacy should be that people have the ability to give or withdraw their consent to be governed, and that governments and other governing and decision-making structures honour the decisions of the people.[9] Agreement with this does not necessarily bind us to one universal application of democratic political legitimacy, to one particular set of structures or even processes. For example, while there is now broad agreement that multi-party elections at the level of national, central, or federal government are usually one of the expressions of democratic political legitimacy, these views are not shared by all democratic countries when it comes to local government. Some countries such as Canada and Ghana have opted for non-party elections for local government on either an informal basis (e.g., Canada) or on a formal basis (e.g., Ghana). Others such as the U.K. and South Africa have accepted multi-party local government elections. Such differences in political culture and the expression of political legitimacy are, in large measure then, differences of the history and cultural context for each of these countries, rather than any corruption of some mythical *one true* expression of democracy. Hence, while there can be a broad agreement on a core set of criteria by which the presence or absence of democracy can be determined (e.g., government legitimately elected, etc.), historical and cultural variations are possible in how that democracy (including political legitimacy) is expressed and experienced.

Democracy incorporates and accepts (indeed perhaps depends upon) diversity, difference, and plurality. This is a key point to recognize in this present analysis of traditional leadership and local government, because traditional leadership/traditional authority and the contemporary state now have different bases of legitimacy. These differences could be, and have been, interpreted as proof that traditional leadership/authority is totally incompatible with contemporary democratic government. If such an argument were extended to local government, then the participation of traditional leadership in democratic local government could be seen as being undesirable. Such an argument, in my view, does not take into account the complexity and specific cultural context of a number of democratic post-colonial states in Africa and elsewhere. Any discussion of the desirability and possibility of the participation of traditional leadership/authority in democratic local government and governance, has first to examine these different bases of legitimacy.

Legitimacy can be based on different arguments (or logics), and these can vary over time[10] between and within cultural and historical contexts. So for example, the legitimacy of the contemporary (or post-colonial) state in Africa derives primarily from three sources, all of which are secular: the nationalist struggle for independence; democracy; and constitutional legality.[11] Constitutional legality can derive from the post-colonial or colonial period in degrees that vary from state to state. In one sense, the contemporary African states are the successors to the colonial states created by the European imperialist powers of the nineteenth and twentieth centuries, just as the United States and Canada can be seen as post-colonial states to Great Britain's colonies in North America. The post-colonial state inherited and has to deal in one way or another with a considerable amount of constitutional and legislative instruments from the colonial state period.[12] In this sense, at least in the initial period of independence, the post-colonial state is usually the successor to the colonial state. Much of the colonial state's legislative and constitutional framework continues to influence that of the post-colonial state in either positive or negative ways. Thus, the post-colonial state demands obedience to those aspects of the colonial laws and constitutional framework that it deems acceptable because these are seen to be acceptable or legitimate in legal and/or constitutional terms.[13] In short, whatever evaluation of the colonial state the post-colonial state might have, it may continue to accept a particular law or constitutional measure or principle on its own legal merit. Legality, thus, may be the legitimacy basis of the continued usage of a colonial measure, even if the colonial state period as a whole has reduced or no legitimacy in the eyes of the post-colonial state and its citizens because of the lack of democracy that imperial or colonial rule means.[14] The post-colonial state also uses the legal system to legitimate its behaviour. Appeals by government are made to the citizenry to be "law-abiding."

The post-colonial state could also appeal to democracy and the nationalist struggle for independence as two more primary-level bases of its legitimation. Of course, this assumes that the post-colonial state represents itself as the democratic result of the nationalist struggle for independence. This could be seen as a mechanism by which the post-colonial state distances itself from the essentially undemocratic past of the colonial state. Sometimes military coups and governments have shrunk the *democratic* legitimacy of the post-colonial state to only that of the achievement of independence and legality. However, where the democratic content of the post-colonial state has been preserved or re-invented, the post-colonial state is able to base its claims to legitimacy on having its government *duly* elected by their people.

All of these democratic claims by the post-colonial states are ultimately rooted in the concept and practice that the citizens really do have the ability to select and to change their governmental leaders through elections held at specified intervals. To expand on a point made earlier, while this particular conception is now widely held throughout much of the world as being the core meaning of democracy, there is considerable debate on how to put democracy into practice. Should the times between elections be fixed (e.g., every four years?) or flexible (e.g., no more than five years apart)? Which governmental leaders should be elected and which should be appointed: executive? legislative? judicial? administrative? or military? There are considerable differences amongst the democracies on these basic questions of democratic legitimation. Should traditional leaders be added to this list of categories of government leaders[15] who might be elected in order to ensure their legitimacy in the contemporary democratic state including local government, or is there a legitimate case for chiefs not to be elected by every citizen?

A significant part of the answer to this question lies within the nature of the legitimacy of traditional authority. Two key points need to be made about the bases of the claims to political legitimacy by traditional leadership in the era of the post-colonial democratic state. First, such legitimacy claims by traditional leaders are in very large measure (if not entirely) different from those of the state itself. Second, the traditional leaders' legitimacy potentially could be added to the legitimacy *pool* of the contemporary state, especially for matters of local governance and development.

This is a point that was and/or has not been lost on a number of colonial and post-colonial states.

Traditional leaders have three distinct claims to legitimacy in the contemporary era. First, traditional leaders can claim to be the carriers of political authority and legitimacy that is derived from the pre-colonial period. Traditional leaders occupy structures supported by constitutions and laws[16] that, while they may have changed in varying degrees by the colonial and post-colonial states, still retain a core of customary legitimacy that predates the imposition of colonialism. In other words, traditional leaders have a special historical claim to pre-colonial roots; i.e., the first period of African independence before it was lost to colonialism (primarily during the 1800s). Traditional leaders can point to the antiquity of their particular office and make the argument that since it was founded (either directly or indirectly through an office that was pre-colonial) in the pre-colonial period, their particular *traditional* authority represents those indigenous, truly African values and authority that existed before the changes imposed by the colonial system began to take effect.[17]

Such customary constitutions of traditional leadership may be seen as the constitutions of the grassroots, i.e., of the local-level rural and often urban people. These customary constitutions form part of rural and often urban local governance that people encounter as they grow up, perhaps even before they engage with the rural local government of the post-colonial state. Traditional leadership and its customary constitutions is the form of rural local governance in which the vast majority of rural Ghanaians are first politically socialised, and thus imbibe their first political values.

The second distinct claim to legitimacy by traditional leaders in the post-colonial democratic state is that based on religion. To be a traditional leader is to have one's authority, one's power legitimated by links to the divine, whether the sacred be a god, a spirit, or the ancestors. For a traditional leader to function, that office must maintain and demonstrate its link to the divine. In Africa, the divine basis of traditional legitimacy pre-dates the imposition of colonialism. This timing thereby reinforces the other distinct basis of legitimacy for traditional leaders. In much of Africa, these religious beliefs were established before the introduction of Islam and Christianity, but in some cases these later religions have been added to, or superseded, the earlier religious beliefs. If one distinguishes between states in which a religion is present as a system of belief and one in which the state has formally adopted the religion as part of its legitimacy, then there are few states in Africa that have state religions and, thus, the differences in the bases of legitimacy which were argued above hold. It should be added, that the absence or presence of any religion does not detract from the ability of a state to be democratic.

The third distinct claim to legitimacy by traditional leaders is that of pre-colonial-rooted culture. The historical and religious legitimacy claims[18] can be interpreted as contributing to the view that traditional authority and leadership has deep roots in indigenous culture. Traditional leaders thus may be seen as the *fathers* and *mothers* of the people. Traditional leaders use regalia, dance, ceremony, music, cloth, etc., to display physically their cultural legitimacy. Traditional leaders may be recognized, as they are in Ghana, as very significant transmitters of culture by their peoples, themselves, and by the state.

There are thus, it is argued, two different sets of roots of legitimacy present within a contemporary post-colonial state such as Ghana. The legitimacy roots of the traditional authorities pre-date those of the colonial and post-colonial states and were not incorporated to any significant degree into the sovereignty claims of the colonial and post-colonial states. As will be seen in the next section, at best these states have been ambiguous as to what degree this differently-rooted legitimacy (and hence also sovereignty[19]) could or should be mobilized or co-opted in aid of the goals of the colonial and post-colonial states. It would appear that legitimacy, sovereignty, power, authority, and influence may be divided in post-colonial states containing traditional authorities. While the overwhelming share of sovereignty, power, and authority is held by the Ghanaian post-colonial state, traditional leaders hold (figuratively), significant amounts and types of legitimacy, authority, and influence. There has been perhaps some recognition in these states by their leaders that they are dealing with states having not just one ultimate source of sovereignty, but rather states which have two different-rooted, asymmetrical sources of sovereignty. If the two different sets of roots (i.e., sources of legitimacy) are seen as being capable of producing different genes or characteristics, then it is possible to conceive of the different roots producing a stronger, more productive tree. If rural local development is imagined to be a tree, then it needs a combination of rural local government and traditional leadership for a stronger rural local governance.

If legitimacy is not seen as a zero-sum, winner-take-all situation, then the different bases of legitimacy that the state and traditional leaders have need not be an obstacle to the achievement of development and democratization by rural local and central/national governments of African post-colonial states. Where there is little co-operation, little co-ordination, and little recognition of the differing bases of legitimacy between the local government of the state and traditional leaders, rural local government itself will carry out its policies and projects as best it can, often without all of the desired or even necessary resources. However, if there is a strategy of adding the legitimacy resources that traditional leaders have to those of the state's rural local government, then it should be possible to mobilize more quickly the compliance, co-operation, and other resources of those people who are both citizens of the state and subjects of the traditional leader with local government. Of course, this strategy will only apply to people who believe in the legitimacy of the traditional leader. From a rural local government policy management perspective, the issue here is not whether people accept the legitimacy of local government, but rather how the addition of legitimacy resources from traditional leaders may increase the compliance and enthusiasm of people for legitimate development projects and policies, thereby increasing the capacity of rural local government in promoting development as well as increasing the cultural fit of democratic local government structures amongst the peoples of African states.

RURAL LOCAL GOVERNANCE AND TRADITIONAL LEADERSHIP UNDER THE COLONIAL STATE AND POST-COLONIAL STATE IN GHANA

In Ghana, the relationship between both the colonial and post-colonial states and traditional leadership with regard to rural local and other government has been uneasy and ambiguous, but it is one in which the state has expressed a constant political and policy interest since the imposition of colonialism, and again since independence. Four ways of measuring this rural local governance relationship will be used in this chapter. First, there is the recognition that traditional leadership formed a layer of government that the colonial state found in place and with which the post-colonial state then had to manage its relations. Thus the first issue, and a continuing issue at that, has been how first the colonial state and then the post-colonial state has attempted to regulate the exercise of authority and power by traditional leaders. The second and third measures concern local government administration and finance. Fourthly, the Houses of Chiefs system is the latest significant policy initiative of the Ghanaian post-colonial state to manage its relations with traditional leaders at the levels of rural and urban local government.

The underlying political canon of the state is revealed by legislative and constitutional instruments (ranging from ordinances to laws to constitutions): these represent formal manifestations of political power shifts. Thus, the analysis of legislative and constitutional instruments can, therefore, illuminate the dynamics of political relationships between both the colonial state and the post-colonial state and traditional leaders with regard to rural local governance.

The creation of the British colonial state in what is now Ghana was uneven and complex. Although there had been a European presence in southern Ghana from the late fifteenth century (an area known then as the Gold Coast), the process of British colonization did not seriously start until 1874. At that time a British Order in Council created the Gold Coast Colony.[20] In 1901, following a war with the Asante, the British formally extended northwards their colonial control of Ghana to what became known as the Ashanti Protectorate and the Northern Territories.[21] In 1922, British administration of the area known as British Togoland was formally recognized by the League of Nations.[22] Complete British colonial rule was maintained over these territories until a system of dyarchy (or joint rule) between the British colonial state and Kwame Nkrumah's nationalist Convention People's Party (CPP) was started in 1951. Britain formally withdrew in 1957, handing over its former colonial state to the Ghanaians who made it into a post-colonial state.

RURAL LOCAL GOVERNANCE AND TRADITIONAL LEADERSHIP: DETERMINING THE AUTHORITY TO GOVERN

A central problem that the colonial and post-colonial states had with regard to traditional leaders, has been how to handle the issue of determining what authority to recognize for them in local governance. The pre-colonial states had their own structures and processes for determining who was recruited to political office and how that authority was to be exercised. Such structures and processes also included explicit customs outlining in what circumstances an office-holder (or "chief[23]") could lose his recognized leadership status; subjects did not hesitate to initiate "destoolment proceedings against a chief to impeach and remove him or her if their actions were not acceptable under customary law (Arhin 1985; Hailey 1938; Ward 1948). However, the question of recognition of traditional leadership in rural local and other government has long proved difficult and attention-demanding upon those who have controlled the colonial and post-colonial states. It is an important one because it involves the state in attempting to articulate its legitimacy claims to govern with those of the traditional leaders whose legitimacy claims exist outside the control of the state.

Prior to 1874, Britain had been not very concerned with rural local government in those small territories on the coast that it controlled. For example, in one case the British empire did allow one of its officials to act as a judicial assessor in the territories of the Fante and other pre-colonial states that signed the Bond of 1844 with Britain. However, this was restricted to judicial practice, applying British legal practice in those territories for serious cases. While this marked to some degree the extension of the British colonial state into the rural local government of these pre-colonial states, Britain did not see this as an extension of British sovereignty over these pre-colonial states (Ward 1948, 186–87). Thus, the issue of the colonizing state extending its authority to determine the political status of the leaders of these pre-colonial states, did not arise as a central policy question until the 1870s.

From the 1870s onwards to the end of the First World War, Britain set about establishing the British colonial state in what is now Ghana, spurred on by imperial competition for colonies and the attacks against the Asante kingdom in 1873–74, 1896 and 1900. In 1874, Britain incorporated much of southern Ghana (i.e., along the coast and somewhat into the interior) into the British colonial state as the Gold Coast Colony. Britain then sought to exert its overall control over the area, but allowed considerable autonomy to the now-traditional leaders in the exercise of rural local government. The 1878 Native Jurisdiction Ordinance (Gold Coast Colony)[24] and the 1883 Gold Coast Native Jurisdiction Ordinance were examples of the colonial state's legislative attempts to control the jurisdiction of traditional leaders in the Gold Coast Colony and to influence, but not necessarily to determine, in the first instance, the selection and removal of traditional leaders. According to section 29 of the 1883 Gold Coast Native Jurisdiction Ordinance, the Governor-in-Council could suspend or dismiss a chief if he proved incompetent or unsatisfactory to the colonial state. However, traditional leaders were not compelled to seek recognition from the governor before they could exercise their jurisdiction, which was mainly in rural areas. Lord Hailey argued that this distinction seems "to recognize that the right of jurisdiction was inherent in the chief, though the extent of its exercise might be subject to regulation" (Hailey 1938, 468). The colonial state thus recognized that traditional leaders had their own source of authority and were not mere creations of the colonial state. These ordinances were evidence that the colonial state recognized that in the Gold Coast Colony if the British colonial state was to govern most effectively in its own terms of minimizing expenditures and maximizing colonial state control,[25] then it must recognize the autonomous legitimacy and authority of traditional leaders, especially in rural local government where traditional leaders already had their institutions covering the ground.[26] While the British colonial state had made bold claims for the extension of its sovereignty in its 1874 Order in Council, when it came to the Native Jurisdiction Ordinances of 1878 and 1883 the British colonial state was more circumspect in implementing its claims to sovereignty in the case of recognizing or withdrawing its recognition of traditional leaders; under the 1883 Ordinance, the colonial state limited itself to the power of removing traditional leaders. How people become a traditional leader or chief was something conceded to the realm of traditional leadership. This does seem to suggest that the British colonial state implicitly recognized that some elements of legitimacy, authority, and even sovereignty still accrued to the traditional leaders.

The 1904 Chiefs' Ordinance was designed to enhance the authority of traditional leaders in the Gold Coast by having the governor officially recognize them as chiefs. This measure was optional and was not necessary for a traditional leader to act as a chief. It was designed to enable traditional leaders to enforce the laws of the colonial state (Hailey 1938, 470). When the 1927 Native Administration Ordinance (Gold Coast Colony) replaced the 1883 ordinance, the colonial state once more did not make recognition by itself a mandatory pre-condition to the exercise of authority and power by a traditional leader in the Gold Coast Colony.

While many of the traditional leaders of what became the Gold Coast Colony (i.e., the areas to the south of the core of the Asante kingdom) had been allies of the British in a series of wars against the Asante from the 1820s to 1901, the Asante kingdom had repeatedly fought the British Empire and its colonial state. In fact the British governor, Sir Charles MacCarthy, literally lost his head in defeat to the Asante army at the Battle of Asamankow on 21 January 1824. The British colonial state perceived the Asante kingdom to be a threat even as the British Empire defeated the Asante kingdom in 1874, 1896, and 1900–01. Even as late as the early 1920s, the British Imperial General Staff sent enquiries to the Northern Territories as to whether there were any Asantes who were likely to rise in rebellion. This perception of threat to the British colonial state by the Asante kingdom may well explain, *inter alia,* the harsher control exercised by the British colonial state over Asante traditional leaders compared to those exercised over the traditional leaders in the coast who had been allies of the British. After defeating the Asante in 1896, the British Empire exiled the Asante king and his court, eventually to the Seychelles Islands which are right across Africa and well across the Indian Ocean. In 1901, the British colonial state annexed the Asante kingdom. Finally in 1924, the British Empire allowed the Asante king, Prempeh I, to return to his former capital Kumasi, not as king but only nominally as the paramount chief of Kumasi. Only in 1935 did the British colonial state formally allow the restoration of the office of the Asante king – the Asantehene – and the creation of a form of the Asante kingdom.

Before this restoration and its reflection of confidence by the British colonial state in its overall ability to control Asante traditional leaders, the British colonial state closely regulated the ability of Asante traditional leaders to govern. The 1902 Ashanti Administration Ordinance stated that a traditional leader could not act as a chief until the governor had granted formal recognition to him. Contrary to the legislative instruments used in the Gold Coast Colony, in the Ashanti Protectorate security concerns seem to have made jurisdiction inherent not in the traditional leaders but in the colonial state. The colonial state went further and selected pro-British candidates as traditional leaders, even though these people were not customarily eligible for these offices (Busia 1951, 105). The Asante responded in 1905 with a campaign to destool or remove traditional leaders not considered to be legitimately selected according to custom, or who did not follow legitimate, customary law in their rule. The colonial state forced people to support those uncustomary traditional leaders, even to the extent of fining some and deporting others (Busia 1951, 105–6). This policy continued with the colonial state's 1924 Native Jurisdiction Ordinance (Ashanti). While section 2 stated that a traditional leader was to be "a person elected and installed in accordance with native customary law," the newly installed traditional leader still had to be recognized by the colonial state before he could exercise his powers and authority. Furthermore, the colonial state still refused to recognize Prempeh I as being king.

The colonial state's policy of exercising direct control over traditional leaders and hence much of rural local governance in colonial Ghana, spread from the Ashanti Protectorate to all parts of colonial Ghana during the 1920s through to the last stages of colonialism. Indeed, this policy continued into the post-colonial period until the inauguration of Ghana's Third Republic in 1979. The 1932 Native Authority Ordinance for the Northern Territories and the Northern Section of Togoland as well as the 1932 Native Administration Ordinance for the Southern Section of Togoland, again specified that traditional leaders were to be selected according to custom, but that they were not to act as chiefs until they had been recognized by the governor (Hailey 1938, 476–79). Likewise, the 1935 Native Authority (Ashanti) Ordinance stated that the Asante king and all other traditional leaders were to be selected and enstooled according to custom, but had to wait for the governor's confirmation before they could exercise their jurisdiction. While this ordinance marked the restoration of the office of the Asante king, the Asantehene, and the limited restoration of the Asante kingdom, the ordinance also noted that the governor could withdraw recognition at any time (Busia 1951). The 1944 Native Authority Ordinance (Gold Coast Colony) also required that the traditional leaders in the Gold Coast Colony on the coast had to be selected and inaugurated according to custom, but that they could not exercise their *Native Authority* jurisdiction until they had been recognized by the governor, and only if the traditional leader acted in conformity with the policies of the colonial state. Like the 1935 Ashanti ordinance, the 1944 Gold Coast Colony ordinance also allowed the colonial state – in the form of the governor – to withdraw recognition of a traditional leader acting as a Native Authority at any time (Hailey 1938, 341).

During this time at the height of indirect rule, to be a recognized traditional leader acting within the framework of the Native Authorities of the colonial state meant that such a traditional leader controlled and administered a significant amount of rural local government: courts, police, jails, treasuries, local market regulation, administrative fees, local roads, cemeteries, and all manner of other local matters. All of this rural local government by traditional leaders was supervised by the colonial state. This pattern of control over traditional leaders acting as agents of rural local government continued in the last period of British-only colonial rule[27] and into the dyarchy period of the colonial state when the British were increasingly sharing colonial state power with Kwame Nkrumah, his Convention Peoples' Party, and the other nationalists. During this latter period, Nkrumah as prime minister kept this policy of control over traditional leaders acting within the colonial state while he reduced their formal powers in local government,[28] but he did not eliminate the offices of traditional leaders nor did he remove them from other aspects of rural local governance and, in fact, he helped create new institutions such as the Regional Houses of Chiefs[29] for traditional leaders at independence which have been continued and expanded throughout the post-colonial period.

After independence in 1957, Nkrumah's government continued the colonial state's policy of implicitly conceding that traditional leaders had independent claims to legitimacy, but that the state needed to control them. For example, the First Republic's 1961 Chieftaincy Act provided that a traditional leader was not legally a chief until he was so recognized by the local government minister by having the chief's name entered on the chiefs list of the minister. The minister could revoke such recognition at any time if the minister deemed it to be "in the public interest." The 1963 Chieftaincy (Amendment) Act further strengthened the hand of the post-colonial state in dealing with traditional leaders. The minister had absolute discretion in referring any chieftaincy question to the judicial commissioner, even if it meant withdrawing it from an ongoing consideration by a rural or urban Traditional Council.[30] The Nkrumah governments realized the importance of controlling traditional leaders, who they were and what they could be allowed to do by the post-colonial state because they had seen how some key Asante and some other traditional leaders had supported another electoral party that challenged the Nkrumahists for control of the post-colonial state, and also because the Nkrumah governments realized the support that the traditional leaders had, especially in the rural areas (Andoh 1987; Rathbone 2000).

The military government which overthrew the First Republic in 1966, the National Liberation Council, withdrew recognition from a number of chiefs that had been recognized by the government of the First Republic, alleging that they had been created in non-customary ways (Ray 1996). The civilian government of the Second Republic (1969–72) that followed in 1969 continued to intervene in the determination of traditional authority status. Although Art. 153 of the constitution of the Second Republic of Ghana (1969) indicated that "the institution of chieftaincy together with its Traditional Councils as established by customary law and usage is hereby guaranteed," section 48 of the subsequent 1971 Chieftaincy Act added two qualifications. First, a person was not recognized as a chief until his name appeared on the newly created National Register of Chiefs that was to be maintained by the National House of Chiefs. The second condition was that a person could not carry out any functions of a chief until he was recognized by the Minister. Moreover, section 52 of the Act allowed the Minister "in the interests of public order" to prohibit by executive instrument any person exercising the functions of a chief if he was not considered a chief in the eyes of the state, direct such person to move out of the area, and even prohibit other persons from treating him as a chief. In 1972, the next military government issued the National Redemption Council (Establishment) Proclamation, 1972, which suspended the 1969 constitution but kept in force and effect the 1971 Chieftaincy Act (Article 23).

The post-colonial state's attempts to claim final sovereignty and inherent jurisdiction are not surprising. First, as has been earlier stated in this chapter, the post-colonial state inherited the constitutional framework of the later colonial state, a framework that was intrinsically western in scope and which recognized a supreme political authority – that of the state. Moreover, having inherited a framework that gave the newly independent state "ultimate" control, there seems little reason to expect that the state would voluntarily "share" its new sovereignty. Finally, and especially in the case of Nkrumah's nationalist government, the institution of chieftaincy was not only considered undemocratic, but many traditional leaders were as well viewed as the willing partners of the previous colonial state.

The Third Republic (1979–81), however, produced a marked policy shift in the area of the determination of traditional authority status. ARTICLE 177 of the constitution not only guaranteed the institution of chieftaincy but also stipulated that Parliament did not have the power to confirm or withdraw recognition from a traditional leader. The power was instead conferred on the Houses of Chiefs system which was to act in accordance with customary law and usage, and the Supreme Court which could with leave hear matters under appeal from the National House of Chiefs.

This policy shift was maintained during the Third Republic and the first few years of the Provisional National Defence Council rule (1981–93) but was changed in 1985 in response to the increasing number of violent chieftaincy disputes (Ray 1996, 62). The Chieftaincy (Amendment) law, 1985 (P.N.D.C.L. 107), stipulated that state recognition by way of a notice published in the Local Government Bulletin was necessary for a person to be deemed a chief. This was followed by the 1987 Chieftaincy (Membership of Regional Houses of Chiefs) (Amendment) Instrument (L.I. 1348) which authorized and recognized the establishment of new paramount chiefs in the Brong-Ahafo Region and their inclusion into the Regional House of Chiefs, and the 1989 Chieftaincy (Specified Areas) (Prohibition and Abatement of Chieftaincy Proceedings) Law (P.N.D.C.L. 212) which "in the interest of peace and public order" prohibited any type of proceedings in the matter of nomination, election, enstoolment or recognition relating to specified chiefs in specified areas.

The constitution of the Fourth Republic (1992), written by the Consultative Assembly which contained many chiefs and persons eligible to become chiefs, resembled the constitution of the Third Republic in the area of determination of traditional authority status, (Ray 1996, 63). Like the 1979 constitution, ART. 270 of the 1992 constitution stipulates that Parliament cannot interfere in the recognition process of chiefs; this power is conferred on the House of Chiefs system and the Supreme Court which can hear matters under appeal from the National House of Chiefs. The same article indicates that the "institution of chieftaincy, together with its traditional councils as established by customary law and usage is hereby guaranteed." Persons convicted of high treason, high crime, offences against the security of the state, fraud, dishonesty or moral turpitude are disqualified from becoming chiefs (ART. 275), but in all other aspects the eligibility requirements of a chief are rooted in tradition. ARTICLE 277 defines a chief as "a person, who, hailing from the appropriate family and lineage, has been validly nominated, elected or selected and enstooled, enskinned or installed as a chief or queenmother in accordance with the relevant customary law and usage."

As has been argued elsewhere (Ray 1996, 64) the wording of the guarantee of the institution of chieftaincy in the constitutions of the Third and Fourth Republics, reveals the state's realization that chiefly legitimation is rooted outside the former colonial state and the contemporary post-colonial state. "Customary law and usage," not the state's directives, legitimates the system of chiefly offices. Moreover, the number of constitutional and legislative instruments produced by the state over the colonial and post-colonial periods in an effort to control (or at least influence) the determination of traditional authority status is an indicator that state leaders knew that they lacked unchallenged authority and legitimacy with regard to rural local government and other aspects of the state.

RURAL LOCAL GOVERNANCE AND TRADITIONAL LEADERSHIP: LOCAL GOVERNMENT ADMINISTRATION

Traditional leaders have been involved in rural and urban local government right from the start of the colonial state through to the present in the post-colonial state. The degree and nature of that involvement of traditional leaders in rural and urban local government has varied considerably, but it has continued.

The 1883 Native Jurisdiction Ordinance (Gold Coast Colony) of the colonial state allowed paramount chiefs, or headchiefs as they were then termed, and their councils to have the option of making bylaws dealing with such local government functions as the building and maintenance of roads, forest conservation, the prevention and abatement of nuisances, the provision of burial grounds, and the regulation of burials. The governor had the ability to disallow bylaws not in keeping with the colonial state's laws and policies. Traditional leaders were given the right to fine or imprison those of their subjects who broke the allowed bylaws.

The bylaw powers of the paramount chiefs were expanded by the 1927 Native Administration Ordinance for the Gold Coast Colony. This time no limits were put on the local government subject matter of the bylaws to be made by the chiefs as long as they were consistent with the laws and policies of the colonial state. The ability of the paramount chiefs to enforce these bylaws was reinforced as they now were able to operate their own Native State prisons.[31] The utilization of traditional leadership in rural local government during this early colonial period reflected not only a recognition of the legitimacy of traditional leaders, but also the financial benefits to be gained by minimizing the number of colonial administrators by substituting the already existing governing institutions of traditional leadership and the expectation that traditional leaders could use bylaws, etc., to force their subjects to engage in compulsory, unpaid labour to construct and maintain roads needed by the colonial state.[32]

Partially elected urban government with limited chiefly participation on the Town Council was proposed by the colonial state for the coastal Gold Coast Colony in the 1924 Municipal Corporations Ordinance. The colonial state dropped this ordinance "… as it was felt by many that an elected mayor would be a dangerous rival to the head chief, and that relationships between the Town Council and the tribal authorities would be very complicated and difficult" (Ward 1948, 323).

The British colonial state's initial suspicion of the Asante after the 1900–01 Yaa Asantewaa uprising was also reflected in the more limited nature of what was accorded to traditional leaders in the Ashanti Protectorate compared to the Gold Coast Colony. The colonial state under the provisions of the 1902 Ashanti Administration Ordinance did not allow traditional leaders to pass bylaws, rather it compelled traditional leaders to perform such local government functions as road construction and maintenance and enforcing sanitary rules in villages. Traditional leaders could fine and otherwise compel their subjects to follow these rules and regulations. The 1909 Ashanti Cemeteries Ordinance compelled traditional leaders, under penalty of fines, to create and maintain cemeteries. By 1924, the colonial state's suspicions of Asante chiefs was ebbing. Under the 1924 Native Jurisdiction Ordinance (Ashanti), headchiefs, later known as paramount chiefs, with their councils were given the jurisdiction to make bylaws and maintain prisons, subject to colonial supervision and approval. The 1925 Kumasi Public Health Board Ordinance was established to regulate public health matters in what was and is the *de facto* capital of the Asante kingdom. The Kumasi Council of Chiefs nominated two of the ten board members. The other members were five from the colonial administration, two members of British colonial interests and a non-Asante African.

The 1930s and 1940s saw the colonial state continue to grant more local government powers to traditional leaders through the 1932 Native Authority Ordinance (Northern Territories and the Northern Section of Togoland), the 1932 Native Administration Ordinance (Southern Section of Togoland), the 1935 Native Authority (Ashanti) Ordinance, and the 1944 Native Authority Ordinance for the coastal Gold Coast Colony. In the case of the Southern Section of Togoland, the colonial state attempted to end the geographic fragmentation of the sixty-nine traditional leadership divisions by offering those divisions which amalgamated more local government powers and, consequently, less control by the District Commissioner, as well as the right to have their own tribunals/courts. These would increase the chief's status and generate revenue for the chief through the court's fines (Hailey 1938, 479–80). The 1935 Ashanti Ordinance allowed traditional leaders to make local government bylaws and regulations on such subjects as the movement of cattle, building construction, and the control of liquor (Busia 1951). In the Gold Coast Colony, the colonial state used the 1944 ordinance to both expand the local government jurisdiction of the traditional authorities, and to also allow the colonial authorities to force the chiefs to make and enforce bylaws that the colonial authorities thought to be necessary, but which the traditional leaders had not implemented or enforced. For example, while traditional leaders had passed bylaws on eliminating cocoa pests, traditional leaders did not enforce these laws which would have cut into the short-term wealth generated by cocoa. Instead, the colonial state itself had to take the necessary, but unpopular action on cocoa pests (Hailey 1938, 468–69; Ward 1948, 340–41).

While the colonial state had come to see traditional leaders as subordinate allies in the operation of local government, just before and during the colonial dyarchy Nkrumah and his CPP saw this and came to regard traditional leaders as potential obstacles to the nationalist struggle for an independent Ghana achieved by democratic means. Moreover, since traditional leaders were not elected by universal adult suffrage, the question arose that if the post-colonial state was to have democratically legislative and executive institutions from Parliament down to rural local government, how did traditional leaders (who by the nature of their institution were not elected by all of their subjects on a regular basis) fit into this type of democracy at the national level and at the level of local government?[33] With regard to local government, during the colonial dyarchy, as Nkrumah gathered more electoral support and power, he implemented a number of ordinances that dismantled direct control by traditional leaders of rural and urban local government, but which allowed chiefs to have one-third of the seats in the new Local Government Councils compared to two-thirds of the council members who were elected. These local government councils administered in their areas of jurisdiction matters as diverse as public order, building, education, forestry, animals, and agriculture. The 1953 Municipal Council Ordinance, dealing with the major urban centres, reduced traditional leadership membership of the municipal council down to one-sixth. The paramount chief of the area was the non-voting president of the municipal council. In 1957, the participation of traditional leaders in the municipal councils was again reduced.[34]

The post-colonial state has continued to centralize local government under its control with varying degrees of traditional leadership participation in local government structures. After independence, Nkrumah, on the one hand, used the Local Government Act to remove traditional leaders from their seats on the local government councils. On the other hand, he used the 1958 House of Chiefs Act and the 1961 Chieftaincy Act to reassure traditional leaders that the institution of chieftaincy and their powers to deal with customary matters was guaranteed, as well as to establish the regional houses of chiefs[35] in which they could debate and deal with customary matters in both rural and urban local governance.

After Nkrumah's overthrow in 1966 by the military, the National Liberation Council (NLC: 1966–69) replaced Nkrumah's local government councils, but not the regional Houses of Chiefs, with nominated management committees. The NLC's 1969 Local Government Amendment Decree changed the membership of the management committees to include three traditional leaders out of a total membership of thirteen. When the NLC handed over power to the elected Second Republic (1969–72), the 1969 constitution specified that all three levels of local government have chiefs as participating members. Up to half of the Local Council members could be traditional leaders. At the next level up, one-third of the District Council members could be traditional leaders. The Regional House of Chiefs was entitled to appoint two of its members to the Regional Council.

The Second Republic was overthrown by a military coup in 1972. A series of military regimes governed Ghana from 1972 to 1979. While various changes in local government took place during this time, on the whole the military governments continued the Second Republic's practice of including traditional leaders as members of the various local government structures.[36] So, too, the constitution of the Third Republic (1979–81) assigned a minority of seats to traditional leaders in the Third Republic's local government structures: Local Councils, District Councils, and Regional Councils.

On 31 December 1981, the Third Republic was overthrown by the Provisional National Defence Council (PNDC) (1982 – 7 June 1993) led by Flt. Lt. J. J. Rawlings.[37] Initially the PNDC abolished the various councils and instituted a system of management committees augmented by People's Defence Committees and Worker's Defence Committees at various levels.[38] However, in 1988, under major internal and external pressures, the PNDC instituted what may yet prove to be a major shift in the post-colonial state's strategy for local government in Ghana. The new District Assemblies were to be the first level of local government in both rural and urban Ghana.

Control of local government was to be decentralized from the capital, Accra, to the District Assembly (D.A.). Various powers and revenues were to be transferred from the headquarters of the various ministries in Accra to the District Assemblies. While two-thirds of the District Assembly members were elected, one third were appointed by the PNDC after consultations with various interest groups, including traditional leaders. The 1992 constitution of the Fourth Republic (1993–present) incorporated the District and Metropolitan Assemblies into its system of local government. Seventy per cent of their members are elected. Thirty per cent are appointed by the president after consultations with recognized interest groups including traditional leaders (Art, 242 of the constitution, Ayee [1994], 113–14). Contrary to some expectations there is not a set quota for chiefs in the District Assemblies, but all or nearly all have some representation of traditional leaders. Traditional leaders are also represented on other local government bodies. Each of the Regional Houses of Chiefs selects one of their members to serve on the Regional Police Committee. The same is true for the Regional Prisons Service Committee. Two seats on each Regional Co-ordinating Council are reserved for members of the Regional House of Chiefs.

Traditional leaders have been incorporated directly into local government administration by both the colonial and post-colonial states. While Nkrumah did remove traditional leaders from participating in elected local government councils, all the other post-colonial governments have directly incorporated traditional leaders as members of state-run local government. Even Nkrumah had to accept the continuing existence of traditional councils and the creation of Regional Houses of Chiefs in order to have local governance structures that had the legitimacy to deal with customary or traditional aspects of Ghanaian society.

RURAL LOCAL GOVERNANCE AND TRADITIONAL LEADERSHIP: LOCAL GOVERNMENT FINANCE

The ability of traditional leaders to control local government finance has followed a similar pattern to their control over local government administration: reductions in their power, a refocusing of their powers into the Houses of Chiefs system, but not their total elimination. Both the colonial and post-colonial states have adopted that strategy. Both the colonial and post-colonial state seem to have recognized that the legitimacy of traditional leaders that exists for many of their subjects precluded such possibilities into the present.

In the Gold Coast Colony, the 1883 Native Jurisdiction Ordinance marked one of the formal shifts in the financing of local government from chiefs. While in the pre-colonial periods the political leaders of the pre-colonial states, etc., could raise their own finances by tribute and fees, subject to their own constitutions and power, the 1883 Ordinance limited the now traditional leaders to fees for their designated services as set by the governor. The 1927 Native Administration Ordinance (Gold Coast Colony) reinforced the principle of local government fees for traditional leaders being set by the colonial state. Paramount chiefs were allowed to establish stool land treasuries, but these were subject to control and audit by the colonial state. The 1924 Native Jurisdiction Act also allowed Asante paramount chiefs to establish stool treasuries, subject to colonial control and audit. The revenues generated by this system of court fees and stool revenues proved inadequate to support the traditional leaders and to carry out development (Hailey 1938, 471–72). In response the British colonial state tried to correct this situation by creating new sources of revenue for the traditional leaders and by revamping the system of treasuries for the traditional leaders that the colonial state would more closely monitor and/or partially administer.[39]

Nkrumah's 1951 Local Government Ordinance and his other legislation dismantling the State Councils and Treasuries of the chiefs during the last period of colonial rule, the dyarchy, removed the ability of traditional leaders to raise finances through their own local government structures as well as their participation as members (as a minority at most) in the new elected or appointed local government bodies which had their own sources of finance. In short, they moved from playing an executive role in local government finance to being council or committee members. Furthermore section 74 of this 1951 ordinance also started the principle of dividing stool land revenues between the chieftaincy and the local and central governments. Over time, more and more of the revenue derived from the lands of the chieftaincies and control over such revenues has shifted from the traditional leaders to the post-colonial state.[40] ARTICLE 267 of the Fourth Republic's 1992 Constitution states that all revenues derived from chieftaincy land will be paid to the post-colonial state's Office of the Administrator of Stool Lands. Nearly half of these royalties from chieftaincy lands is allocated to the District Assemblies, with smaller amounts going to the Traditional Councils, the traditional leaders, and also to the Office of the Administrator of Stool Lands.

The post-colonial state provides all of the funding for the Houses of Chiefs system.[41]

Family house of President Kufuor in Kumasi, Ghana. This house is less than five hundred metres from the Asante king's Manhyia Palace (photo by D. Ray).

RURAL LOCAL GOVERNANCE AND TRADITIONAL LEADERSHIP: HOUSES OF CHIEFS

The *Houses of Chiefs* system consists of three levels: the National House of Chiefs, the ten Regional Houses of Chiefs, and the more than one hundred and sixty Traditional Councils at the district and sub-district level. Together they form a blanket of rural and urban local government that covers Ghana from east to west and from north to south.

Each Traditional Council is composed of the president, who is the paramount chief or equivalent,[42] and such other lower-level chiefs as divisional chiefs, paramount queenmother, and other chiefs according to custom. The president of the Traditional Council has a seat in the Regional House of Chiefs. Each of the ten Regional Houses elects five members to the fifty-member National House of Chiefs. Each House of Chiefs elects its president and other executive members who form the Standing Committee (i.e., executive committee) to each house. Besides the Standing Committee, each house has a number of other committees. The Stool and Skin Lands[43] Committee deals with disputes and other questions over chief-held land: the allocation of land in an agricultural society is an important governing function. The Research Committee investigates the background to a variety of chief-recognition and other issues. The Judicial Committees determine and give judgement on issues of recognizing who is and who is not a chief, or what type of chief a claimant may be. Each house meets twice a year or more as needed. The committees meet as needed, usually twice a year.

The National House of Chiefs was created in 1971 by an Act of Parliament (The Chieftaincy Act, 1971, Act 370) and has most recently been entrenched in the 1992 constitution of the Fourth Republic (Chapter 22, ARTS. 270–73) as part of the state's official policy of recognizing and guaranteeing the institution of chieftaincy (ART, 270). This constitution gives seven major functions to the National House of Chiefs.

First, the National House of Chiefs is to act as an advisory body to the state, including all government bodies under the constitution, that deal with "any matter relating to or affecting chieftaincy" (ART. 272(a)). This is a very broad and consolidated mandate that covers all manner of traditional authority matters in the social, political, and economic realms of chieftaincy governance and customs and their interaction with the entire range of post-colonial state activities. Since there are chiefs or other forms of traditional leadership in virtually every homestead, hamlet, village, town, and city in Ghana, the scope of the National House of Chiefs' authority can be better understood.

Second, the National House of Chiefs was to develop and codify a unified system of customary law and also to codify the rules of succession for every chieftaincy in Ghana (ART. 272(b), 1992 constitution). The creation of a codified, unified system of customary law, would involve extensive efforts by many researchers over many years with the co-operation of many chiefs with various, sometimes differing, interests and interpretations of their own several systems of customary law.[44] Were this to be done, it would have been possible to establish a uniform code of customary law. This could have been administered in rural local court by traditional leaders, assisted by legal assessors, under state supervision and whose sentences could have been appealable to a state-run appeal court, as has been the case in Botswana. In the case of Botswana, something like 70 per cent of all cases are brought before the chief's courts, which use the codified customary law and operate in the main indigenous language. These courts are thought to be so popular because they are more accessible, more understandable, and less expensive to use than the regular state courts.[45] However, the National House of Chiefs has lacked the resources, etc., to implement this part of its mandate.

Similarly, the National House of Chiefs has lacked the resources, etc., to undertake the codification of customary laws on the succession and impeachment processes for each of the thousands of chiefs in Ghana. The state's Chieftaincy Division in conjunction with one of the Regional Houses of Chiefs did compile such a document, but the report was not released, reportedly because of disputes over the processes from those traditional authorities who had not been interviewed or who disagreed with the report. However, in the late 1990s, a new attempt at such codification of political succession was started. The National House of Chiefs received funding from the Konrad Adenauer Foundation[46] to start a pilot study in 2000 on questions of customary political succession procedures in several regions. As of the end of 2002, the draft results were still being studied by chiefs who were the subjects of the report.

Thirdly, the National House of Chiefs was empowered by the constitution to evaluate traditional social practice. The House was not only to determine which customary practices were *outmoded and socially harmful,* but was also to develop and implement strategies to eliminate such harmful traditions (section 272 (c)). The politicians of the post-colonial state appeared to be moving responsibility for the changing of social customs that dated to the pre-colonial period from their sphere of action to that of the traditional leaders in the National House of Chiefs. The state was shifting this responsibility to the chiefs because the state expected that since chiefs dealt with customary rule and law (i.e., political and legal custom), the Houses of Chiefs system would also be the appropriate structure to deal with social customs.

The Houses of Chiefs have discussed a number of important social custom issues such as the cost of funerals, widowhood, and the treatment of certain girls and women under the rules of certain aspects of the traditional religions, such as the trokosi and witch camp practices. In the case of funerals, the Houses of Chiefs did condemn what has become the high cost of funerals in Ghana and recommended that Ghanaians adopt less elaborate and expensive funeral practices.[47]

The National House of Chiefs does not have the legal power to prohibit what it deems to be undesirable customary social practices or the legal power to punish those who continue to carry out such undesirable traditional customs. In these senses, the Houses of Chiefs are not legislative or judicial bodies, but rather they are forums for public debate of issues that might not otherwise receive much public attention. Furthermore, when the members of the National House of Chiefs or one or more of the Regional Houses of Chiefs agree on the need to modify or eliminate a social custom, the traditional leaders lend their legitimacy and political and social authority to the issue's resolution. As traditional leaders in the Houses of Chiefs are convinced to change their opinions on social and other issues, in turn they carry out important public education with their subjects on social issues, and indeed on other issues. The National and Regional House of Chiefs can thus play an important role in helping to change public opinion. Without this change, the government would have trouble getting its own members of Parliament, let alone those of the opposition parties, to outlaw or legally modify an undesirable practice. Indeed, if such a law were to be passed without the necessary shift in the opinions of the citizens, it might even be very difficult to get the police to enforce the law, as may well have been the case with the anti-trokosi law.[48]

Fourthly, the National House of Chiefs is in charge of giving official recognition to those that the House determines to be chiefs. In order to do this, the House maintains an official list of chiefs, the National Register of Chiefs (ART. 270 (3b), 1992 constitution) that was established in 1971 (Chieftaincy Act, 1971, act 370, section 50). This national registry keeps track of the status of those traditional leaders who are recognized by the National House of Chiefs as chiefs by recording when they are installed as chiefs, when they are impeached and deposed, when they abdicate, or when they die. The National House of Chiefs uses the government of Ghana *Gazette* to communicate these changes to the state, citizenry, and others. This political communication of who is and who is not a chief has been the exclusive responsibility of the National House of Chiefs since the start of the Fourth Republic's Constitution on 7 January 1992.

Related to this is the fifth function of the National House of Chiefs: making the next-to-final determination on chieftaincy questions (Arts. 270 (3a) and 273, 1992 constitution). For example, the question may arise as to who is the legitimate chief in a particular chieftaincy. Disputes may arise at a number of points in the processes for the selection and deselection of traditional leaders, i.e., nomination, election, selection, installation, or impeachment. The legitimacy or validity by which a traditional leader obtained or lost his/her office may be challenged on the basis of custom, which may not be widely known and which requires specialized knowledge. The particular issue may first be examined at the Traditional Council, then taken to a judicial committee of the Regional House of Chiefs, then taken to a judicial committee of the National House of Chiefs, and finally appealed to the Supreme Court of Ghana.

The sixth function of the National House of Chiefs is to undertake various tasks that Parliament refers to the House (Art. 272 (d)). Thus the House has a mandate to not only advise Parliament, but also to carry out actions as Parliament requests.

The seventh function that the 1992 constitution assigns to the National and Regional Houses of Chiefs is to choose members as representatives to a variety of national and local state bodies. For example, the president of the National House of Chiefs is one of the twenty-five members of the Council of State (Art. 89 (2b)). One indication of the importance that the designers of the state constitution accorded to chieftaincy, is that the president of the National House of Chiefs is the only membership category that is automatically and necessarily a member of the Council of State. This Council advises the president on important issues ranging from parliamentary bills to key appointments in the state, such as the Electoral Commission, which controls the political succession process of the post-colonial state, or the Public Services Commission, which controls most of the major staffing decisions for the administration of the post-colonial state (Arts. 70, 90–92). The Regional Houses of Chiefs are each entitled to appoint, for example, one representative to such local government bodies as their Regional Police Committees or Regional Prisons Committees, and to appoint two representatives to the Regional Co-ordinating Council which is chaired by the regional minister (Arts. 204, 209, 255).

CONCLUSIONS AND POLICY IMPLICATIONS FOR RURAL LOCAL GOVERNMENT IN GHANA

The overall pattern that is suggested by this analysis is that the control exerted by the state over traditional leaders in local government has varied, but that the state continues to find traditional leaders to be part of Ghana's political reality. At different times both the colonial and post-colonial states have not only appeared to recognize the legitimacy of traditional leaders, but have also employed different strategies to mobilize or co-opt this legitimacy to aid in the achievement of their development goals. At other times, however, they have viewed the legitimacy of traditional leaders as a threat (to either their own sovereignty or public order) and have attempted to minimize (but never completely eliminate) the sovereignty and legitimacy of the pre-colonial rooted political entities.

What then are the policy implications? While the on-going relationship of the post-colonial state at the level of local government is one in which the state wishes to control traditional leadership, the state does not seem to wish to eliminate traditional leadership at the local level. This policy tension seems to reflect the need of the post-colonial state to accumulate more legitimacy resources, so that it can more effectively manage and develop at the local government level, by co-opting the different legitimacy resources of the traditional leadership. Indeed, these differently rooted legitimacy resources of the traditional leaders would seem to exist only as long as these are part of the traditional authority structures, and do not seem to be transferable to the post-colonial state. Without the presence of traditional leaders, their legitimacy resources cannot be present.

What are some practical strategies for mobilizing this legitimacy (or credibility) of traditional leadership in aid of the development and democratization efforts of local government? First, it is useful to distinguish between government and governance. Government can be considered to be composed of those formal constitutionally and legislatively designated structures, processes, and political culture (including legitimacy) of the state. Governance could be considered to be comprised of government plus those political activities and culture (including legitimacy) which may be technically outside the formal legislative and constitutional activities of the state, but which have effects on the activities of formal government. Such effects might be felt in the realms of development projects or the political culture of democracy. Governance, thus, could be said to include both the formal activities of the state as well as those unofficial activities and attitudes of the people living within the state. In short, we could talk of governance as the governing style of a country. These distinctions apply to all levels of governing in the state, including that of local government. We could see this distinction as actually expanding the field in which traditional leadership could play a role with regard to local government.

The first set of options focuses on those that involve traditional leaders with local government. Traditional leaders might be involved in the legislative or executive functions of local government. Reserved seats for traditional leaders in which executive or legislature might be apportioned on the basis of several mechanisms. Local, regional, provincial, or national government might appoint the traditional leaders to these local government bodies. Such positions could be filled by elections in traditional leadership forums such as the local equivalent of traditional councils, regional houses of chiefs, provincial houses of traditional leaders, national house of chiefs or national council of traditional leaders. Another selection method could be to have the traditional leaders elected to the reserved seats during the regular local government elections. Variations and combinations of the above selection techniques are, of course, also possible. A second general possibility with regard to traditional leadership participation in the legislative and executive bodies of local government, might be for individual traditional leaders to run as ordinary individual candidates in the regular local government elections. A third option in this regard would be to have traditional leaders take over these executive and legislative bodies of local government for their areas. The first two options of this set (i.e., reserved seats and traditional leader as individual candidate) represent two different versions of traditional leaders contributing their legitimacy to local government. The third option is likely to be strongly opposed on practical administrative grounds, but especially on the basis of arguments for democracy, given the emergence of the democratic state which demands that all levels of its government conform on the whole to the core value of universally-elected governments. This question needs to be debated more extensively, but it may be undesirable for the interests of traditional leaders since such an option might well create a backlash against traditional leaders, including calls for the abolishment of traditional leadership.

Traditional leaders could be allocated seats for administrative or supervisory functions of local government. This is the case in Ghana for a number of regional bodies such as the regional commissions, committees and councils for lands, prisons, police, and regional co-ordination.

Traditional leaders could also serve on advisory bodies of local government such as joint committees of local government; traditional leaders that focus on specific policies. Such policy areas could include (or have included) the environment (e.g., sacred groves, forests, rivers, etc.), health (e.g., anti-HIV/AIDS campaigns, child vaccination campaigns), social practice (e.g., funerals, etc.), gender (e.g., the role of queenmothers and other female chiefs, or even male chiefs, in dealing with gender questions, women and development, or gender roles), fund-raising for education, health, and other development projects, etc. Local government could establish new citizen participation bodies that focus on traditional leaders, or else expand existing ones to include traditional leaders.

There are of course quite a range of possibilities in terms of the second option, the involvement of traditional leaders in local governance. Traditional leaders could be involved informally in individual development programs, policies, and projects organized by local government, communities, and non-governmental organizations.

Where appropriate, this participation could be more formalized. Customary values could be mobilized by traditional leaders in support of development, as in Zimbabwean reforestation (Daneel 1996). Traditional leaders themselves could organize development projects. Traditional leaders could mobilize customary values to endorse and participate in civic education programs in support of democratic values and citizen participation in elections for local and other levels of government. Traditional leaders could organize meetings of their subjects, as with the *kgotlas* in Botswana, to discuss local government and other development projects and policies.

There needs to be active (and where necessary pre-emptive) measures by traditional leaders to resolve customary disputes in their own individual customary jurisdictions so as to maintain social, economic, political, and customary justice as well as local community peace, order, and good government; all of the above being necessary for development activities to take place in their localities. However, where and when customary disputes in one traditional leadership jurisdiction cannot or have not been solved to the satisfaction of all involved, or involve more than one traditional leadership jurisdiction, then traditional leadership conflict resolution mechanisms of the state such as Traditional Councils at the sub-district/district level, or Regional Houses of Chiefs and Provincial Houses of Traditional Leaders at the regional/provincial level, or even the National House of Chiefs or National Council of Traditional Leaders at the national level need to be in place and have the operational capability (e.g., judicial committees of the houses of chiefs), the constitutional and legal authority to operate, the political will to act, the legal and administrative support of the local, regional, and national governments to enforce legitimate decisions, as well as the necessary resources of staff, transportation, communication, and other funding necessary to carry out their responsibilities. Thus, the relationship between traditional leaders and local, regional, and national government is interactive: traditional leaders can legitimate the state by acting on behalf of the state objectives of development and democratization, while the state sets the terms of traditional leaders' legitimacy in the contemporary era and also provides new frameworks and resources within which traditional leadership can operate.

ACKNOWLEDGMENTS

This research was carried out with the aid of a grant from the Social Sciences and Humanities Research Council of Canada (SSHRCC).

This research was carried out with the aid of a grant from the International Development Research Centre (IDRC) of Ottawa, Canada.

Grants from the University of Calgary's University Research Grants Committee (URGC) contributed to the awarding of the SSHRCC and IDRC grants.

I would like to acknowledge gratefully the contributions of Laura Durham (Canada), Meghan Dalrymple (Canada) and Morgan Nyendu (Ghana) who were my research assistants and graduate students. I would also like to thank my academic colleagues in Ghana as well as the tradtional leaders, state leaders and people of Ghana for their help, kindness and friendship. I would also like to thank Peter and Ama Shinnie who persuaded me to go to Ghana and who have been such a constant source of advice, help and friendship.

REFERENCES

Amenumey, D. E. K. 1986. *The Ewe in Pre-colonial Times*. Accra: Sedco.
Andoh, A. S. Y. 1987. "The Asante National Liberation Movement of the 1950's in Retrospect." In Enid Schildkrout with Carol Gelber, eds., *The Golden Stool: Studies of the Asante Center and Periphery*. New York: Anthropological Papers of the American Museum of Natural History Vol. 65, Part 1: 173–83.
Apter, D. 1972. *Ghana in Transition*. 2d rev. ed. Princeton: Princeton University Press.
Arhin, K. 1985. *Traditional Rule in Ghana: Past and Present*. Accra: Sedco.
———. 1991. "The Search for 'constitutional chieftaincy'." In K. Arhin, ed., *The Life and Work of Kwame Nkrumah*. Accra: Sedco, pp. 27–54.
Arhin, Kwame, Donald I. Ray, and E. A. B. van Rouveroy, eds. 1995. *Proceedings of the Conference on the Contribution of Traditional Authority to Development, Human Rights and Environmental Protection: Strategies for Africa*. Leiden, Netherlands: African Studies Centre.
Asamoa, Ansa K. 1986. *The Ewe of South-Eastern Ghana and Togo on the Eve of Colonialism*. Tema: Ghana Publishing Corporate.

Austin, D. 1964. *Politics in Ghana 1946–60*. London: Oxford University Press.

Austin, D., and Luckham, R., eds. 1975. *Politicians and Soldiers in Ghana 1966–1972*. London: Frank Cass.

Ayee, Joseph R. A. 1994. *An Anatomy of Public Policy Implementation: The Case of Decentralisation Policies in Ghana*. Aldershot, UK: Avebury.

Bank, Leslie, and Roger Southall. 1996. "Traditional Leaders in South Africa's New Democracy," *Journal of Legal Pluralism* 37/38: 407–30.

Baynes, Kenneth. 1993. "Legitimacy." In Joel Krieger et al., eds. *The Oxford Companion to Politics of the World*. Oxford and New York: Oxford University Press, 533–34.

Boahen, A. 1987. *African Perspectives on Colonialism*. Baltimore, Md.: Johns Hopkins University Press.

Boahen, A. Adu, J. F. Ade Tidy, and Michael Ajayi.1986. *Topics in West African History*, London: Longman.

Busia, K. A. 1951. *The Position of the Chief in the Modern Political System of Ashanti: A Study of the Influence of Contemporary Social Changes on Ashanti Political Institutions*. London: Oxford University Press for the International African Institute.

Catchpole, Brian, and I. A. Akinjogbin. 1983. *A History of Africa in Maps and Diagrams*. London: Collins Educational.

Chazan, N. 1983. *An Anatomy of Ghanaian Politics: Managing Political Recession, 1969–1982*. Boulder, Colo.: Westview Press.

Chilcote, Ronald H. 1994. *Theories of Comparative Politics: The Search for a Paradigm Reconsidered*. Second Edition, Boulder, Colo.: Westview Press.

Commonwealth Local Government Forum (CLGF). 1995. *Commonwealth Roundtable on Democratisation and Decentralisation*. Harare, 27–29 June 1995, London: Commonwealth Local Government Forum.

Connolly, W. In David Miller, ed. 1987. *Blackwell Encyclopedia of Political Thought*. Oxford and New York: Basil Blackwell, 279–80.

Daneel, M. L. 1996. "Environmental Reform: A New Venture of Zimbabwe's Traditional Custodians of the Land," *Journal of Legal Pluralism* 37/38: 347–76.

Foucault, M. 1980. *Power/Knowledge: Selected Interviews and Other Writings, 1972–1977*. Edited by Colin Gordon. New York: Pantheon.

Fynn, J. K. 1971. *Asante and its Neighbours 1700–1807*. London: Longman.

Gyandoh, S. O., and J. Griffiths. 1972. *A Sourcebook of the Constitutional Law of Ghana*. Vol. 1 (Part 1). Accra: University of Ghana, Faculty of Law.

Hailey, Lord. 1938. *An African Survey: A Study of Problems Arising in African South Of the Sahara*. London: Oxford University Press.

King, Preston. 1987. "Sovereignty." In David Miller, ed. *The Blackwell Encyclopedia of Political Thought*. Oxford and New York: Basil Blackwell: 492–94.

Kwamena-Poh, M. A. 1972. "History." In David Brokensha, ed., *Akwapim Handbook*. Tema: Ghana Publishing, 33–57.

McCaskie, T. 1995. *State and Society in Pre-Colonial Asante*. Cambridge: University Press.

McIntosh, Alastair. 1995. "The Rural Local Government Debate in South Africa: Centrist Control of Local Development." In P. S. Reddy, ed., *Perspectives on Local Government Management and Development in Africa*. Durban: University of Durban–Westville.

Metcalfe, G. 1964. *Great Britain and Ghana: Documents of Ghana History, 1807–1957*. London: Thomas Nelson and Sons for the University of Ghana.

Naidu, R. A., and P. S. Reddy, eds. 1997. *Metropolitan Government and Development: Present and Future Challenges*. Durban: Konrad Adenauer Stiftung and the Democracy Development Programme.

Ninsin, K. 1985. *Political Struggles in Ghana 1966–1981*. Accra: Tornado.

Ninsin, K., and Francis K. Drah, eds. 1991. *Ghana's Transition to Constitutional Rule*. Accra: Ghana Universities Press.

Nkrumah, K. 1957. *The Autobiography of Kwame Nkrumah*. London: Thomas Nelson and Sons.

Nsarkoh, J. K. 1964. *Local Government in Ghana*. Accra: Ghana Universities Press.

Nugent, P. 1995. *Big Men, Small Boys and Politics in Ghana: Power, Ideology and the Burden of History 1982–1994*. London: Pinter.

Oloka-Onyango, J. 1997. "The Question of Buganda in Contemporary Ugandan Politics," *Journal of Contemporary African Studies* 15, no. 2:173–89.

Oquaye, M. 1980. *Politics in Ghana, 1972–1979.* Accra: Tornado.

Rathbone, Richard. 2000. *Nkrumah and the Chiefs: The Politics of Chieftaincy in Ghana 1951–60.* Oxford: James Currey.

Ray, Donald I. 1986. *Ghana: Politics, Economics, and Society.* London: Frances Pinter.

———. 2000. Chiefs Net: TAARN (Traditional Authority Applied Research Network web site still "under construction") (with the assistance of Meghan Dalrymple) (www.ucalgary.ca/UofC/faculties/SS/POLI/RUPP/taarn/taarn.htm).

———. 1998. "Divided Sovereignty: Managing Chief-State Relations in Ghana." Paper presented to the Department of Sociology, University of Alberta, Edmonton, 2 February.

———. 1996. "Divided Sovereignty: Traditional Authority and the State in Ghana," *Journal of Legal Pluralism* 37/38: 181–202.

Ray, Donald I., and S. La Branche. 1998. "Foucault's Chiefs: The Question of Legitimacy in Chief-State Relations in Ghana." Presented to the Canadian Political Science Association Conference, Ottawa, 2 June.

Ray, Donald I., and T. Quinlan. 1997. "Chieftaincy Studies – The Traditional Authority Applied Research Network (TAARN): CHIEFS NET." Paper presented to the Human Sciences Research Council of South Africa (Centre for Science Development), 6–22 August 1997 and delivered by D. I. Ray to the University of Durban–Westville, 7 August ; the University of Natal–Durban, 11 August, Rhodes University, 14 August, University of Witwatersrand, 20 August; Human Sciences Research Council, Pretoria, 21 August; University of Pretoria, 22 August.

Ray, Donald I., K. Sharma, and I. I. May-Parker, eds. 1997. *Symposium on Traditional Leadership and Local Government: Gaborone, Botswana, 23–26 September, 1997.* London: Commonwealth Local Government Forum.

Ray, Donald I., and E. A. B. van Rouveroy. 1996. "The New Relevance of Traditional Authorities in Africa: An Introduction," *Journal of Legal Pluralism* 37/38: 1–38. [*The New Relevance of Traditional Authorities to Africa's Future,* special double issue edited by E. A. B. van Rouveroy and Donald I. Ray.].

Reddy, P. S., ed. 1995. *Perspectives on Local Government Management and Development in Africa.* Durban: University of Durban–Westville.

Shinnie, Peter, and Ama Shinnie. 1995. *Early Asante.* Calgary, Alta.: Department of Archeology, University of Calgary.

Venson, Pelonomi, ed. 1995. *Traditional Leadership in Africa: A Research Report on Traditional Systems of Administration and their Role in the Promotion of Good Governance.* London and Cape Town: Commonwealth Local Government Forum and the Institute for Local Governance and Development.

Ward, W. 1948. *A History of Ghana.* London: George Allen and Unwin.

Watkins, Frederick M. 1968. "State: The concept." In David L. Sills, ed. *International Encyclopedia of the Social Sciences* 15, s.v. "state": 150–57.

Wilks, I. 1989. *Asante in the Nineteenth Century: The Structure and Evolution of a Political Order.* Cambridge: Cambridge University Press.

Woodman, G. R. 1988. "Unification or Continuing Pluralism in Family Law in Anglophone Africa: Past Experience, Present Realities and Future Possibilities." *Lesotho Law Journal* 4, no. 2: 33–79.

Wright, Carl. 1997. Preface to *Symposium on Traditional Leadership and Local Government: Gaborone, Botswana, 23–26 September, 1997,* edited by Donald I. Ray, K. Sharma, and I. I. May-Parker. London: Commonwealth Local Government Forum.

Zips, Werner, and E. A. B. van Rouveroy, eds. 1998 *Sovereignty, Legitimacy, and Power in West African Societies: Perspectives from Legal Anthropology* (African Studies Series, Vol. 10). Hamburg, Germany: LIT.

NOTES

1. I am grateful to Professor Valerie Haines for sharing with me her work on the sociology of canons during our time as annual fellows at the Calgary Institute for the Humanities in 2000–2001.

2. For further discussion of this point, see Ray 1998.

3. Chiefs in Ghana are based in villages, towns and cities, each with its attached rural area. Chiefs are organized into hierarchies (most of them based on the pre-colonial situation) which incorporate sub-sets of urban and rural areas.

4. The history, structure, and nature of these pre-colonial states are increasingly well documented. See, for example, the following: Amenumey 1986; Asamoa 1986; Boahen 1987; Boahen, Ajayi and Tidy 1986; Fynn 1971; Kwamena-Poh 1972; McCaskie 1995; Shinnie and Shinnie 1995; Ward 1948; Wilks 1989. For a useful overview using maps, see Catchpole and Akinjogbin 1983.

5. For a summary of this process, see Ray 1998, 49–50.

6. See Andoh 1987; Arhin 1991; Rathbone 2000.

7. The dyarchy was a transitional period from the colonial state to the post-colonial state.

8. For a variety of analyses of these governments, see Apter 1968; Austin 1964; Austin and Luckham 1975; Chazan 1983; Ninsin 1985; Ninsin and Drah 1981; Nugent 1995; Oquaye 1980; and Ray 1986.

9. These democratic values should be examined within national and local government as well as a variety of other structures, including traditional authorities and such civil society organizations as religious organizations and community associations.

10. See, for example, Baynes 1993 or Connolly 1987.

11. Arguably, there are religious and monarchical/estate exceptions, but overall this pattern would seem to be present.

12. See Ray 1996 for an elaboration of this argument. The degree to which the post-colonial state accepts this inheritance over time is another question.

13. For example, the written constitution of Canada was initially derived, in large measure, from the British North America Act of 1867 that was passed by the British Parliament.

14. By definition, since colonial rule means government by an external force, the wishes of the people are not necessarily (or even usually) followed by the imposed government.

15. The question of whether chiefs belong to the state or civil society needs to be addressed with respect to what is meant by *government leaders*.

16. The fact that these laws and constitutions may or may not have been written does not detract from their legal, historical, cultural, or intellectual validity. It is worthwhile noting that countries like Britain and Canada have had custom and convention as a considerable part of their constitutions.

17. The historic cultural and religious claims to legitimacy by traditional leaders in the era of democratic, post-colonial states are subject to the overriding principle of consent of the people to these claims. If people do not agree to be bound by these claims, there seems little that traditional leaders (or the state) can or should do to demand that they be honoured in special ways.

18. In turn, these claims may provide the basis for traditional leaders to make legalistic claims to legitimacy within the post-colonial state, as also sometimes happened during the colonial period.

19. See Ray 1996 for an elaboration of this argument, especially the linkage between legitimacy and sovereignty.

20. United Kingdom, 6 August 1874. "Order in Council for determining the mode of exercising the power and jurisdiction acquired by Her Majesty within divers countries on the West Coast of Africa near or adjacent to Her Majesty's Gold Coast Colony" in Metcalfe 1964, 368–69.

21. United Kingdom, 26 September 1901. "Ashanti Order of His Majesty the King in Council" Gold Coast Government Gazette, 1 January 1902 in Metcalfe 1964, 521–23; United Kingdom, 26 September 1901. "Northern Territories Order of His Majesty the King in Council" Gold Coast Government Gazette, 1 January 1902 in Metcalfe 1964, 523–24.

22. League of Nations, Mandates Section, 20 July 1922. British Mandates for the Cameroon, Togoland and East Africa" London in Metcalfe 1964, 590–92.

23. The difficulties of identity terminology need to be recognized here, especially in the transition from the African pre-colonial period with its various types of leaders, including kings, to the colonial state which downplayed their titles and transformed *kings* into *chiefs*. Indeed, this is the English-language term now commonly used by Ghanaians of all social ranks and by the Ghanaian state's constitution when referring to one or more traditional leaders. For a further discussion of the political uses of terminology, see, for example, Arhin 1985; Ray and LaBranche 1998.

24. Metcalfe notes that this ordinance was not implemented (1964, 390).

25. See, for example, the Earl of Kimberley's letter to Governor Ussher, 19 November 1880 in Metcalfe 1964, 402.

26. Ibid.

27. See, for example, the Gold Coast Colony and Ashanti (Legislative Council) which was in Order in Council, 1946 and the Gold Coast (Constitution) Order in Council, 1950. Both measures were colonial constructions.

28. 1951 Local Government (Gold Coast) Ordinance; Gold Coast, 27 March 1952, "The State Councils (Ashanti) Ordinance, No. 4 of 1952"; Gold Coast, 1952, "The State Councils (Colony and Southern Togoland) Ordinance, No. 3 of 1952"; Gold Coast, 14 December 1955, "The State Councils (Ashanti) (Amendment) Ordinance, No. 38 of 1955"; Gold Coast, 7 February 1957, "The State Councils (Ashanti) (Amendment) Ordinance, No. 3 of 1957"; Gold Coast, 1 March 1957, "The State Councils (Colony and Southern Togoland) (Amendment) Ordinance, No. 8 of 1957."

29. The Houses of Chiefs are discussed below in their own section.

30. The Judicial Commissioner was eventually replaced by the judicial committees of the National House of Chiefs and the Regional Houses of Chiefs. The Traditional Council is the grassroots level of the Houses of Chiefs system. See the Houses of Chiefs system section below.

31. Native States were the government units of traditional leadership in the colonial period that later became the Traditional Councils whose presidents were usually paramount chiefs. See below section on the Houses of Chiefs.

32. See Governor Freelings letter to the Earl of Carnarvon, 10 February 1877 in Metcalfe 1964, 387.

33. See Nkrumah 1957 (esp. p. 120); Rathbone 2000, 22–23.

34. 1951 Local Government (Gold Coast) Ordinance, Gold Coast, 27 March 1952; "The State Councils (Ashanti) Ordinance, No. 4 of 1952"; Gold Coast, 1952, "The State Councils (Colony and Southern Togoland) Ordinance, No. 3 of 1952"; Gold Coast, 14 December 1955, "The State Councils (Ashanti) (Amendment) Ordinance, No. 38 of 1955"; Gold Coast, 7 February 1957, "The State Councils (Ashanti) (Amendment) Ordinance, No. 3 of 1957"; Gold Coast, 1 March 1957, "The State Councils (Colony and Southern Togoland) (Amendment) Ordinance, No. 8 of 1957"; Municipal Councils (Amendment) Ordinance (No. 2) of 1957; Nsarkoh 1964: 5–6.

35. See the Houses of Chiefs section below.

36. Local Administration (Amendment) Decree (NRCD 138) (1972), cited by Ayee, 22, 54, 91; Local Administration (Amendment) Decree (NRCD 258) (1974), cited by Ayee, 22, 54, 92; Local Government (Amendment) Decree (SMDC 194 of 1978), cited by Ayee, 54.

37. Rawlings was also elected President of the Fourth Republic in 1992 and 1996. He had also been Chairman of the Armed Forces Revolutionary Council from 4 June to 24 September 1979. He was thus head of the post-colonial state of Ghana from June–September 1979, and 31 December 1981 to 7 January 2001.

38. Ray, 1986; Ayee, 113–14 and PNDC Law 14 (June 1982), cited by Ayee, 109.

39. See, for example, the following ordinances: 1931 Native Administration Amendment Ordinance (Gold Coast Colony), 1939 Native Administration Treasuries Ordinance (Gold Coast Colony); 1932 Native Treasuries Ordinance (Northern Territories and Northern Section of Togoland). Similar measures were applied in the Ashanti Protectorate, Hailey 1938, 346, 472–75.

40. See also, for example, the 1958 Ashanti Stool Lands Act, 1961 Local Government Act, the 1971 Chieftaincy Act, the regulations, etc., transforming such stool land revenues to the District Assemblies in 1988 as well as the Fourth Republic's 1992 constitution.

41. This is analyzed in the next section.

42. In a few Traditional Councils, the presidency rotates amongst the paramount chiefs (if there are several) or amongst the divisional chiefs.

43. In southern Ghana (which was formerly heavily forested), special wooden seats called stools are part of the regalia. This forms the physical manifestation of a chieftaincy's legitimacy. Similarly, in northern Ghana, which is a cattle-raising area, each new chief sits on a cattle hide or skin. Hence, since land is seen as being attached to a full-fledged chieftaincy, the terms *skin land* or *stool land* mean land attached to a chieftaincy.

44. Woodman (1988) has a very perceptive analysis of what happens to customary law when it is codified and brought under state law.

45. Interview Commissioner Patricia D. Matenge, Customary Courts Commissioner, Tribal Administration Department, Ministry of Local Government, Lands and Housing, Gaberone, Botswana, 26 September 1997. See also Sharma 1999.

46. This is the outreach arm of the German Christian Democratic Party, which has had a longstanding interest in traditional authority in Africa.

47. In much of Ghana, funerals are complex, expensive ceremonies that take place over considerable periods of time and involve large gatherings of family, friends, and dignitaries. Funerals are seen as important statements of the achievements and worth of the deceased and their families. Much prestige is at stake.

48. Interview with Justice Emile Short, Commissioner for Human Rights and Administrative Justice, Kumasi, 28 June 2000.

CHIEFS: POWER IN A POLITICAL WILDERNESS

CHAPTER 5

ROBERT THORNTON

ROBERT THORNTON is a professor of social anthropology at the University of the Witwatersrand, Johannesburg, South Africa. He is currently engaged in research on issues around "political and cultural power at the margins of the South African state." This comprises examination of local government and chiefs in the South African lowveld (northeastern South Africa) in the Provinces of Mpumalanga and Limpopo, on traditional healers, faith healers, and party politics in a region that is, in many ways, on the "margin" of the increasingly centralized, urban-based political order of the post-apartheid state. Previous research includes work in the history of anthropology (nineteenth century ethnography of South Africa, a book on *The Early Writings of Bronislaw Malinowski*), ethnicity, theory of culture, ritual, and religion. He studied at Stanford University (BA 1972, Anthropology) and at the University of Chicago (MA 1974 and PhD 1978, Anthropology). He taught at the University of Cape Town (1979–89), and University of the Witwatersrand, Johannesburg (1992–present), with a year at the Institute for Advanced Study in Princeton (1989–90) and at the Center for Historical Analysis, Rutgers University, U.S.A. (1990–91). PhD research was conducted in Tanzania, resulting in the book *Space, Time and Culture among the Iraqw of Tanzania* (1980).

ASKING THE WRONG QUESTIONS

The role of chiefs and kings in the contemporary South African political arena is one of the most difficult to describe or to make sense of (Kessel and Oomen 1997). One recent writer comments:

> The involvement of traditional leaders in decision-making processes is one of the most intractable problems facing [the South Africa government].... [T]he possible involvement of non-elected traditional leaders in democratic structure is highly complex. [Since] traditional leaders are not elected, and if they are accorded special treatment, why no other members of civil society such as religious, union and cultural leaders? (de Villiers 1994, 11)

The word *chiefship* (or *traditional authorities*, *indunas*, *kings*, and so on[1]) is itself in dispute and has no single common referent. Opprobrium has been heaped on the word itself since chiefs were incorporated into the Apartheid government structures in the 1950s. In the current political and administrative climate, it makes little sense to consider as a single group all those who call themselves *chiefs*, *kings* or *indunas*. Partly for simplicity, I use both common terms *chiefship* or *traditional authority* to label all aspects of contemporary South African political leaders who partly derive their office from tradition, and partly from their appointment under the Bantu Authorities Act of 1951. This category itself has little descriptive validity and contains great variation, but it is a significant institution in the political landscape.

The chiefship does exist in the sense that it is recognized by the constitution, has various regional instances, and is believed by many to constitute a single category. Thus, while all chiefs have varying degrees of legitimate claim to traditional authority based on descent or election by community elders and councillors, all also exist only by appointment of the State President under South African statutory law. In the interim constitution of 1994 [ART. 181–84] traditional authorities were recognized and granted some powers despite the objections of the ANC negotiators. The latter believed, probably correctly, that there were insurmountable problems in integrating the institution into a democratic constitutional order that complied with the Universal Bill of Human Rights promulgated by the UN. Both Nelson Mandela himself, and the Congress of Traditional Leaders (Contralesa) lobbied for a role for chiefs. Chiefs were thus given a role *ex-officio* in local government, and permitted to *comment* on matters affecting tradition and customary law as it affected local communities (de Villiers 1994, 11; Kessel and Oomen 1997, 573–77). At the end of the 1990s, however, after nearly a decade of intensive discussion, negotiations, and efforts to make this work, it was still not clear what role chiefs could or would have in future, or how their *powers* were to be understood or constituted.

The history of the institution from the nineteenth century up to the present, and its function, has been amply documented (see Kessel and Oomen 1997; Bothma 1976; Hammond-Tooke 1974, 1984, 1993). But the questions that remain have to do with what sorts of power do chiefs have, and how is it to be understood. Hammond-Tooke raised this question in his 1975 book on the chiefs in Transkei in the 1960s, namely, is it "command" or is it "consensus" that gives the chief his power? That is, does the continuing power of chiefs derive from the bureaucratization of the chiefship in this century (command), or is it something older and more traditional (consensus)? Chiefs themselves have complicated the issue by obscuring it in order to remain flexible and adaptable in changing circumstances. As Kessel and Oomen say in 1997:

> Chiefs have proven that the institution is adaptable to changing times. If traditional leaders are perceived as non-partisan, they can play a valuable role in local communities, e.g., in the sphere of conflict resolution and justice. But if chiefs remain dependent on government patronage, they can easily be manipulated by the government of the day. The central issue remains unresolved: do chiefs derive their legitimacy from state recognition or from popular support? (585)

This chapter attempts to answer these questions by taking a different approach. It argues that the chiefship relies on an entirely different form of power that exists, in effect, parallel to the ordinary governmental system based on statutes and deriving ultimately from the idea of the state. It is significant here that chiefs seem to continue to assert that their power is *not political*. What does this assertion mean in the face of their obvious and continuing power on the ground and in action? The leader of Contralesa, Patekile Holomisa, has consistently declared that the power of chiefs is different from, but relevant to the political system of the state. In arguing for their recognition in the constitution, he said:

> Under the present dispensation of multi-party democracy, characterized ... by division, the traditional leader still commands respect.... Any political party which allows itself to incur his wrath is more likely than not to fare badly in terms of getting mass support for its policies and/or development projects.[2]

Thus, chiefship was held to influence political parties, but not to be of the same nature or quality. In constitutional talks, Contralesa envisioned an advisory role that would not involve them directly in *politics*. They accused the politicians of not understanding the nature of their role, and wanted

> ... to advise ... provincial and national parliaments on how to accommodate this unique type of leadership which so many of the educated and political elite tend to misunderstand and to misrepresent.[3]

Thus, if this is taken seriously, the logic of chiefly power is sufficiently different to make questions about their legitimacy, command, or consensus unanswerable simply because these are the wrong questions. Trying to define the chiefship with the concepts of statutory law and within the parameters of the state is like trying to play a game of draughts (American *checkers*) with a set of chess pieces: it can't be done despite many similarities. It is manifestly true that there are many political similarities in the two systems, and that they have functioned together within a common polity. Despite this, I argue here that the differences are sufficiently great, and of a sort that makes them function effectively in parallel with each other, like layers in a complex political community.

There is a great temptation to see the chiefship as a system of African tyranny opposed to the (ideally) emancipatory quality of state-mandated democracy. Many South Africans see these as two cultures, an African and a European one. Jan Smuts and many politicians of his generation saw them as different stages of a political evolution. Recent commentators like Mahmood Mamdani see the two as two aspects of the dual state derived from Frederick Lugard's colonial policies of the dual mandate or divide and rule. These approaches miss the point, it seems to me, and if the fundamental questions still remain unanswered at the beginning of the twenty-first century after more than a century of pondering the issue, it may well be that they are in fact the wrong questions.

POSING SOME PROBLEMS

The primary question that must be asked is "what kind of power do chiefs have?" For the most part, in South Africa today, as in the past, the *chiefship question* has been asked in terms of it relationship to the state. The nature of the state has changed somewhat from its colonial or *creole* origins, but the burning question has remained the same: How can the local power of the chief be integrated into the overarching state system of political power? As a first approximation in answering this question, we must recognize that the chiefship represents not just questions of political process, but rather questions of identity and the assertion of local autonomy against the globalizing and modernizing power of the state. Despite local differences, all chiefs seem to insist first of all that they represent land and people, not in general democratic terms, but rather as *s*pecific and local embodiment. This presents fundamental problems to the universal and abstract order of the modern state, and it is these problems that must be addressed first before any questions of interactions between the two can be addressed.

Each region of South Africa, however, has a distinctly different history, and chiefship differs so radically from one region to another that it is scarcely the same institution across the entire country. There is significant variation even between neighbouring chiefs in the same region. Legally, however, and in the new constitution, the chiefship has been treated as a single *broad church* of so-called *traditional authorities*. While the very term *traditional authority* suggests its own vagueness, there is little that can be said empirically about the structure and function of the institution as a whole in contemporary South Africa. Most of what is written about it, moreover, refers either to archival and historical material, or to political issues of the day. There is almost no fieldwork or survey work on it. This is, in large part, due to the political opprobrium cast on the chiefship during apartheid, when many of them served as administrators of apartheid policy in the rural areas. From the foundation of the Republic of South Africa in 1962, chiefs were all considered as part of government, under the supreme titular authority of the State President. While this introduced some legal regularities within the state's administrative structures, it fomented dissent on the ground. In the face of the local dissensus and centralized efforts to co-opt and control it, the chiefship became adaptable and protean.

The general opinions held by South Africans about the institution and persons of the chiefship are Manichean in their division between good and evil, light and darkness. For some, the chief is the symbol of African unity and, therefore, of its collective good. It stands for the essential goodness of the African past before it was corrupted by Europe, and by modernity.

> The traditional leader is the epitome of the lifestyle of his community. He is the symbol of unity; he is the father figure; he is

the tier of cases and dispute arbitrator; he is the lawmaker; he is the custodian of culture, tradition, and custom; he is the custodian of communal land; he is the overall administrator; and above all he is the commander in chief of the armed forces. He is in a position to mobilize the youth and have them attack his perceived enemies or to defend himself against attack.[4]

On the other hand, the chiefship also represents, for others, a past that oppressed women, children, and youth in its demand for labour, for control of sexuality and reproduction, and its insistence in most cases on a male monopoly on political power. In more recent times, the chiefship is tainted fatally, in the views of many by its collaboration with apartheid, and by its role in the enforcement of government-planned development schemes known as *betterment*, and by their conservatism in the face of the liberation struggle of the 1970s and 1980s.

The institution of chiefship is divided in other ways as well. Some provinces possess traditional authorities in the persons of kings, chiefs, and headmen while other provinces do not. In effect, the territory of South Africa is divided between those provinces which have chiefs (Northern, Northwest, Mpumalanga, Eastern Cape, KwaZulu-Natal, Free State) and those that do not (Gauteng, Western Cape, Northern Cape). Although there were once traditional authorities in the regions now occupied by the Gauteng and Western Cape, the vast metropolitan centres of Cape Town and Johannesburg that dominate them have long since overwhelmed *traditional* rural communities and their chiefs. This is the case, too, in the former Natal, dominated as it is by Durban, but since its effective fusion with KwaZulu, the hierarchy of Zulu chiefs with the Zulu king at its head is now held to include all of the province in its domain.

Even where the chiefship exists, however, it does not command respect among so much as a majority of local people, its ostensible subjects. Many simply do not recognize its authority, nor worry much about its moral, legal, or economic standing. It is largely irrelevant among youth, migrant workers who live mainly in the cities, or women. And there are other factors that decrease its relevance. Until now, those who have begun to argue for a cultural independence, or at least recognition of a *coloured* and/or Griqua identity, have not seen their leaders in the same terms as the leaders of the Bantu-speaking Black traditional authorities. Moreover, there is apparently no counterpart to African traditional authority in the Indian communities, or in the many smaller communities of identity such as the Greeks, the Chinese, the Jews, the English, or Afrikaners. Nevertheless, in KwaZulu-Natal, the Zulu King, Zwelethini, has declared that he is king of the entire province, including, in his words, "Jews and English." There have in the past been Whites who held the office of chief under a different historical situation. Joaõ Albasini among the Tsonga in the North, and Theophilus Shepstone in Kwa Zulu were effectively chiefs, for instance, in the later- nineteenth-century, although both were officially designated *Chief Native Commissioners* for form's sake. With a strong degree of continuity with these cases, under apartheid the (white) State President was de jure head of all traditional leaders. Nevertheless, today it is clear in popular belief that only Black *tribesmen* can be chiefs or occupy a place in a hierarchy of traditional leadership. This presents insurmountable problems for any policy of non-racialism, and contradicts principles in the South African constitutional article on fundamental human rights.

Moreover, the very concept of *chief* seems to require a *tribe* who consents to be ruled by a chief, that is, his *sechaba* (Sotho/Tswana) or *isizwe* (Zulu/Nguni), and the existence of tribes in contemporary South Africa is itself a doubtful proposition. It may be that king, chiefs, and headmen can exist without tribes, but their political functions then become anomalous. The allegiance to the notion and office of the chief appears to divide South Africa neatly between an urban domain and a rural domain, although these domains are largely conceptual rather than clearly spatial. In the age of democracy, the defenders of chiefship eschew democratic election, arguing that a chief is born of royal blood, not elected. While government bureaucracy and legally appointed commissions ponder how land should be distributed, chiefs maintain that it is only they who can allocate land as the common heritage and rightful property of their own communities, their *tribes*. This link to both people and land is essential to the chiefship. As S. P. Holomisa remarked in a statement concerning the aims of Contralesa:

> The founders of Contralesa had come to realise that the resilience of the institution of traditional leadership in the face of the onslaught from colonial and apartheid governments and the homeland administrations, was due to the fact that the institution was deeply rooted in the people and the soil of Africa; it would endure as long as the two continued to exist.[5]

Finally, and in a way that sums up all of the other contrasts and oppositions that the notion of the chief lies between, the debate around chiefship swings wildly between the two poles of traditional and modernism, and between the *European* and the *African*.

WORKING TOWARD THE RIGHT QUESTIONS

The idea of chiefship must be discussed, then, in two modes: the one as ideology and belief, the other as institution and practice. There is a vast gulf between the ideology of chiefship and its practice, and there is a continuous debate among those who believe in its viability as an institution and those who do not. Most of the battles over the chiefship, including that leading up to the final draft of the constitution, are fought in terms of ideology rather than with reference to knowledge of how (and if) the institution really exists on the ground, or *works as claimed*. For one thing, there has been very little empirical work done since the middle of the century; for another, most participants in these debates seem to prefer the ideology to the reality. Ideologically, the idea of the African chiefs sums up for their supporters all that was golden and good about the pre-colonial age of African innocence. For these visionaries, the chief was both the origin and instrument of all goodness for his people, a protector, a father, a shepherd, a hero, a warrior, a law-giver, a judge as full of wisdom as Solomon, and an able administrator of his peoples' collective wealth in cattle and pastures. In this idyllic vision of the past, the chief was in tune with the natural time of the seasons so that he set the times for ploughing and planting, and determined the times for initiation of the boys and girls into the statuses of men and women. The chief declared the time of meetings for his people to decide on matters of importance at the *imbizo* or *kgotla*. Fully aware of the needs of his people, it was the chief who allocated space for dwellings, for agriculture, or rituals and ceremonies, and for grazing the cattle. Romantic vision of this sort usually marks the nostalgic celebration of institutions that no longer exist, or at least seem to signal its imminent demise. Like the brothers Grimm, and other folklorists and romantics of the later eighteenth and early nineteenth centuries who salvaged the last of Europe's peasant oral literature, in practice, surprisingly, the chiefship in South Africa is not merely alive; it is growing. Despite the contradictions and difficulties, the current existence of the office has been recognized by virtually all political actors. The 1996 constitution recognizes a role of chiefs, formally called *Traditional Authorities* in the new South Africa.

The contradictions inherent in the institution arise principally from its conflict with the principles of bureaucracy and the principles of modernism in administration. Conflicts arise also because of the persistent and fundamental localism that chiefship implies when this flies in the face of global cultural patterns, consumerism, and universalistic principles such as the Universal Bill of Human Rights proposed by the United Nations and espousedat least in publicby virtually all levels of political organization in South Africa today. Significantly, it also contradicts the powerful urban nouveau bourgeoisie that constitute the core of the ANC now that it is in power. For them, chiefship is an anomaly, an embarrassment, obsolete and an obstacle to their plans for centralized state control of modernization. For the locals and the subjects of the chiefs, the chiefs are increasingly becoming the focus of black resistance to the ANC government. The institution, the personnel, and the ideology of chiefship as it is represented in the so-called "*rural* areas of South Africa, cannot be reconciled with these principles, desires, and demands of the constitution or the state or the expectations of urban bureaucrats and party ideologues. In other words, there is no logical or administrative solution to the problems it poses. This does not mean that it will disappear, any more than it means that globalization, modernization, and bureaucracy will disappear. It appears inevitably that they will both continue to exist in South Africa for the foreseeable future, and that they will simply present opposite sides of a political conundrum.

TAKE ME TO YOUR LEADER

In the Bushbuckridge area, the chiefs are a variegated bunch. The extent and nature of their powers differs tremendously, depending, it would appear, largely on personal aptitude, interest, and energy.

Chief Malele is elderly. His teeth are severely rotten, and his tongue searches the gaps ceaselessly, his lips moving as if he were speaking. He seems to have nothing to say. The court building dates from the 1930s. A faint, naive painting in brown of a lion with the name Kgosi Masego appears over the door. The buildings are painted in a colonial, public-works department style in cream and brown. At the front is the chief's court with a raised dais and panelled wooden box in which the chief sits. In front of this are incongruous bright blue plastic stacking chairs lined up in haphazard rows. Behind this there are a few offices and a small kitchen area. All of the rooms are empty, the walls bare, but all are spotlessly clean.

Although he claims that there is no power in the chiefship anymore, he tells us that there are "no problems." He is defeated and tired. The compound around the court is deserted, although the floors are polished and the building is clean. His office is empty of anything but government-issue furniture, the same furniture that stands in the courts and offices of Chief Masego in Relane, Chief Moletele, Chief George Masego in Thabaholo, and Chief Setlhare in Green Valley. There are no pictures, calendars, or certificates on the wall, nothing on the desktop. As he opens a drawer, I can see that there is nothing inside it either. He even has to go out of the room to find an ashtray; he brings it back: an old, old sardine tin, at least decades old. He is smoking a cigarette that is already nearly burnt to the filter, but he has been gone for less than a minute. He saves his cigarette butts to relight them later. When we arrive, at around half past nine, we are asked to wait. "He is still washing himself at home and will be here when he is ready." We suspect that he is still asleep, and when he does arrive he does indeed look as if he has just got out of bed. Our interview is frustrating and confused: he has little to say. At the end of the interview, we find that a group of old men about his age have gathered in the courtroom and behind the building. They gather around a small fire in the back of the court, next to the outdoor toilets, to roast meat on a small fire. They are most of his councillors and *indunas*. In the middle of day, they quietly roast their meat while a woman brings a large plate of *mielie pap* to eat with the meat. We are invited to join, but are served out of a separate plate of meat and pap. While we eat, Hudson Malele, the chief's brother, who is also the secretary to the chief and to the Tribal Authority, quietly tells us that he would be happier elsewhere. "In fact," he says conspiratorially, "I am looking for a job." He makes only R360 a month. "Even if I can get a job with a pick or a spade, I would be happy," he confides. "At least it would be a job and I would have respect." When the meat is gone, the men leave in their bakkies and cars, and the chief walks to his home across the road.

By contrast, Chief George Mashego of Thabaholo gives every impression of being an energetic businessman. The court buildings are modern, and his house across the street is clean and neat, built in the style of the surrounding township brick houses, but painted and plastered. There is no quaint picture of a lion with the name of the Tribal Authority over the door. A modest Toyota sits in the driveway. As we approach, a member of the council greets us. They are friendly, even jolly. I explain my business, and they say the chief is in, but busy. Just then he comes out of the court building. He is stern and distant in front of his councillors and clients. He tells us we must make an appointment with his secretary if we wish to see him. He gives me a disapproving look when I say in a friendly invitational tone that I had met him briefly at the shops in the Acornhoek Plaza some weeks before, and walks quickly towards his house for his lunch. Inside, the secretary phones him to arrange an appointment with me for an interview. The phone is new, and works, on a desk full of papers, in an office full of life and business. Although the secretary's hands shake almost uncontrollably from alcoholism, he is not drunk. There are trucks in the driveway of the court building getting supplies to carry out some work for the *sechaba*, the chief's people, and the people seem to be occupied in every room of the building. On the wall across the reception area, a local architect has posted sample plans for houses, business, and churches in a jazzy, contemporary style that is clearly recognisable as the 1980s style of the (old) white, northern suburbs of Johannesburg, and of the trend-setting areas of Soweto. His contact numbers are on the sheet. An undertaker and several other businesses also advertise their services in the waiting room.

Chief Moletele's establishment in Buffelshoek is again different. My assistant and I ask for instructions to get to the chief, and are eventually directed to his house. The house is a large A-frame suburban style, evidently built in the sixties, but is dilapidated beyond repair. There is no one home. Behind it, there is a mud-brick building with a tin roof and an open fire. Smoke curls out from under the tin, and we greet an old woman that emerges from the blackened interior. "No," she tells us, "the old chief Moletele is dead, and his son is now chief." Goats clamber over the patio, with its cement planters in the form of Grecian urns, and the driveway is littered with cow dung. The barbed wire security fence that once surrounded it has rusted and fallen. Down the road, we are greeted in the old court buildings. Johannes Ntilela and his brother Isaac, are the secretary and assistant secretaries of the Tribal Authority. They are friendly and speak excellent English, as well as Afrikaans, SeSotho and XiTsonga. We are there to make an appointment to see the chief, we tell them, and a time is duly and efficiently agreed to even though they do not have contact with the chief. They assure us he will have the time. The buildings are dilapidated, and a Tribal Authority bus quietly rusts on its axles next to the building. There is no glass in the windows, which are shuttered with boards. The court has a long veranda on the front, more in the style of old *voortrekker* houses or Indian shops of the last century. Both the court and the few outbuildings behind it are painted the same cream and brown of Chief Malele's ageing buildings. There is a huge mango tree in the middle of the fenced yard around it. It has clearly been here a very long time. Outside the fence and down the road a short distance is a brand new chief's court, but this has not yet been occupied. Chief Moletele was not available on the two days that I went to see him. On the second, the acting chief gave us an impressive interview in complex and nuanced English that was so heavily accented by his native SeSotho (more accurately, SePulana) that it was difficult to understand. He clearly had done a great deal of reading in English, but had had little opportunity or need to speak it, and certainly did not do so regularly. His brother, the chief, on the other hand, had not been educated, and had succeeded to the chiefship in 1990 after their father's death.

If Chief George Masego looks like a businessman, Chief Setlhare looks like a cleric or a worried academic. He dropped out of university to become a chief on his father's death in the later 1980s and seems careworn and unhappy with his lot. There are people in his offices, but unlike those in Masego's offices who seem to be there with a purpose, those in Setlhare's office look aimless, ready to wait, and vaguely supplicative. The furniture comes from the storeroom of South African bureaucracy of the 1950s: heavy wooden tables, with a row of wooden filing boxes along the back of the desk. Several bound and dog-eared logbooks lie around on the table. One of them is a "visitor's book" which I am asked to sign. It has only one page of signatures, about fifteen in all, for the year of 1996, but it is already July. There is nothing else in the book, though it too is dog-eared and dirty. There are health posters and calendars on the walls, however, and up-to-date notices of community meetings and events. The court building is perhaps a decade old, and the old, previous building stands unused next to it in the fenced enclosure. Chief Setlhare, himself, is young and thoughtful.

All of these chiefs and their establishments, as different as they are, once belonged to the same homeland government of Lebowa, and today all are members of the Congress of Traditional Leaders of South Africa (Contralesa). All of these chiefs are Sotho, and all belong to the Pulana *tribe*, administering different parts of the same *tribal trust land*. There is still a remarkable variety amongst them. This variety can perhaps best be explained with reference to the ways that each has faced the political and cultural problems that confront them. These problems, however, are perhaps best termed "conundrums" since there are no clear solutions to any of them. If there were simple answers to the problems, surely all would more or less conform to a single style or method of dealing with them. The fact that they do not conform either to each other, or to some bureaucratic norm, suggests a casting around, a search, and an adaptive diversity to a complex environment.

THE POLITICAL CONUNDRUM:
TRADITION AND AUTHORITY

In fact, *traditional authorities* in South Africa are neither *traditional* nor *authorities*.[6] They are not authorized by tradition as they are currently constituted, and they do not constitute *authority* in the normal (Weberian) sense of the term since they are not *legitimate* power. They are not *legitimate* because they have, at the moment, almost no basis in current South African law, and they are not *powers* since the chief or *induna* have little authority deriving from other capacities or positions, such as wealth derived from employment or business, or respect for their *honour* or fear for possible control of spiritual and occult powers. Thus, *traditional authority* is a misnomer. Nevertheless, there are many such persons playing this role however ambiguously it is defined.

But Max Weber makes an error when he attempts to subsume *traditional, charismatic,* and *rational* authority under a common rubric or types of legitimate domination. At least in South Africa, traditional authority and charisma are not types of *domination* at all, and the forms and processes by which these forms of power exist are incommensurate with the modes of rational bureaucracy. The latter depends on the issuance of a command, and the written registration of this in the form of legal codes and procedures. Power of this sort – the sort most of us take for granted, based on models of European and American constitutions and politics – takes place in formal architectures of bureaucracy, while the other two do not. The reasons for obeying a bureaucrat have nothing to do with the reasons for obeying a chief, or for respecting the will of a charismatic individual. It is Weber's overall ambition to construct a fully rationalized theory of "economy and society" that forces this classification, not the empirical forms of its exercise.

In the Bushbuckridge area, the chiefship seems to function in fact rather like an NGO. The South African NGOs fulfillled functions that government either refused to fulfill, or was incapable of fulfilling. It is similar with the chiefs today. Formally, deprived of a significant role in the local government councils, they continue to exist for their believers and clients, and fulfill functions and carry out duties that government is not able to do, or is prevented from doing for one reason or another. Circumcision schools are a prime example of this. The chief is formally required to open a circumcision school in Sotho tradition. The chiefs, too, claim to maintain a sort of quality control over the circumcision schools and attempt to police the authenticity of the customary practices of the schools. In this role, the chiefs are exercising their role as cultural arbitrators and guarantors of tradition. In a multicultural state committed to the principle cultural diversity, it is not possible for state offices to exercise control over an institution such as circumcision schools in which some of the principle traditions of the *tribe*, *people*, or *sechaba* are passed down. In this, they hold a secure position that will be required so long as people continue to send their children to circumcision schools. Fulfilling this function, though, involves them in a role that is neither governmental nor fully voluntary. They collect fees for their services and they give advice; effectively selling it, in fact, in a way that would be seen as *consultancy* in any other context. The institution of the chief, then, has gradually merged with the institutions called NGOs that are not quite government, and not quite voluntary cultural or recreational organizations either. At the same time, the chiefship also functions as an avocational focus for a group of people who are culturally conservative and who wish to emphasize their ethnic and local identity by associating themselves with the chief. Indeed, taking on a position analogous to the NGO effectively saves the chiefship from death by neglect, and bolsters considerably its position in the community. This is not, however, the role that the chiefs would wish to see themselves in.

THE CULTURAL CONUNDRUM

The history of the institution of the chiefship in South Africa shows a process of mutual accommodation and incorporation. As in other aspects of South African history, the cultural problems that had to be faced were: how to be African in the context of European encroachment and in a European-dominated global system, on the one hand, and how to be European in the African landscape and in and amidst an African and Africanizing population. This pair of implicit problems presented themselves with equal force to black Africans and to white people from Europe who were permanently resident in Africa, although in different forms. For the black chief, king, or other political leader such as an *induna* or a chief's councillor, the problems of *being African* consisted of maintaining traditional forms of domination over women and juniors, as well as labour tenants, vassals, and allies, in the presence of a number of European-derived, or European-managed political orders that also presented themselves. Ever since the seventeenth century, this was a problem to the *captains* of the *Hottentots*, or Khoe. They struggled to maintain authority over children, youth, and women who often saw better, or at least different and exciting opportunities in the Dutch settlements. The histories of Krotoa, and of Saartjie Baartman, are famous cases in point, but there are many others. Eventually, it was an unequal struggle, and all Khoe who survived were incorporated into the Dutch Creole society that emerged in the place of the Khoe bands that had previously occupied the lands of the Cape province. The same process occurred again and again as settlers moved east and north. Each chief or person of authority, usually but not always male, had to consider how to maintain *traditional* forms of power and order in the face of new forms and orders that presented themselves at their doorsteps, and that eventually engulfed them entirely. With the exception of the Khoe and the Bushman, the struggle to maintain African ways was often successful. This involved finding ways to maintain tradition, often entirely within the overarching order of the farm, and the new patrimonial authority of the European farmer and his wife. In most cases this was accomplished by two systems of spatial management. In the first, the African-indigenous one, spatial management was based on a culturally conceived meaningful landscape in which rights of usufruct were allocated by the chief. In the second, which overlay the former, *farms* as tracts of land were surveyed with instruments and plotted in cadastral survey maps entirely without reference to the African modes of spatial management. The first depended upon *tradition* while the second was entirely self referential, and depended on texts and maps (a special kind of text) and on a technical method of geographical measurement that yielded numbers and written representations. The former set of spaces represented a way of *being African* with reference to the landscape, and formed its space around social power of chiefs and men, gender and use of land by cattle herdsmen, planters, gatherers, and hunters. The latter divided the landscape into rectilinear polygons and assigned these spaces to families of farmers or *boere*. An implicit double-landscape – the one divided into chiefdoms and kraals, and the other divided into farms, homes, and locations – permitted each system to coexist despite the other. The government land acts and the native (or Black) administration acts of the twentieth century, beginning immediately after union and carrying on until the end of apartheid, attempted to disaggregate (that is, to segregate) these two overlapping concepts of the land-cum-political-space. They sought to regularize and control – that is, routinize and bureaucratize – the varying concepts of landscape, power, and identity that were implicit in the two spatial conceptual systems.

Nevertheless, the two spatial orders continue to coexist, and are a key element in the structures of local power, knowledge, and resources that permitted parallel, relatively autonomous, though densely overlapping and interacting systems of culture and power, to coexist in South Africa. Neither the *African* nor the *European* modes ever fully succeeded in eclipsing the other and, thus, gaining hegemony, but neither has been able to fully insulate or isolate itself from the other. Apartheid, of course, was in part a forty-year-long gargantuan effort to do precisely this – to eclipse the African political orders by its own form of state bureaucracy – but, as we know now, it failed to achieve most of its goals, including this one.

The ambiguous power of chiefs today is the consequence of this struggle that took place in a deeply ambiguous landscape governed by (at least) two overlapping and interpenetrating regimes of power, kept separate by radically different understandings and practices of *power*. These different regimes came into conflict, of course, because there is physically only one actual surface to the earth and only one human population. They remained contrastively in isolation from each other, because their modes of understanding that unique physical reality were widely divergent. Hence, the continuity and ambiguity of power, but also the continuing ambiguity and tenuousness of state power, especially at the margins.

THE RIGHT QUESTIONS: LAND AND POWER

The link between power and land in southern Africa is not the instrumental one that exists in the West. It is not within the power of the chief to exercise sovereignty over a territory, as it has been in European political practice of empires, states and republics since Roman times. Rather, the link derives from a concept of land and space that empowers the chief.

Rather, the chief must be autonomous on his land. Coming *from the land* confers autochthonous identity, but also confers isolation from other figures of authority or power; that is, autonomy. It is the importance of autonomy that makes the segmentary system so appealing to those who live within it. Each segment claims its own autonomy. Autonomy in this sense is power. It is not that the segments lack a head (that is that they are *acephalous* or leaderless) but rather that the leader is internal to each segment. Co-operation is not coordinated from a person higher than each autonomous segment and, therefore, outside of each as a paramount or transcendent authority. Instead, each segment is ideally a model of all others and, therefore, autonomous from them in its completeness. Each segment is, ideally, an isomorphic pattern with respect to other segments, and the recognition of this fact of similarity is enough to justify the identity of each with respect to any of the others. None of them "has what the other has not," and each is whole with respect to other segments at its level. The logic is not a logic of command and, therefore, of causation executed through verbal command, but rather of identity and isomorphism. While this logic has been recognized as a mechanical form of solidarity by Durkheim and others, the significance of autonomy within this system as a form of power has not been recognized. Instead, the autonomy of the segments has been perceived as a *lack*. Power, always conceived as hierarchical and verbal, did not exist in these systems (except at the lower level), since there was little development of hierarchy. Instead, the automorphic mechanical solidarity that existed was interpreted either temporally as a *stage* prior to the development of *true* power (hierarchy, verbal command), or morally as lacking in *fibre*, *ambition*, *order* or, quite simply, *power* itself. Instead, there was a different understanding of the nature of power at its extremes.

It is not that there is no power of command in southern African societies. Rather it is the nature of power and command at the extremes of the continuum. At the top, in the Western-Weberian model, the ultimate power is the power to command; that is, to be the source of "the word." Religious models have supported this pattern since *God* or *The Creator* is held to be the source of all moral commands, as well as the source of the command required for physical creation itself. The Weberian commander (that is, the person at the top of the political hierarchy) has no choice but to command. Without the command, that is, without creating speech acts that can be construed as commands and conceivably be *followed* as orders, the leader is not a leader. The *commander* without a command ceases to be a commander by a very simple grammatical logic: one cannot be a woodcutter without wood, anymore than a commander can lack command.

In African models, a commander does not occupy the centre of power. The chief who may command holds this position, but he may also choose not to command. The drunken king may be incapable of command, but he is still king irrespective of any temporary incapacity. By the same logic, the deposed chief typically must be killed, since he remains a chief even without "a say" in anything. His chief-ness is in his being, not his words, and not his verbal *power* over followers who execute his commands. His words may, of course, have *power*, but this is not the power to command individuals to perform empirical actions ("do something"), but rather to *be* something (through performative acts such as "you are now a man," "you are now no longer kin"). The power of the African chief's word is also the power to heal, or to harm. This is not accomplished through the command to followers to heal or to harm, but by his merely saying that there will be health or danger *in the land*. The category of *the land* includes the beings of his followers and thus affects them, but does not cause their action as effects of his command.

The chief's word is an act in itself, not necessarily a command that exists (or does not exist) by virtue of the actions of others. A command that does not cause any follower to act as a consequence of that utterance, is not held to be a command, or is held to be a command in abeyance. It does not go away by virtue of not being obeyed immediately, but rather becomes a *standing* order that continues in its potential to cause others to act as a consequence of it. However, a command that receives no objective observable obedience is normally regarded as not a command: it contains no power if it fails to cause others to act according to it. The command – and thus the power of the command – is contingent upon its being followed. It is the empirical act of followership that is the symptom of power rather than the existence of *commands*. The command that is not followed is not, in principle, a command. The follower that follows a command, however, makes that command powerful rather than the other way round. In the African model, however, the word of the chief is *sui generis* powerful. It does not require obedience to be of significance. Its value is in its having been uttered by the chief. Thus, a chief may exist even when no one follows his commands, but he may not exist without a tribe that acknowledges his existence as chief. It is their recognition of the chief as chief, rather than their obeisance to his command, that makes him chief, and that makes him powerful.

Since *the land* always underwrites this form of power as *being*, the chief is the prime autochthon (even when displaced) and the prime disposer of the resource which supports his and his followers' *being*, in theory, even when he no longer commands the land as physical resource, but (as in much of South Africa) as the representative of *land* or of lands now gone, or even of mythical lands of origin, the source of a once-upon-a-timeautochthony which virtually all African people south of the Sahara seem to accept as fully natural. Without this faith in the landscape, even the imagined landscape, as *origin*, the African model of political power collapses. Power in Africa is thus deeply rooted in specific cultural landscapes rather than in specific verbal *dicta* (such as the Code of Hammurabi, or the constitution in Pretoria). These are the imagined landscapes of autochthonous origin, rather than origin in "the word," or by consequence of the command. The notion of origin in the landscape thus powerfully underwrites an ontological theory of power that can operate together with a verbal-action theory of power, but which is fundamentally irreconcilable with it. The land is not just a productive resource, a token of economic value, an instrument of production (*pace* Marx) in some or other mode, but is first of all the foundation of power itself; power, that is, as being of and in the land as a product of autonomous creation.

Authochthony and autonomy are thus closely related in this theory of power. The chief is both autochthonous and autonomous. He represents the land and is of the land, while at the same time embodying a kind and quality of power that is not controlled by others' forms of power. That is, it is autonomous in its own domain, and this is what gives the chief the right to distribute land to his followers. Only the chief *holds* the land and *is* the land, while at the same time being relatively free of other influences of witches or spirits that might undermine the judgment of others who would presume to distribute land. This autonomy must be protected, however, from the influence of others, and the chief's autonomy is constantly at risk. Similarly, his claim to autochthony depends upon his bond to the people who constitute his following. This dependency on *the people* by means of which he is a chief, however, cannot be called "legitimacy" in the strict Weberian (or Parsonian) sense since it is not based on written rules of contract, or on laws in terms of which his power is guaranteed. The acceptability of the chief as chief is more ambiguous than this, since it depends upon specifically unwritten consensus. Thus, the chief is a chief by virtue of his place in a field of influence that is constituted by consensus, and breach of that consensus can undermine and ultimately destroy his ability to act as chief. In a very real sense, the role of chief is defined and given *power* by the very nature of the ambiguity and unspoken-ness of the verbal consensus that constitutes it. This same ambiguity and unspoken-ness – that is, the *diffusion of influence* and the power of ambiguity on which it rests – is also its weakness with respect to Western systems of law that attempt to make the ambiguities explicit, and which attempt to routinize influence through bureaucratization of the office.

The bureaucratic chief is no longer a chief, since his powers cease to be ambiguously constituted by *diffused influence* and become instead explicit. As such, they fall under the control of the command and are linked into the chains of written command on which bureaucracy uniquely depends. When the chief loses his autonomy, he can no longer be thought of as autochthonous. His powers are defined in an entirely different way. Lugard may have realized this in some way when he designed the system of "indirect rule," but the architects of apartheid's Bantu Authorities Act certainly did not. The architects of the act imagined that the chiefs would be easily brought into the bureaucratic system of central government. In fact, they could, but practically and philosophically the real basis of their power changed.

In practice, however, the two systems of power are sufficiently different that they could continue to function in parallel, mostly without knowledge of each other. The institution of chiefship during most of the twentieth century in South Africa functioned by virtue of what Sahlins has called the "working misunderstanding." Accordingly, both traditionalists and bureaucrats could assume that the chief was constituted in terms of their own making, while the same actions and events could be explained culturally in two quite different ways. Historically, this allows us to account for the re-emergence of the chiefship as a viable African institution after years of apartheid. Just as the two systems of understanding the landscape continued to exist as if they were different conceptual *layers* within the same landscape, the chiefship could continue to exist in terms of two culturally distinct systems of thought about its nature. This has meant that even though the chiefs were bureaucrats under the Bantu Authorities Act, they continued to be conceptualized among their followers in the *traditional* way. One system depended on writing and registration of genealogies in the government ethnologist's offices, while the other depended on the *secret* of unspoken, ambiguous influence. This effectively maintained the separate identity of the two systems of thought. Both possibilities of power – a bureaucratic one and a traditional one – continued to exist and could be exploited to different degrees as historical conditions required. This is what we have seen in the late 1990s in South Africa as the conditions of apartheid gave way to the conditions of a new South Africa, a new modernity, and a new demand for an autonomous African identity.

This did not do away with the paradoxes of how best to be African within a European legal-bureaucratic system, or how to enforce a European logic of human rights and constitutionality within an African landscape, landscape, and sense of identity. The paradox remains, and will continue to drive the history of the chiefship into the future.

The contrast between chiefly power and the power of governments or states is a contrast between a model of power based on *diffusion of influence* versus a model based on *chains of command*. The chief's power is a diffused power that is largely unspoken, but that lies within a fabric of *secret* powers that belong to the healers, the witches, the masters of initiation schools, and to the chief himself. All of these people have secret powers that are held to be able to influence each other as well as other members of society. These powers are secret not because they are explicit knowledge that is deliberately not shared (as a secret would be in command-based systems of power), but because they cannot and do not directly control others through means of spoken commands. They are unspoken not necessarily because they are secret, but they are secret because they cannot be spoken and thus remain unknown until some manifestation of them in everyday life is apparent. Thus, they remain ambiguous and implicit. The role of tradition is important in the *traditional system* not so much because it draws on the past or represents a continuity with the past, but because it is implicit and ambiguous. Its very ambiguity is its *power* since it cannot ultimately be gainsaid, and because it is held to be pervasive. But since mere ambiguity cannot directly cause action, action comes from deep sources of shared knowledge that we call "culture," or which Bourdieu chooses to call "*habitus*." This conception of power provides explanation in all cases since it can be held to be responsible for all eventualities, but does not cause any event in particular. The ambiguous, pervasive influence of secret power is responsible for all events in general. Unlike the command which must be stated explicitly and which constitutes a concrete act (the speech act), the power of the chief and other *influential* persons always remains in potential until events themselves make these powers manifest.

ACKNOWLEDGMENTS

This work was partially carried out with the aid of a grant from the International Development Research Centre, Ottawa, Canada. Part of this chapter was originally delivered as a paper presented to the Annual Meeting of the American Anthropological Association, 23 November 1996.

REFERENCES

Bothma, C. V. 1976. "The political structure of the Pedi of Sekhukhuneland," *African Studies* 35.
de Villiers, Bertus. 1994. The New Constitution: Framework and Protection of Human Rights. Occasional Papers. Johannesburg: Konrad Adenauer Stiftung, July. [In Mothibe papers collection, in library of R. Thornton].
Hammond-Tooke, W. D. 1974. *The Bantu-speaking Peoples of Southern Africa.* London: Routledge & Kegan Paul.
———. 1975. *Command or Consensus: The Development of Transkeian Local Government.* Cape Town: D. Philip.
———. 1984. *Descent Groups, Chiefdoms, and South African Historiography.* Johannesburg: University of Witwatersrand, African Studies Institute.
———. 1993. *The Roots of Black South Africa.* Cape Town: A. D. Donker.
Holomisa, S. P. [n.d.] Memorandum: The identity of the Congress of Traditional Leaders of South Africa, its aims and objectives. [Amended typescript.] [In Mothibe papers collection, in library of R. Thornton].

Kessel, Ineke van, and Barbara Oomen. 1997. "One Chief, One Vote: The Revival of traditional authorities in post-Apartheid South Africa," *African Affairs* 96: 561–85. [Reprinted by the Van Vollenhoven Institute for Law and Administration in Non-Western Countries, Reprint 98/2, Leiden University, Netherlands.]

Shils, Edward. 1981. *Tradition.* London: Faber and Faber.

Spiegel, A. D., and E. Boonzaier. 1988. *Promoting Tradition: Images of the South African Past South African Keywords: The Uses and Abuses of Political Concepts.* Cape Town: David Philip.

Weber, Max. 1968. *Economy and Society,* 2 vols. Edited by Guenther Roth and Claus Wittich, translated from *Wirtschaft und Gesellschaft* [1951]. University of California Press.

NOTES

1. The term "induna" also refers to sub-chief, or "headman, although many so-called indunas prefer to think of themselves as chiefs, or at least to understand their role in the same terms. Thus many former indunas are also calling themselves chiefs. Only formally recognized chiefs receive salaries from government, however. Many erstwhile chiefs are also vying for the title King, especially in the context of current legislation and constitutional guarantees that the institution will be permitted to survive, and even prosper with government stipends. Only when referring specifically to the Zulu king do I use the term king, usually with the qualifier Zulu.

2. Holomisa, S. P. n.d. "Memorandum: The identity of the Congress of Traditional Leaders of South Africa, its aims and objectives," p. 3 [amended typescript]. [In Mothibe papers collection, in library of R. Thornton.]

3. Holomisa, "Memorandum," op. cit., 3.

4. Holomisa, "Memorandum," op. cit.

5. Holomisa, "Memorandum," op. cit.

6. That is, in terms of the more or less standard definition of *tradition* (for example, Weber 1968; Shils 1981; Spiegel and Boonzaier 1988), and of *authority* (Weber 1968).

LOCAL GOVERNANCE IN LESOTHO:
THE CENTRAL ROLE OF CHIEFS

CHAPTER 6

TIM QUINLAN AND MALCOLM WALLIS

TIM QUINLAN is now associate professor and research director of Health Economics and AIDS Research Division (HEARD) at the University of Natal–Durban, South Africa, and was formerly an associate research professor in the Institute for Social and Economic Studies at the University of Durban–Westville, Durban, South Africa. An anthropologist by training, at the University of Cape Town, he completed a master's degree on the transformation of land tenure in Lesotho and his Ph.D. thesis entitled: "Marena a Lesotho, Chiefs, Politics and Culture in Lesotho." He is the South Africa Country Team Leader of the IDRC-funded TAARN research project.

MALCOLM WALLIS is professor and head, School of Governance, University of Durban–Westville, Durban, in South Africa. He is a member of IASIA.

INTRODUCTION

Public debate in Southern Africa about traditional authorities generally revolves around two positions. On the one hand, chiefs are regarded as outdated forms of authority and, therefore, they should have no role in government. An extension of this argument is that the institution of chieftainship is a hindrance to evolution of political democracy and, therefore, the institution should not be recognized by the national government at all. On the other hand, chiefs are regarded as significant forms of authority, particularly in rural areas, and therefore they have a role to play in the government of a modern state. An extension of this argument is that the institution of chieftainship stands alongside the bureaucracy of a modern state and, therefore, the institution needs to be transformed to the effect that chiefs become line functionaries within local government structures.

The debate is long-standing and unresolved. Chiefs have never been as malleable as the national government of the day or the populace might wish. Here, we examine a familiar historical pattern: national governments always prescribe roles and functions, but this has been an intractable problem in the case of traditional authorities. We use Lesotho as a case study of how many chiefs continue to be popularly legitimate authorities in rural communities, just beyond the reach of the national government, despite efforts, first, by colonial governments and, later, by successive national governments to transform them into functionaries of the state.

We argue that chiefs and national governments are always enmeshed in each other's intentions such that neither party ever succeeds in supplanting the other. The institution of chieftainship has been transformed over time in Lesotho, partly as a result of government interventions, but the new forms have never been in the image of the government of the day. We assert two principles for understanding the existence of the chieftainship in Lesotho. First, the appearance of a dual structure of government in Lesotho is deceptive, and any analysis that proceeds on this basis must confound itself. Such analysis inevitably overemphasizes the difference between the structures at the cost of ignoring the historical process by which both traditional and modern forms of government have evolved together. Secondly, the notion of traditional authority is misleading, for the form and role of chieftainship in Lesotho has changed over time. In other words, we question any analysis that presumes a traditional–modern dichotomy with regard to the existence of a chieftainship in Lesotho.

WHAT IS A CHIEFTAINSHIP?

If one were to ask "what is the chieftainship?" (*serena* in Sesotho), many Basotho would hesitate to answer. Few people would adopt such a distanced stance as is implied in using the word *serena*; indeed, it is rarely used in conversation. But if one were to ask "what is a chief?" an answer would be given readily. People describe the chieftainship as *Marena a Lesotho,* literally *the chiefs of Lesotho*. There are many *marena*, approximately 1,558 (Mazenod 1984)[1] – one for every thousand citizens. Although there are formal distinctions of rank between chiefs (e.g., district chief, ward chief), and between them and headmen (*bo ramotse*), all are popularly acknowledged by the title *morena*.

Individual chiefs are identified by name, for that relates the person genealogically to predecessors and indicates that the office is a hereditary one. Chiefs are also identified by the area they live in, which allows description of the chieftainship as a set of offices with jurisdiction over settlements. However, the chieftainship is not a static entity. Agencies within and beyond Lesotho have shaped the chieftainship, giving it a heritage which stretches back to pre-colonial African societies, across the world to Europe, and which includes political and economic developments in South Africa.

A stereotypical description portrays a pyramid structure with the office of king at the apex under which there are strata of chiefs and headmen down to a broad base of councillors. This structure is based on a territorial division of authority; small areas administered by headmen are encapsulated in larger and larger territories of succeeding strata of chiefs to the point where the king is vested with authority over the whole country. This description reflects the influence of colonial and post-colonial governments in shaping Lesotho society. However, it obscures the interaction between indigenous and colonial authorities in creating the chieftainship in Lesotho.

There was mutual effort by leaders on both sides to create a hierarchical structure of chiefs, but they had different premises and aims. Whereas colonial officials sought to define authority on the basis of territories, the indigenous leaders sought to incorporate this basis within a model of kinship. Political authority was to be structured according to individuals' genealogical position in relation to the founder of the Basotho nation, Moshoeshoe I. In sum, chiefs in the past and today proclaim the chieftainship as a dynastic form of authority (Hamnett 1975; Mazenod 1984).

However, subsumed within both models, there are pre-colonial and novel concepts that emphasize personal relationships between chiefs and subjects, and the subordination of chiefs' authority to the material and symbolic needs of the populace.

Table 1: The pyramid description of the chieftainship

Paramount Chief/King (Morena emoholo/Motlotlehi)	(1)
District Chief (Morena oa setereke)	(10)
Ward Chief (Morena [oa sehloho])	(14)
Sub-Ward Chief (Morena)	(556)
Village Headman (Ramotse)	(1,002)
Councillor (Letona)	$(?)^2$

(Source: Mazenod 1984)

The chieftainship is akin to the hub of the wheel, kept in place by the spokes that are the relationships between chiefs and subjects. In sum, the chieftainship is the focal point of society, around which, and through which, Basotho define the nation, the country, and their place in it. As we shall see, this popular understanding of the chieftainship has hindered succeeding governments' ability to govern in the rural areas.

In view of the above, how should one describe the chieftainship in Lesotho? Each description reveals significant features and important agencies in its development, but no single description is adequate. The descriptions indicate a complex political process in which there have been conflicting notions of what the chieftainship is, and what it should be. There is tension between the impetus to define a hierarchy of political authority over and above the populace, and that which seeks to keep political authority grounded in citizens' everday concerns and activities. It is this tension which reveals the life and complexity of the chieftainship. The chieftainship is always coming into being, for it has yet to be drawn entirely in the image of any of its makers. The stereotypical description of the chieftainship is illustrated in table 1. The numbers in brackets indicate the approximate number of incumbents.

The emphasis in this chart is on territorial differentiation of authority.[3] The paramount chief or king has dominion over the whole country. Territorial sub-divisions demarcate areas of jurisdiction of subordinate chiefs, down to a spatially defined unit: the village. This description reflects Lesotho's development as a geo-political entity. It is a state that occupies a defined area of land. Within the country there are now ten administrative districts, but the boundaries of chieftainships do not coincide with them in several instances. Within these districts there are smaller demarcated areas, known as wards and sub-wards, while numerous villages dot the landscape.

A British imperial hand is evident in these developments. Following the creation of the Basutoland protectorate in 1870, British officials proceeded to establish an administration on the basis of territorial units. At the time, this territory was described in terms of three loosely defined areas under the authority of three chiefs, the senior heir to Moshoeshoe I and two of his brothers, and one area governed by a magistrate (Lagden 1909, 462). All were in the lowland regions while the vast mountain interior was simply described as "very rugged ground" (ibid.).

By 1884, when Basutoland became a Crown Protectorate, the borders of the country had been demarcated. By 1904, the interior had been demarcated into seven districts (Berea, Maseru, Leribe, Quthing, Mafeteng, Mohales Hoek and Qacha's Nek). At the turn of the century, Butha Buthe and Mokhotlong were simply small police camps which would later be administrative nuclei for districts that would be demarcated during the 1940s. This practice continued after independence. In 1978, the district of Thaba Tseka was carved out of existing districts, following the growth of a small town, Thaba Tseka, as an administrative centre in the central mountain region (Ferguson 1990, 76, 80).

Colonial officials encouraged spatial demarcation by which senior chiefs were proclaimed as district chiefs and their subordinates were placed in sub-divisions of these areas (wards and sub-wards). Alarmed by the proliferation of chiefs, and by conflicts over territorial claims, the colonial government rationalized the structure during the 1930s, following the Pim Report of 1933 (Hailey 1953, 69; Hamnett 1975, 35–36). A limited number of district, ward, and sub-ward chiefs and headmen were recognized in a government gazette and, thereafter, only these individuals and their heirs were to be accorded official status as authorities. That heritage is evident today. People can readily point out the areas under the authority of particular headmen, and how each area is encapsulated by wards and districts.

However, the colonial description subsumes another description that is based on a patrilineal model of authority that was elaborated by the chiefs themselves. This model originated with Moshoeshoe I who strove to build the Basotho nation into a coherent entity that could challenge the intrusions of colonial settlers. He appointed sons ("Sons of Moshesh" is a common term in the early literature and in local parlance) and brothers subordinate to himself, with authority over particular settlements and immigrant groups. Oldest sons inherited the positions of their fathers, and their brothers were appointed as subordinate chiefs to govern smaller communities within the broader community of the oldest sibling.

This *indigenous* hierarchy invoked a pre-colonial model of society. Agnatic relationships formed the framework for the transfer of wealth and authority, nominally specified by the link between father and eldest son. Lineages, interconnected through marriages, provided the skeleton for defining individuals as members of a group and for their identity vis-à-vis other groups. Oral genealogical records that traced male ancestors back to a single legendary ancestor, like branches of a tree to a trunk, provided the basis for identifying clans and the relationship between members of different groups.

This model was useful to draw people into the Basotho polity. It defined real and imagined relationships between the many groups on the high veld and, in the context of colonial intrusion, it could be used to unite those groups into a corporate entity. Moshoeshoe's half brother, Mopeli Mokhachane, for example, brought his own following into the Basotho fold following the numerous conflicts with colonial settlers during the 1840s and 1850s. Thereafter, he was acknowledged as a chief under the authority of Moshoeshoe's third son, Masopha (Damane and Sanders 1974, 96–97; J. de Miss. Ev. 41 (1866): 46). Characterization of a chief as a father figure, and of his role as a personal leader, indicates that there was a distinctly indigenous premise to political authority which was the antithesis of the colonial perspective that tended to place an overwhelming emphasis on territoriality. Humans were the fundamental resource rather than territory. However, elaboration of authority on this premise alone proved to be short-lived in the face of persistent colonial pressure.

Encapsulation of a population within the territorial borders of the protectorate simply created a group for which political organization had to be developed. Within these confines, Moshoeshoe's agnates elaborated the kinship model of authority to their advantage. The Laws of Lerotholi provide an apt illustration. The laws were written after Lerotholi became paramount chief in 1891. They are ostensibly a "declaration of Sotho law and custom," but they have also been a means for senior chiefs to codify a system of authority in the image they desired (Hamnett 1975, 37–40). They were also strongly influenced by colonial officialdom and the missionaries. The rules for succession, for example, coincidentally justified Lerotholi's position as the paramount chief that had been previously contested. The pertinent rule (Duncan 1960) states that:

> The succession to chieftainship shall be by right of birth; that is, the first born male of the first wife married; if the first wife has

no male issue then the first born male child of the next wife in
succession shall be chief.... Provided that if a chief dies leaving no
male issue, the chieftainship shall devolve upon the male following
according to the succession of houses.

The significance of this rule belies the fact that Lerotholi was the oldest son of Letsie
I's second wife, and heir apparent because his father's first wife had borne no sons.
The question of who would succeed Letsie had been raised before Moshoeshoe died,
and the latter had tried to stipulate that the heir should be a son born to the daughter of
Letsie's first wife. Hamnett (1975, 39–43) has also described similar instances in later
years when succession to the paramountcy was questioned, when different principles
had to be applied, and, on occasion, when attempts were made to change the laws to
suit the desires of the incumbent paramount chief.

Hamnett (1975, 38) described the application of the kinship model as "heredity
modified by expediency." A few principles were elaborated, but the model always
contained ambiguities that could not be resolved. Hamnett (1975: 25–35) explained
these ambiguities through what he calls the "retrospective" and "circumspective
models." The former refers to the way Moshoeshoe was seen as a founder of a
dynasty, with his four sons forming the basis of cardinal lineages. Taken as fixed
points of reference, these lineages determine forever the structure of the chieftainship.
In each succeeding generation, the eldest son of each incumbent would inherit the
position of chief, and together they would form a closed elite group of chiefs. If these
chiefs decided to appoint other agnates or supporters as subordinate chiefs, inheritance
to the positions would follow along the same lines as for the principal chiefs.
However, the model also contained the seeds for chiefs to use the circumspective
model. If Moshoeshoe could place his younger sons as chiefs, then other chiefs in
each succeeding generation could do the same. In other words, in each generation a
chief acted as a new founder of a lineage.

Hamnett provided a convincing explanation of the origins and dynamics of what
was known in Lesotho as the "placing system," by which chiefs were appointed and
how the number of chiefs proliferated accordingly. In 1938, the colonial government
formally began to rationalize the chieftainship through statutory proclamations.
The formal process was to last twenty years. The number of chiefs was reduced, and
the statutory authority of chiefs was curtailed and made subordinate to the colonial
government (Ashton 1952, 186; Hamnett 1975, 35). The proclamations were a means
for the colonial government to clarify territorial areas of jurisdiction, to specify the
number of these chiefs in these areas, and to subordinate the authority of chiefs to

colonial institutions. However, senior chiefs were very involved in the process, such that individuals whose genealogical ties were closer than others to Moshoeshoe I and his immediate heirs, were confirmed as authorities, thereby re-affirming their status as senior chiefs. Other chiefs and headmen whose genealogical status did not dovetail with this rendition of the patrilineal model, generally lost their legal status as authorities.

In sum, the chieftainship was shaped into a more coherent form than it had in the past as a result of the combined actions of senior chiefs and colonial officials. One needs to be circumspect, however, about any suggestion (Ashton 1952; Jones 1951; Hamnett 1975) that the chieftainship was fixed into a particular form by the 1950s. The possibility of a neat synchronization of the kinship and territorial models, for example, is unlikely in view of the different premises of their creators and the ambiguities in the kinship model. Hamnett's argument that the political system was reconstructed suggests new tensions as much as resolution of old ones. Furthermore, as much as institutions may be shaped by elites, it is improbable that something so central as the chieftainship could be reconstructed without significant interventions by its subjects. In a different vein, the ethnographic record obscures as much as it reveals. The explanations of Hamnett (1975), Ashton (1952), and Jones (1951), limited the agents who were taken into consideration and compacted the social process, such that the chieftainship could be presented as a finished product.

Our point is that ethnographic description of Lesotho's chieftainship has alluded to, but obscured a dialectic that can be broadly defined as a struggle over, and a struggle for, the institution. The former struggle has been well documented, for it has involved the visible interventions of government officials and senior chiefs. The struggle for the chieftainship is less visible, however, for it is to be found in the interactions between the rural populace and chiefs, notably those in the lower echelons of the hierarchy. As the circumstances of rural life change, so the rural populace reassesses what chiefs do, and acts to keep the chieftainship relevant to its needs. The rural populace's struggle to ensure that the exercise of authority reflects their changing needs, means that the chieftainship is never fixed, but always coming into being. We discuss this dialectic below through reference to the political history of Lesotho before and since independence in 1966.

THE MAKING OF THE CHIEFTAINSHIP

In the nineteenth century, Moshoeshoe and his agnates could not have created an *indigenous"* hierarchy of authority on the basis of kinship unless it resonated with their followers. That hierarchy, as we have seen, invoked prevailing social norms of patriarchal authority. Nonetheless, the formal principles of patrilineality and patriarchy provided only a framework for political authority. The practice of authority required chiefs to substantiate the personal relationship between leader and follower that was implied by these principles. In other words, while the kinship model emphasized command over people rather than territory, so too it demanded personal allegiance of people to a chief. The critical issue for chiefs was how to build up and sustain the allegiance of followers. The key was control over, and access to land. On the one hand, chiefs established their authority by enabling followers to gain access to land. On the other hand, followers sanctioned that authority only if chiefs demonstrated capability to provide land.

This process is reflected in village names. Many villages have a prefix "Ha," followed by a personal name, thereby indicating their origins. The nucleus of a village would be an original homestead established by a man and his wife/wives. In time, sons would establish their own homesteads in that place and, with immigration of friends and affines, the hamlet would grow into a village. Authority in the hamlet was defined in relation to the founder, who would be regarded by the other residents as the *father* (*Ramotse*) of the settlement, and whose name would identify it. Elevation to status as a chief depended on the person's capabilities to found settlements. For instance, as people came to settle in the mountain region, a notable leader, Lelingoana Sekonyela, first established his own village, Malingoaneng (literally, "where Lelingoana's people live"), then he appointed his sons as chiefs and sent them with small followings to establish other villages. Similarly, he allowed a Batloung group to settle in the area, and acknowledged its leader as a chief under his overall authority. As each community grew and new hamlets were established, these chiefs appointed their own kin, or acknowledged village founders as subordinate authorities. In each case, the subordinate authorities were *fathers* to their own subjects, and Lelingoana was the paternal authority over all who acknowledged his status as a chief.

This articulation of the kinship model of authority was different to that of the colonial officials, even of Moshoeshoe and his agnates. The key element of the territorial model is settlement as a physical construct. The colonial government demarcated chiefs' authority on the basis of the location of villages and people.

To chiefs, settlement was a social construct that expressed the identity of a group over which a chief had authority. While the colonial government's perspective was to define the relationship it wanted between itself and the chiefs, the chiefs sought to define the relationship between themselves and their subjects. While the colonial imperative was to demarcate boundaries of authority, the chiefs' imperative was to define the *locus standi* of authority from which it could be elaborated.

The key element of the dynastic model is distinction in social status. The principle of agnatic descent was a means to distinguish status, but it was interpreted in different ways. The colonial imperative was to differentiate authority through hierarchal divisions, in order to place the colonial representative of the British monarchy at the apex. The chiefs' imperative was to confirm their positions at the centre of their subject groups. Even though the placement of agnates in subordinate positions established a hierarchy, it also expanded the social boundaries of the group in a way that always indicated the centre whence the group originated, namely the senior chief. However, this historical process has occurred in conjunction with attempts by other government agencies to define these *boundaries*.

CHIEFS AND INDEPENDENCE:
THE FIRST TWO DECADES

Like the colonial government, post-independence governments of Lesotho have influenced the chieftainship through legislation, development initiatives, and resource allocation, but chiefs have also influenced the nature of the state. For example, the Chieftainship Act of 1968 (Kingdom of Lesotho 1968, Act 22) attempted to achieve a number of objectives, such as making provision for tenure, the exercise of functions, and discipline. However, the impact arising from implementation of that legislation has to be seen in the context of its acceptability to the chiefs and communities themselves. A similar point can be made about other policies and legislation in areas such as land and local government. In several cases, and especially between 1966 and 1986, chiefs played prominent roles in party politics at national level; for example, the prime minister during that entire period was also a minor chief.

The government elected just before independence was dominated by the Basotho National Party (BNP) under the leadership of Chief Leabua Jonathan. It remained in power until the military coup of 1986. The BNP made little effort during its two decades in power, to create a democratic political order. The national elections held in 1970 were seen by many observers as a turning point in the country's history, for the result was that the BNP remained in power despite evidence that they had been defeated at the polls by the opposition Basutoland Congress Party (BCP) led by Ntsu Mokhehle. What Khaketla (1971) called a "coup" occurred with the support of the police and paramilitary in order that the BNP should not lose power.

The significance of these events for the chieftainship is that the BNP was the party seen as representing the chiefs (particularly those in the lower echelons) and the Roman Catholic Church, whilst the BCP had stronger ties with the commoners and followers of Protestantism. For example, at any one time, the BNP cabinet contained a number of chiefs and they were often in the majority. Furthermore, the interim National Assembly which was nominated and established in 1973, included all twenty-two principal chiefs (Bardill and Cobbe 1985, 137). This unelected body remained as the country's legislature until Jonathan's government was overthrown. However, this link between the chiefs and the BNP became blurred as time went by because of wider patterns of social and political change. Bardill and Cobbe (1985: 147), for example, noted that the political and economic power of the chiefs:

> rests far less today on their traditional status and far more on their position as salaried functionaries of the state, as well as on their agricultural and commercial ventures. One result of these developments is that the chieftainship in general no longer provides the same source of interparty friction as it did in the past.

The fact that the BCP achieved an election plurality in 1970 suggests that the BNP's traditional base was crumbling, so that even if it retained the support of chiefs, it lost ground amongst rural communities, even in remote mountain areas (Ferguson 1990, 109). An additional complication is that Lesotho became independent as a constitutional monarchy and has remained so. However, the political events mentioned here have not left the system of kingship unscathed. In particular, King Moshoeshoe II, the ruling monarch throughout the BNP period, was frequently in conflict with the government. This constitutional conflict also alienated him from those chiefs who were benefiting from participation in the various arenas of political power.

In parallel with these political shifts, the question of the future of the chieftainship found its way onto the policy agenda of the BNP regime. Two examples will be given here. The first is the Chieftainship Act of 1968, which was passed at a time when the position of elected local government was being eroded. These cannot be seen as unrelated trends since the collapse of the nine District Councils, which were part of the colonial legacy, was an element of the BNP strategy to undermine the BCP (which, for the first years of independence was stronger locally than nationally: it controlled all nine councils). The BNP aim, in effect, was to eliminate the limited local democracy that colonialism had introduced, leaving the way open for a system of local administration in which field officers (such as District Administrators) posted by the central government were to work in collaboration with the chiefs. The Chieftainship Act was part of this strategic framework as it formalized the position of chiefs beyond the point reached by the colonial administration. In that sense, it continued a trend of bureaucratizing the chieftainship, without taking away its hereditary base, and without contradicting the *Laws of Lerotholi*, which had hitherto provided the legal basis for chieftainship.

The second example concerns the administration of land. The Land Act of 1979 (Kingdom of Lesotho 1979, Act 17) ostensibly reduced the powers of chiefs to control access to, and use of land. Historically, Basotho have had inalienable usufruct rights to land. Land was held in trust by the paramount chief on behalf of the nation. The chiefs then allocated parcels of land which families could use but not own. The system came in for widespread criticism from donor aid agencies on the grounds that it was being abused and was not promoting productive use of land. The Act introduced land committees of which chiefs would merely be a part. However, this seems to have been an attempt to satisfy donors and, as we discuss shortly, chiefs were able to conduct affairs much as they had in the past (Kingdom of Lesotho 1987, 44). There have been two reasons for this outcome. On the one hand, there was little attempt by government to enforce the changes. On the other hand, the realities of local power relations made it difficult for the government to usurp the entrenched, local authority of chiefs.

For the chieftainship, the first two decades of independence saw processes of change at work, some of which were the direct result of government policies. In some instances, the chiefs found themselves embroiled in conflict. At times, this was a result of party politics whilst occasionally there were aspects of state policy to be considered. What is clear is that the system of local governance by chiefs demonstrated a substantial capacity for survival despite considerable pressures to prescribe and represcribe their authority.

CHIEFS, THE MILITARY, AND THE PROCESS
OF DEMOCRATIZATION

The 1986 military coup heralded a seven-year period of military government, during which Major General Lekhanya and, later, Colonel Ramaema held the reins of power (Southall and Petlane 1995). For the military, the chieftainship was not a priority. However, legislation was introduced in 1986 (Kingdom of Lesotho 1986, Order no. 9) which concerned district administration, local institutions, and the chiefs (Mapetla and Rembe 1989, 36). Advisory development councils were created at district and village levels, within which chiefs were accorded significant roles; for example, they were to chair the councils. The powers of these bodies were modest, however, and did not force major changes on the chiefs, nor did they enhance the principle of democratic government.

The end of military rule came in 1993 when the BCP under Ntsu Mokhehle won an overwhelming victory in national elections; the opposition parties did not return a single candidate. Notably, the new government quickly adopted a new constitution (Kingdom of Lesotho 1993). The new constitution addressed the position of the chiefs, but the main emphasis was on the office and role of *principal chiefs*. Sections 54 and 55 established a senate composed of the twenty-two principal chiefs and eleven other senators – not necessarily chiefs – nominated by the king. Whilst these provisions appeared to give this category of chief a national role, the constitution also limited the powers of the senate, such that the latter could be easily overridden by the National Assembly itself. There are parallels here with the House of Lords in the U.K. The senate could express its views and some notice might be taken of them, but it was not in a position to exercise real power.

The twenty-two principal chiefs were also members of the College of Chiefs, a body charged with the task of overseeing the processes associated with succession to the throne, including possible designation of a regent under certain circumstances, such as the king having not attained the age of twenty-one or considered infirm.

The constitution had little to say about chiefs in general. It merely stated that chiefs would continue to enjoy the status they had before 1993, with the rider that Parliament may make regulations (Section 103). However, in view of some of the criticisms that have been made of the chiefs because of the undemocratic nature of the institution, it is significant that the constitution provides for continuity rather than abolition or diminution of their powers. For example, Rugege (1993) argued that the chieftainship was undemocratic and had to go. The gist of his argument, which reflected the perspectives of vocal individuals within Lesotho's intelligentsia, was that the chiefs have been instruments of state power and closely linked to the BNP. For example, in relation to the Chieftainship Act of 1968, he argued that "the main function of chiefs today is to assist the coercive arms of the state, especially the police" (Rugege 1993, 419).

Notwithstanding these arguments, the incoming government adopted a pragmatic position. Part of the reason for this may have been the preoccupation with crisis management, including threats to the regime itself. Whilst acknowledging that the legislation (notably the Chieftainship Act) needed to be changed, there was no likelihood of radical change. Interviews with key informants in the Ministry of Local Government and elsewhere in Maseru early in 2000 indicated that there were problems which need to be dealt with (chiefs are not systematically trained, are often corrupt, morale is low, etc.). But the official view seemed to be that chiefs will continue to play a role for a long time to come, at least in rural areas. A standard argument was that very few people want to see the institution scrapped, partly because it performed local functions such as dispute resolution in a relatively cheap manner. To many local observers, there seemed to be no realistic alternative to the chieftainship. With the continuing spread of education this may change, but government did not wish to undertake major reform action unless people are ready for it. The government followed in the footsteps of its forebears, nonetheless, in attempting to modify the institutions and practice of local government.

CHIEFS, LOCAL GOVERNMENT AND DEVELOPMENT

A key problem for the BCP government was the absence of modern democratic governance in the country's localities (towns, districts, and villages). This was seen as undesirable for many reasons, but partly because chiefs were still de facto the sole repositories of local authority below the district level. Soon after forming a government, the BCP made a commitment to the re-establishment of local government. The motives were mixed. The minister of Local Government, in a speech in 1995, argued that this was an essential element of the strategy by which a democratic culture could be cultivated. In addition, there were historical sentiments arising from the fact that the BNP had abolished local government in the late 1960s as part of its assault on the power base of the BCP (Wallis 1999, 97).

However, to date, this re-establishment of local government has not happened. Substantial effort has gone into planning, but the political uncertainties facing the country have derailed the process on several occasions. A split in the ruling party in 1997, for example, followed by a disputed national election in 1998, delayed the process. An account of what has been planned is useful, nonetheless, for indications of the difficulties and the changes that may occur.

Legislation to re-establish local government was passed in 1996 (Kingdom of Lesotho 1996, Act 7 of 1997). This followed a detailed policy formulation process (White Papers, workshops, mission reports, etc.,) assisted by consultants funded by the United Kingdom government (University of Birmingham, 1995). With regard to the chieftainship, a consultant from Botswana with substantial experience of local government in that country was invited to assist.

The 1997 Act empowers the minister of Local Government to declare areas to be served by a variety of councils. These are community councils, rural councils, urban councils, and municipal councils. The composition of these local authorities is based on election, but in each case a minority of positions is reserved for chiefs other than principal chiefs. To quote section 4 of the Act:

> In accordance with the provisions of this Act there shall be constituted the following Councils:
>
> - a Community Council shall consist of not less than nine elected members, but not exceeding fifteen elected members, and not exceeding two gazetted chiefs (other than principal chiefs) who shall also be elected;
>
> - an Urban Council shall consist of not less than nine elected members, but not exceeding thirteen elected members, and not exceeding two gazetted chiefs (other than principal chiefs) who shall also be elected;
>
> - a Municipal Council shall consist of not less than eleven elected members, but not exceeding fifteen elected members, and not exceeding three gazetted chiefs (other than principal chiefs) who shall also be elected;
>
> - a Rural Council shall consist of not less than thirty-seven members, but not exceeding forty-five members representing each of the Community Councils, within its jurisdiction as follows:

- the chairman of a Community Council;
- a member of a Community Council elected by the councillors from amongst them;
- three gazetted chiefs (other than principal chiefs) who are members of a Community Council and elected from amongst the chiefs who are members of a Community Council.

Two important issues emerge from these provisions, both of which have caused concern amongst the chiefs. The first is the exclusion of principal chiefs, the assumption being that they will play a role at national level through membership of the senate. This will detract from their local responsibilities in their *wards* (which, it needs to be remembered, do not coincide with local government boundaries). National policy makers, however, have expressed a desire to review the position and to make the requirements of senate attendance less demanding. Nonetheless, difficulties can be expected, as the allowances paid for attendance may be lost as a result of any revision. Early in 2000, there was talk of scrapping the upper house. Were this to happen, a more local focus for these chiefs would be expected; in discussion with key informants, the possibility of a co-ordinating role linking central and local levels was suggested.

The second issue is really a twofold problem. The first element to it is that the chiefs will occupy minority positions in all councils, and the second is that they will experience what they tend to see as the indignity of having to stand for election in competition with one another. The Act, in its schedules, lists a number of functions for the new bodies in which chiefs are likely to be interested, such as land/site allocation, grazing control, burial grounds, and minor roads. There is a sense in which the chiefs find themselves in a twilight zone wherein they continue to function as authorities, but in the knowledge that their significance as authorities within local government administration will diminish. To reinforce this point, it is possible that the Chieftainship Act of 1968 will be amended to reconcile it with the Local Government Act.

A related area of concern for chiefs and government continues to be land. At the end of 1999, a Commission of Inquiry was established to look again at this issue (Kingdom of Lesotho 1999). Of the fifteen members of the Commission, one was a principal chief (the influential and popular chief of Thaba Bosiu who was well known for his active involvement in affairs of state). Other stakeholders more strongly represented, in terms of numbers at least, included the development councils, farmers, and commercial interests. The terms of reference, in summary, were: to evaluate the land tenure system in relation to equitable access, security of tenure, land productivity, and efficient administration; to determine ways of resolving problems including dispute resolution mechanisms (both judicial and administrative); to examine the present arrangements for inheritance; assess the fragmentation of land through sub division; to look at relevant institutions including the planned and anticipated restructuring of local government; to review and recommend revision of legislation; and to recommend a national land policy. Whilst the terms of reference made no direct reference to the chiefs, it was clear that their roles would come under scrutiny as they were key actors in the management of rural land matters.

There are several other issues concerning chiefs and development that have been reflected in debates in Lesotho. One is the extent to which chieftainship is unacceptable as it is associated with gender inequality. Two researchers have argued that it "is essentially a male domain predicated on lineage" (Petlane and Mapetla 1998, 248). However, there are a growing number of female chiefs, and though their status is not totally the same as males, they are reported to constitute 35 per cent of the total number of chiefs in the country (Petlane and Mapetla 1998, 250). This growing trend might be supportive of the chieftainship in the present climate in which greater gender equality is advocated. Another issue is a concern that chiefs need training and capacity building generally. Some interest has been shown by donors (IOD 1998, 7, 34; ISO/SIDA 1987), but little has been achieved.[4] Another pertinent issue is the widespread view that chiefs have an excessive tendency to behave in what is seen as an undisciplined way. Examples are corruption, alcohol abuse, and violence. National officials with specific responsibilities for chieftainship report that these concerns constitute a large part of their workload.

Clearly, the chieftainship is once again being re-assessed by the national government of the day, and found to be wanting. The chieftainship is perceived to be at odds with the current norms and values of local government in a modern, democratic, state. Yet it is also clear that the national government's attempt to prescribe changes to the form and content of local administrations (supported by donor agencies) is not proceeding with ease and is unlikely to do so. We discuss reasons for this state of affairs below, highlighting in the process the contemporary "struggle for the chieftainship." Our focus is on how the populace has articulated the kinship model of authority in recent times, in order to sustain a chieftainship that is relevant to their changing circumstances.

A chief's court dealing with livestock cases in Lesotho (photo by Tim Quinlan).

In sum, we contend that while Basotho continue to define the chieftainship on the basis of historical precedents, they also strive to define the chieftainship on the basis of contemporary needs and economic circumstances in the rural areas. On the one hand, the accumulation of precedents over time enabled chiefs and the colonial government to refine their conception of the chieftainship as an institution with permanent features that would be endorsed in each generation. On the other hand, the way in which chiefs sought to define political boundaries through their subjects indicates a conception of the chieftainship as an organic entity, whose survival depended on its ability to adjust to the changing needs of its subjects. Underlying each model are the key factors of settlement, land and, one must add, livestock, in view of its long-standing economic and cultural significance.

THE MANAGEMENT OF SETTLEMENT, LAND AND LIVESTOCK

Villages are the most common form of settlement in Lesotho. There are a few towns; notably the nine district centres and the capital, Maseru. The majority of the population maintains de jure residence in villages, although many people, particularly men, spend most of their lives working in South Africa. The mining industry has been the most significant employer of labour from Lesotho.

It is the proximity of kin to each other which substantiates the patriarchal framework of authority. A married man is the head of his homestead that is identified by his name. In cases where a married son stays on at the homestead to support a widowed mother, the latter is nominally the head of the homestead in her husband's name. When she dies, the son becomes the head of the homestead which will then be identified, in time, by his name.

Many villages are substantially larger than they were in the past so that kinship is less visible as a framework for the social order. The superimposition of other forms of social and economic networks is evident. There are many schools and churches, for example, as a result of intensive missionary work by the Paris Evangelical Missionary Society, now constituted as the Lesotho Evangelical Church, and by various orders of the Roman Catholic Church. There is also a network of institutions to address civil order, health, and the agricultural economy, which are based in the district administrations of the national government. Therefore, it is not surprising that kinship is not always visible as a framework of rural social order, and that it is irrelevant in many instances. Villagers are materially integrated into a market economy and subject to agencies of the modern nation state. However, neither the state nor the market predominate in the rural social order. They are important forces of social change, but they have yet to dictate the management of settlements.

Basotho have an inalienable right to residential sites and, prior to the 1960s, individuals would approach the relevant chief or headman in whose area he/she wished to stay for permission to build a home. Since the late 1970s, however, site allocation has been, at least in theory, in the hands of Land Committees. Today, these committees also deal with arable land allocations as a result of the 1979 Land Act (Kingdom of Lesotho, 1979) and the 1980 Land Regulations (Kingdom of Lesotho, 1980a). The Land Committees are a means for the state to exercise its authority in villages. They are based on the territorial areas of jurisdiction of chiefs and headmen, but the residents may elect any individuals to serve on the committee. Individuals who wish to build a homestead must approach the relevant committee, fill in the appropriate forms and, following confirmation of title to the land by the Ministry of Interior, they may build dwellings.

The bureaucratic process nominally places site allocation under the authority of government departments. The election of Land Committees provides a platform for rural residents to participate in the management of settlements and, if necessary, to contest the decisions of chiefs and headmen. In practice, however, the Land Committees are no more than a minor modification to established procedures. They are elected bodies, but the chairmen are usually chiefs or headmen. The other members are usually men rather than women. Furthermore, the intention of the Land Act to facilitate settlement planning is still largely ignored. Individuals can build homes and business premises virtually wherever they wish, especially in urban areas, whilst in rural communities chiefs can still be decisive. The Land Committees do not think in terms of town planning; they simply fulfill the bureaucratic functions demanded of them, and intervene only if a site application involves the appropriation of fields or use of natural resources. In other words, the committees define settlement management in traditional terms, in the sense of upholding chiefs' authority to mediate their subjects' usufructory rights to land and its constituent resources. These conditions suggest that the state is only the nominal authority in managing rural settlement. A closer look at settlement issues confirms this impression. The state addresses settlement as a development issue. To this end, the state encourages the establishment of a hierarchy of Development Committees, which are based on the territorial jurisdictions of chiefs and headmen, and constituted by rural residents.

Under the system established by the BNP government, in each area governed by a sub-ward chief or headman, there was a Village Development Committee (VDC). A VDC consisted of elected residents from the area, and it did not need to include the local chief or headman. A VDC was responsible for improving services by initiating projects through funds raised by villagers, by identifying needs for submission to the district administration, and by co-operating with government officials who assist with projects. Project proposals were supposed to be submitted to the relevant Ward Development Committee (WDC) which, in principle, consisted of elected ward residents. In turn, the WDC submitted proposals to the District Development Committee (DDC) which, in principle, included elected members as well as the District Secretary, the district chief and, as observers, the district heads of government departments. The DDC is still responsible for assessing project proposals and for authorizing the relevant government departments to carry them out. As discussed earlier, subsequent governments modified this structure, but in most respects it is still intact.

The formal structure outlines a democratic process in which rural residents are identified as citizens with rights of representation and access to government services, and as participants in development. However, the structure of authority is no challenge to that of the chiefs. Firstly, the government's reliance on local committees reflects a lack of infrastructure and finance which minimizes the potential of these bodies to shape the rural social order as intended. The committees carry out small projects; e.g., building of hygienic toilets (Ventilated Improved Pit Latrines), and improve village water supplies through the assistance of the Village Water Supply Unit. In short, financial restrictions dictate a narrow functional role for the VDCs and their successors. Secondly, villagers endorse this role. To most villagers, VDCs are a means to extract material benefits from a parsimonious government that exists beyond the world of village life. They support VDCs, and they elect people who, they believe, know how to deal with the government.

The way the VDCs are reconstituted is repeated with the WDCs. In principle, a WDC consists of elected persons and is an intermediary body in the system. Accordingly, one would expect it to be a platform for democratic representation in the district administration, and to mesh partisan interests in VDC project proposals with broader plans for the ward as a whole. However, WDCs reflected the way rural residents have manipulated the intent and functions of the VDCs. The members are elected, but in terms of being nominees of various VDCs, Land Committees and chiefs and headmen. On this basis, they fulfilled a limited development role of passing on project proposals to the DDC. The DDC still today nominally integrates principles of political democracy with the practical demands of bureaucracy, but, in practice, public accountability is minimal. The DDC concentrates authority in the hands of civil servants who are not formally accountable to the populace. Moreover, due to its particular focus on development, the DDC emphasizes a top-down and restricted approach.

To summarize, the contemporary management of settlement in rural Lesotho highlights a process of differentiation of authority. The government intervenes to exercise its authority and to subordinate the chieftainship, but in a way which minimizes its presence in rural settlements and affirms chiefs' authority to manage settlement. There are similarities here to colonial interventions to subordinate the chieftainship. The colonial government's efforts to categorize different facets of chiefs' authority is replicated in the post-independence governments' efforts to impose objective criteria for development and democratic representation in rural local government.

This theme is evident in other aspects of the interaction between the government and the rural populace. The ongoing contest between chiefs and national governments has its roots in the rural populace's reliance on chiefs to uphold collective access to, and need for, natural resources, particularly those that sustain livestock. This is especially so in the mountains. People's pre-occupation with livestock is central to the way land categories are defined in relation to each other and to broader economic circumstances of life in rural Lesotho. Chiefs are the pivot on which villagers assess possibilities and constraints for rearing livestock.

The central role of chiefs in the livestock economy is palpable. Access to summer grazing areas beyond village environs is governed by district chiefs, from whom stock owners obtain permission to build grazing posts. Subordinate chiefs control use of grassland within their areas of jurisdiction. Throughout the summer months, chiefs are responsible for ensuring that stock do not graze on cultivated fields and grassland which they have reserved for winter grazing. Chiefs may prohibit grazing in areas that are badly degraded for as long as they feel is necessary. Chiefs are responsible for controlling the number of livestock in the villages during the summer, and can demand their removal to grazing posts. During the winter months, their duties are primarily to protecting specified restricted areas. With the onset of spring chiefs must decide when to restrict grazing in village environs, and when to order the removal of the majority of livestock to grazing posts.

Generally speaking, chiefs carry out their duties assiduously and with the co-operation of villagers. Their authority is demonstrated at the twice-weekly gatherings of stock owners, usually men, at chiefs' homesteads, to conduct the business of livestock management. Trade in livestock, registration of brands, impounding of livestock, their retrieval, and the care of stray animals, are all carried out under the auspices of the chief. This business is usually supervised by men who occupy positions that represent the chiefs' duties (chief's secretary, pound master, *babeisi/bewys* [stock transfer certificate] writer, grazing land supervisors [*batsoari ba maboella*]). In addition, 70 per cent of the pound fines are allocated to the grazing land supervisors, who are men appointed by the chief to enforce grazing restrictions, and the remaining 30 per cent is sent to the national treasury.

The legitimacy of chiefs is expressed in the way decisions are made to restrict winter grazing. Chiefs make the decision, usually in October, on the basis of debates amongst stock owners at public meetings held at chiefs' homesteads. The debates revolve around the welfare of livestock in relation to prevailing ecological conditions, such that many factors are voiced and considered (e.g., condition of village grassland in relation to the alpine grassland; forecasted spring rainfall; the strength of newborn lambs). There have been government regulations on the use of grazing land since colonial times (regularly updated to tie in with contemporary policies), but villagers regard them as simply one factor amongst the many for consideration.

In sum, there is community of purpose and understanding amongst stock owners and chiefs. There is common concern about the deterioration of grazing land, and about the difficulties of rearing a variety of livestock with different survival and regenerative capabilities in a harsh environment. There is also evident tension between the relatively rich and the poor stock owners over government interventions that are seen generally to favour the former. We outline these dynamics below.

Basotho have integrated market-oriented rearing of livestock with their pre-colonial pastoralist heritage. The outcome is a remarkable diversity of livestock, to which are attached a range of economic and cultural values. Cattle are the basis of the pastoralist heritage, but merino sheep and angora goats now vastly outnumber cattle, horses and donkeys, and mules. The preponderance of sheep and goats reflects the importance of Lesotho as a wool and mohair producer for international markets. Cattle, sheep, goats, and horses are mediums of exchange in cultural rituals as well as being commodities.

The critical problem for Basotho owners is how to rear livestock in a harsh environment. Not only is it difficult to rear animals in a country with climatic extremes (winters are severely cold and dry, summers generally very hot), but the different survival capabilities of livestock species and breeds required stock owners to develop different management techniques if their value(s) was to be realized. For instance,

Basotho have modified the transhumance system in recent years. For many years, the alpine grasslands were used during the summer months, and allowed to regenerate during winter and spring when livestock were grazed in village environs. During the last twenty years, stock owners have established winter grazing posts in the intermediate valleys, between villages and the summer grazing areas. These grazing posts are situated no more than three or four hours walk from villages, thereby allowing rapid removal of livestock to the villages whenever the weather deteriorates.

Underlying these changes is a gradual division between the minority who are relatively wealthy stock owners and the majority who are relatively poor stock owners. The former often keep their sheep and goats permanently at grazing posts rather than in villages, on the grounds that forage in village environs are inadequate for their needs. It is the majority of poor stock owners who move their different animals regularly between village, and winter and summer grazing posts because they can ill afford any stock losses. It is this majority that rely on the chiefs to extend winter grazing periods and to ignore government stipulations, in opposition to the minority of wealthy stock owners who tend to support the government's interventions.

The overt cause of this tension is government intervention in the livestock economy. Government policy is to concentrate livestock production in the mountain region, with an emphasis on grassland management, and arable farming in the lowlands. Range Management Areas (RMAs) have been created throughout the mountain region (Dobb 1985; Lesotho National Livestock Task Force 1990; Bainbridge, Motsamai, and Weaver 1991). However, there has been popular opposition to the RMAs since they were introduced in the late 1980s, such that the form and the manner in which they are established is continually being modified (Quinlan 1995). Similarly, a proposed grazing tax (in 1989) was shelved in the face of popular opposition.

Each RMA is the basis for grassland and livestock management programs that are restricted to the residents who live within the circumscribed area. Government officials manage the RMAs. They establish Wool and Mohair Growers' Associations, which are the basis for community participation in range management (Artz 1994). The general expectation is that these associations will take over the management of their respective RMAs. In the meantime the associations are the medium through which stock owners are educated about livestock and grassland management techniques. Members of the associations are elected to management committees which carry out business such as collection of membership fees, arranging for hire of stud animals, and general management of members' interests in producing and marketing mohair and wool. Through these arrangements, rotational grazing and breed improvement schemes have been established. Each RMA is divided up into grazing areas, and stock owners must move their stock to the different areas prescribed by government officials, and to keep stock within the designated carrying capacity levels in each area.

For rural residents, however, the need to manage the grasslands in the face of degradation is only one important concern. Their modification of the transhumance system and the government's interventions involve far more than the preservation of grassland. They involve redefinition of the content and boundaries of the rural political order. The chiefs remain central figures in the rural areas because people still rely on them to maintain their interests in livestock. As arable farming becomes less significant as a source of sustenance, livestock become, more than ever, a critical component of rural livelihoods. By creating winter grazing posts within the areas of jurisdiction of lower echelon chiefs, stock owners are emphasizing that the *locus standi* of authority for use of grazing land lies with their chiefs.

Ironically, the government's interventions are stimulating a contest over the boundaries of chiefs' authority in ways that are likely to exacerbate conflict between the government and the rural population. Simply put, the government is seeking to drive a wedge into the community of interest amongst chiefs and stock owners, but it does not take into account the strength of that community. It is a community grounded in the village, as a manifestation of the complex social relationship between chief and subject. Moreover, it is a community grounded in a context of material poverty in which mutual support is endorsed by the emphasis of the land tenure system on communal access to resources for the collective good.

Nonetheless, there are tensions in this community as a result of government interventions. On the one hand, there is a possibility of conflict between chiefs and the majority who are relatively poor stock owners on the one side, and the government and the minority who are relatively wealthy stock owners on the other. On the other hand, recent changes in the transhumance system indicate a struggle over the way grassland resources are categorized, which involves the subliminal issue of retention of communal right of access to grazing land and, therefore, a struggle over the appropriate form of authority to manage these resources.

Popular support for the chieftainship is likely to continue in this context for two reasons. First, the village is the nexus of any attempt to control use of grazing land, and this dynamic has yet to be recognized by the government. Secondly, the development of winter grazing posts within, and along the territorial boundaries of chiefs' areas of jurisdiction is similar to the period in the past when grazing posts were like satellites around settlements. In other words, the separation of grazing areas from chiefs' areas of jurisdiction is breaking down. As government interventions intrude on their authority over land within these areas, chiefs will be drawn to defend that authority generally, and their subjects' efforts to secure winter forage for their animals in particular. The political problem is that such reinvention of *tradition* is likely to reinforce government scepticism of the chieftainship, and popular disdain of chiefs amongst the rural population. Nonetheless, even if individual chiefs become the subject of disdain as impediments to the interests of the relatively wealthy stock owners and to government concerns, or even as ineffectual defenders of the interests of the majority of poorer stock owners, the chieftainship will be expected to resolve disputes.

This role of conflict resolution goes beyond livestock and land to include what are essentially policing and judicial functions. Family disputes, too, often find their way to the chief, which means that he/she may be seen as performing a social work role. Therefore, the chieftainship will both remain a critical factor in the strategies of people to maintain their cultural and economic interests in livestock and, more generally, in rural lives on a day-to-day basis.

CONCLUSION

Our argument is that any analysis of development management and institutional change in Lesotho cannot afford to neglect the chieftainship. The historical experience outlined here demonstrates the close association of this institution and the emergence of the identity of the Basotho people. This pattern, whilst undoubtedly complicated and distorted by colonial rule, showed remarkable qualities of resilience and sustainability. The reasons for this do not reside in romantic notions of traditional culture and beliefs, but in the realities of rural life. The need for chiefs rests on the fact that they perform a range of essential functions, the termination of which could result in a vacuum that bureaucrats and elected local government would not be able to fill. This is not to argue that bureaucracy and local government are irrelevant; that is clearly not so. What is important, however, is that the role they can play, especially in rural society, is a limited one. Under such circumstances, it makes sense to recognize that the chiefs have to be part and parcel of the system of governance. How best to do this remains a tough question to be answered.

The legacy of colonialism for the Basotho was not merely expressed in the form of the trappings of western forms of governance. Alongside such institutions as public sector bureaucracies and political parties, the chieftainship also emerged very much alive after a century of foreign rule. In the course of that time it had undergone and initiated change for a variety of reasons. For all its imperfections, its demonstrated ability to continue functioning in a sustainable fashion has also enabled it to continue to be a force to reckon with after thirty-five years of independence.

REFERENCES

Artz, N. 1994. "Lesotho's Range Management Area Program: The Evolution of Community Participation and Support." *Journal of the Grassland Society of South Africa.*

Ashton, H. 1952. *The Basuto.* Oxford: Oxford University Press.

Bainbridge, W., B. Motsamai, and C. Weaver, eds. 1991. *Report of the Drakensberg/Maluti Catchment Conservation Programme.* Pietermaritzburg: Ministry of Agriculture, Maseru and Natal Parks Board.

Bardill, J., and J. Cobbe. 1985. *Lesotho: Dilemmas of Dependence in Southern Africa.* Boulder, Colo.: Westview.

Damane, M., and P. Sanders. 1974. *Lithoko, Sotho Praise Poems.* Oxford: Oxford University Press.

Dobb, A. 1985. "The organization of range use in Lesotho, southern Africa: A review of attempted modification and case study." M.Sc. thesis, Washington State University.

Duncan, P. 1960. *Sotho Laws and Custom.* Oxford: Oxford University Press.

Ferguson, J. 1990. *The Anti-Politics Machine: Development, depoliticization and bureaucratic state power in Lesotho.* Cambridge: Cambridge University Press.

Hailey, Lord. 1953. *Native Administration in the British African Territories,* Part V. London: HMSO.

Hamnett, I. 1975. *Chieftainship and Legitimacy: An Anthropological Study of Executive Law in Lesotho.* London: Routledge and Kegan Paul.

IOD. 1998. *Lesotho, Decentralisation and the Establishment of Local Government.* Birmingham: International Organization Development.

ISO/SIDA. 1987. *Possible SIDA Support for Training of District Chiefs, Councillors and Staff.* Stockholm: ISO.

Journal de Mission Evangelique de Paris (J. de Miss. Ev.)

Jones, G. 1951. *Basutoland Medecine Murders.* London: HMSO.

Khaketla, B. 1971. *Lesotho 1970: An African Coup under the Microscope.* London: Hurst.

Kingdom of Lesotho. 1968. The Chieftainship Act. Act no. 22. Maseru: Government Printer.

———. 1979. The Land Act. Act no.17. Maseru: Government Printer.

———. 1980a. The Land Regulations 1980. Legal Notice No. 15, Government Gazette No. 29 of 22 August. Maseru: Government Printer.

———. 1986. Order no. 9 of 1986. Maseru: Government Printer.

———. 1987. Report of the Land Review Commission. Maseru.

———. 1993. The Constitution of Lesotho. Maseru: Government Printer.

———. 1996. The Local Government Act. Act no. 6 of 1997. Maseru: Government Printer.

———. 1999. Legal Notice no. 138 (Commission of Inquiry: Land Policy Review Commission). Maseru: Government Printer.

Lagden, G. 1909. *The Basutos.* London: Hutchinson & Co.

Lesotho National Livestock Task Force. 1990. "National Livestock Policy Implementation Plan." Maseru: Ministry of Agriculture.

Mapetla, E., and S. Rembe. 1989. *Decentralization and Development in Lesotho.* Roma: National University of Lesotho.

Mazenod. 1984. *Marena a Lesotho*. Mazenod.

Petlane, T., and M. Mapetla. 1998. "Gender aspects of female chieftainship in Lesotho." In d'Engelbronner et al., eds. *Traditional Authority and Democracy in Southern Africa*. Windhoek: New Namibia Books.

Quinlan, T. 1995. "Grassland Degradation and Livestock Rearing in Lesotho," *Journal of Southern African Studies* 21, no. 3: 491–507.

Rugege, S. 1993. *Chieftaincy and Society in Lesotho; a study in the Political Economy of the Basotho Chieftaincy from pre colonial times to the present*. Oxford University: D.Phil. thesis.

Southall, R., and T. Petlane. 1995. *Democratisation and Demilitarisation in Lesotho: The general election of 1993 and its aftermath*. Pretoria: Africa Institute.

University of Birmingham. 1995. *Decentralisation of Government Activities and the Establishment of Democratic Local Government in Lesotho*. Birmingham.

Wallis, M. 1999. "Lesotho: Seeking local democracy in the mountain kingdom." In P. S. Reddy, ed. *Local Government Democracy and Decentralisation; a review of the Southern African Region*. Kenwyn: Juta.

NOTES

1. The number of posts is now relatively stable.

2. This position is largely informal, and the number of councillors that a chief or headman has varies considerably.

3. The territorial categorization, particularly in the upper echelons, does not coincide with local designations of senior chiefs as *principal chiefs*, notably in legislation. *Principal chiefs* include the paramount chief, the district chiefs, and most of the ward chiefs, and the local designations refer to the dynastic, kinship model of authority discussed shortly.

4. Some initiatives have been started by the National University of Lesotho.

TRADITIONAL AUTHORITIES, LOCAL GOVERNMENT AND LAND RIGHTS[1]

CHAPTER 7

LUNGUSILE NTSEBEZA

LUNGISILE NTSEBEZA is a senior researcher in the Programme for Land and Agrarian Studies, a unit of the School of Government at the University of the Western Cape, Cape Town, South Africa. Since the advent of democracy in South Africa in 1994, he has been exploring the tension arising out of the roles, functions, and powers of a hereditary institution of traditional authorities in a post-1994 South Africa that is based on principles of democratic decision-making and elected representative government. His current research and analysis focuses on rural local government and the relationship of traditional authorities to elected representatives and how this relationship impacts land tenure and land administration in the rural areas of the former Bantustans. Ntsebeza has held a number of research fellowships at institutions such as the Land Tenure Center, University of Wisconsin; University of York; St. Antony's College, Oxford; and the Institute of International Studies, University of California, in Berkeley, and has published his work as book chapters and a wide range of academic and advocacy journals. He is a member of the South Africa Country Team of the IDRC-funded Traditional Authority Applied Research Network (TAARN) research project.

INTRODUCTION

This chapter examines land tenure and rural local government reform in post-apartheid South Africa, with specific reference to the role, powers, and functions of traditional authorities[2] in the Eastern Cape province. Tenure reform is one of the three main legs of the land reform program that is run under the auspices of the Department of Land Affairs, the others being land restitution and land redistribution. Government policy on the reform of land tenure is outlined in the 1996 constitution:

A person or community whose tenure of land is legally insecure as
a result of past racially discriminatory laws or practices is entitled,
to the extent provided by an Act of Parliament, either to tenure
which is legally secure or to comparable redress (Sec. 25, 6).

Before 1994, there was no distinction between landownership, administration, and management. These were centralized in the central state and, during the apartheid period, Tribal Authorities. As will be clear below, the aim of tenure reform in post-apartheid South Africa is to separate these functions.

The current local government reform policy in rural areas, led by the Department of Provincial Affairs and Constitutional Development, is based on section 151(1) of the constitution, which stipulates:

The local sphere of government consists of municipalities, which
must be established for the whole of the territory of the Republic.

Prior to the first democratic elections in 1994, municipalities existed only in urban areas. These municipalities were made up of elected councillors. There were no municipalities in rural areas in the former Bantustans. Municipal functions such as service delivery were provided by unelected traditional authorities, who acted as representatives of relevant government departments. The aim of local government reform in post-1994 South Africa is to establish municipalities that are made up of elected councillors throughout the country, including rural areas.

The overall aim of the chapter is to contribute to the formulation of appropriate and feasible policies at provincial and national level for implementing land tenure and local government reform. The chapter draws on in-depth field research in the Eastern Cape contained in a case study area, Tshezi.

The key questions addressed by the chapter are:

- What is the history of land tenure and local government in the rural areas of the former homelands in the period up to the demise of apartheid in 1994? What was the role of traditional authorities?

- What policies and legislation on land tenure and local government have emerged (and are emerging) since the advent of democracy in 1994? What, precisely, is the role of traditional authorities in the new dispensation?

- To what extent is the recognition in the South African Constitution of an unelected "institution of traditional leadership," on the one hand, and municipalities made up of elected councillors throughout the country, on the other, promoting and/or hindering current initiatives to implement policy and legislation on local government?

- To what degree does the District Council model of local government for rural areas provide an effective "check" to the previously unaccountable rule of locally (village and Tribal Authority) based traditional authorities?

- What is the response of traditional authorities to post-apartheid policies and legislation on land tenure and local government reform?

In attempting to answer these questions, the chapter, as indicated, draws on in-depth research conducted in the case study of Tshezi. No attempt is made to generalize.

"DECENTRALIZED DESPOTISM"

As indicated, a feature of African administration during the period after colonial conquest and land dispossession, in particular during the apartheid period, was the concentration or fusion of administrative, judicial, and executive power in the tribal authority. This fusion is well captured by Mamdani (1996, 23) in his delineation of what he calls "decentralized despotism," the "bifurcated state" or the "clenched fist," namely, the "Native Authority." This paper uses this theoretical framework to understand the role of traditional authorities in land tenure and local government in South Africa.

Mamdani's book examines contemporary Africa and the legacy of late colonialism. His thesis is wide-ranging and complex. He deals with a number of interrelated themes and notions, to wit, nineteenthcentury pre-colonial Africa and the nature of chiefly rule, notions of customs, tradition, customary law during colonialism, communal tenure, the rural-urban divide, resistance to colonialism, the post-colonial African state, and lessons for post-apartheid South Africa in its attempts to democratize rural areas. This paper, however, concentrates on one aspect of his argument, the Native Authority or clenched fist.

The chief, according to Mamdani, was pivotal in the local state, the Native Authority. Key to his authority was the fusion of various powers in his office, rather than a separation thereof. In his words:

> Not only did the chief have the right to pass rules (bylaws) governing persons under his domain, he also executed all laws and was the administrator in "his" area, in which he settled all disputes. The authority of the chief thus fused in a single person[3] all moments of power, judicial, legislative, executive, and administrative. This authority was like a clenched fist, necessary because the chief stood at the intersection of the market economy and the non-market one. The administrative justice and the administrative coercion that were the sum and substance of his authority lay behind a regime of extra-economic coercion, a regime that breathed life into a whole range of compulsions: forced labour, forced crops, forced sales, forced contributions, and forced removals.

The chief and his personnel, Mamdani asserts, were protected from "any external threat." They were "appointed from above" and "never elected." They had no term of office, and remained therein for as long as "they enjoyed the confidence of their superiors" (Mamdani 1996, 53).

It is this clenched fist that Mamdani sees as central to despotism in colonial and post-colonial rural Africa. Dismantling it is seen by him as a condition for democratic transformation in the countryside of Africa, including South Africa. Mamdani describes a system of "indirect rule" that was used by British colonialists in all their colonies, South Africa included. As indicated, this paper uses Mamdani's thesis to understand and explain land tenure reform, traditional authorities, and rural local government in post-apartheid South Africa.

In the case of post-apartheid South Africa, efforts are made to simultaneously retain and dismantle the clenched fist. An attempt is made to introduce separate, democratically elected structures for local government, on the one hand, and land management, on the other. Quite clearly, at least on paper, this is a major departure from tribal authorities, in which, as noted, these functions were concentrated, and where almost all its officials were appointed by government and the chief, rather than being democratically elected. However, by recognizing unelected traditional authorities, who during the apartheid period in particular, were largely discredited and feared,[4] while remaining vague about its precise role in land tenure and local government, prospects of extending representative democracy to these areas, and implementing emerging policies and legislation become extremely doubtful.

WHO ARE TRADITIONAL AUTHORITIES?

In this chapter, "traditional authorities" is an all encompassing term to refer to "chiefs" of various ranks, who have jurisdiction over rural people. Historically, at least at the point of contact between colonialists and Africans, the majority of the latter were organized into small groups (*tribes*) which had their leaders (*chiefs/iinkosi/ amakhosi/ kgosi*). Some of these groups were large and divided into smaller groups, each under the leadership of a chief. The larger groups were led by a *paramount chief/ikumnkani*. There were also *smaller chiefs* or *headmen/iinkosana*.

What is important for the purposes of this chapter is that these leaders were, at the time of conquest, hereditary. Things started to change soon after colonial conquest and land dispossession. Some of the African groups, led by their leaders, waged wars against colonialists, but were defeated. Whenever colonialists defeated Africans and dispossessed them of their land, they set aside a portion of land for African occupation. In these areas, colonialists adopted the traditional institution that ruled Africans, namely, one based on chieftaincy. They adapted this institution, however, and made it an instrument of *native administration*. Under colonialism, chiefs were expected to owe their allegiance to the colonialists. For this chiefs got a salary.

At the same time, chiefs who resisted colonial encroachment were deposed and replaced with compliant chiefs who were appointed by the colonialists. This marked a major break with the hereditary form of traditional authority. Although Beinart and Bundy (1987) point out that often these appointments were made from members of the chiefly family, a brother or uncle, this did not alter the fact that the government appointments were a departure from the rule, in that the wrong lineage was followed. This practice to appoint chiefs and paramount chiefs reached its peak during the apartheid period where recognized paramount chiefs such as Sabata Dalindyebo in the Eastern Cape, and Sekhukhuni among the Pedi in the (after 1994) Northern/now Limpopo Province were deposed and replaced by government appointees. In other words, the titles were retained, but the incumbents did not follow tradition. What is common, though, between hereditary and government appointed leadership, is that both are not based on election.

Traditional authorities are a highly differentiated lot. Apart from the above mentioned hierarchy; colonialism, segregation, and above all, apartheid divided them economically and socially. In their *civilizing* function, missionaries introduced Africans, including traditional authorities, to Christianity and Western education. Some traditional authorities were educated. When the National Party came to power in 1948 and introduced the Bantu Authorities Act in 1951 as a precursor to preparing Africans to become *self-governing* and *independent*[5] under traditional authorities, the latter needed to be prepared for this task. In the Transkei, for example, a school for the sons of chiefs and headmen was set up in Tsolo. During the apartheid period in particular, when, according to Govan Mbeki (1984) "chiefs" were "in the saddle," there was further differentiation among them. Some became politicians, business people, lawyers, teachers, and a combination of the above. Often, these traditional authorities spent their lives away from the areas of their jurisdiction, or had regents standing for them. They only periodically visited their areas of jurisdiction.

However, a significant portion of them was illiterate/semi-literate, poor, and lived permanently in their areas of jurisdiction. The majority of them used the enormous powers given to them by the apartheid regime to tax rural people, including the poorest of the poor. Some of these traditional authorities have become alcoholics as a result of the amount of liquor they get as part of the tax. Tapscott (1997, 292) has argued that it is this poverty and poor remuneration of traditional authorities at the grassroots level that made them corrupt. While this may be the case, Tapscott does not explain why those traditional authorities that were well off were also corrupt.

Until recently, the terms used for the groups and their leaders were *tribes* for the former, and *chiefs* for the latter. During the late 1980s, when some *chiefs* decided to throw their weight behind the ANC, there was resentment by the enlightened chiefs to the use of the terms *paramount chief, chief* or *headman*, on the grounds that these were pejorative terms that were used by colonialists. They prefer the all-embracing term *traditional authority* or *traditional leader*. Some prefer to use terminology drawn from an indigenous language. This study follows the new trend and uses the all-embracing term *traditional authority*. Where distinctions need to be made regarding rank, the appropriate term(s) are used.

SITUATION IN THE RURAL AREAS OF BANTUSTANS PRIOR TO 1994

The period prior to the democratic elections in 1994 divides into various phases: the pre-colonial times, or more accurately, the colonial encounter; the period before the Union of South Africa in 1910; after union to the introduction of apartheid in 1948; the apartheid period to its demise in the late 1980s; and the transition to the 1994 democratic elections. A thread that goes through this period was the concentration of power, at a village level, in traditional authorities' structures which were formalized during the apartheid period under tribal authorities established in terms of the 1951 Bantu Authorities Act. Traditional authorities, though, did not wield absolute power. They were accountable to colonial, later apartheid regimes. This was South Africa's version of indirect rule.

THE COLONIAL ENCOUNTER

At the time of encounter with colonialists, traditional societies were composed of groups that were under the authority of independent chiefs (traditional authorities). In establishing indirect rule through traditional authorities, colonialists exploited an ambiguity in the relationship between traditional authorities and their people, in particular on the question of accountability and how traditional authorities derived their legitimacy. Some traditional authorities were openly autocratic and feared (Edge and Lekowe 1998, 5–6; Lambert 1995, 270). Peires' analysis of the relationship between chiefs and commoners among the amaXhosa is revealing:

> Royal ideology implied not redistribution but dominion. It sought
> to entrench and accentuate the distinction between chief and
> commoner. Symbolically, the chief was thought of as a "bull" or
> an "elephant" whereas commoners were referred to as "dogs" or
> "black men." … His decisions were regarded as infallible, and any

mistake would be blamed on the "bad advice" of his councillors. Each chief was saluted by a special praise-name, and commoners who accidentally neglected to salute could be beaten.... No commoner could raise his hand against "a person of the blood" (umntu wegazi) even when, as sometimes happened, the chief's sons raided his herds and gardens. (Peires 1981, 32)

Yet there are those who argue that the chief derived legitimacy from popular support. Tapscott, clearly under the influence of Hammond-Tooke, represents this view in noting that

traditional leadership structures prior to European settlement in South Africa ... were not as autocratic and tyrannical as is sometimes suggested. Chief in Xhosa-speaking societies, for example, did not wield absolute and unchallenged power, and their influence was mediated by the community at large – in effect, by civil society. (Tapscott 1997, 292)

By community at large or civil society, Tapscott is presumably referring to the general assembly (*imbizo/pitso/kgotla*), which was attended only by married men. What is interesting is that both Peires and Tapscott are writing about *Xhosa-speaking societies*, yet they differ in their depiction of the relationship between *chiefs* and *commoners*. This, it is contended, demonstrates how complex and ambiguous the relationship was.

The same ambiguity existed with regard to land and how it was owned, allocated, managed, and administered. According to Hendricks, who wrote mainly about Western Phondoland, private ownership of land was unknown in African societies such as that of the amaMphondo.[6] With regard to the relationship between the traditional authority and his people, Hendricks notes:

All members were entitled to the use of plots, the distribution of which was the responsibility of the chief. It is known that the latter usually had the best land and more wives and cattle than other tribesmen, but there was no shortage of land. (Hendricks 1990, 44)

As far as the ownership of land and the power of traditional authorities in land allocation were concerned, Hendricks points out:

It is commonly accepted that all the land belonged to the chief, but he did not wield absolute authority in this regard. He was obliged to consult with his group of councillors and there were clearly stipulated conditions determining where and when he could appropriate land. His rule was therefore not arbitrary and in reality he only had power over unallotted land…. A married male member of the tribe had the right to request a plot of arable land as well as a homestead site. Polygamy was condoned in that one male could house a number of wives in different homesteads. (Hendricks 1990, 45)

The issue of ownership of land seems to have been complex. Peires draws a distinction between ownership and possession. According to him:

> Above all, the chief participated in production through his role as owner of the land. It is important to differentiate between ownership and possession. In pre-colonial Xhosa society, the commoners possessed the means of production but they did not own them.

Peires, though, qualifies the above by quoting the following from a colonial commission: "although it [land] was held in the name of the chief, he had no right to disturb me in my garden." Having said this, Peires nevertheless argues that "ownership was no mere form of words, since it was precisely by virtue of such ownership that the lord was entitled to extract part of the serf's labour." (Peires 1991, 33)[7]

Despite the complexity of establishing the precise meaning of landownership in pre-colonial African society, it would appear that once land was allocated to members, the traditional authority and his councillors no longer had any claim to the allocated land. Even Peires does not suggest that land was confiscated from commoners, once it had been allocated. Whatever these commoners owed to the traditional authority, their labour was extracted in exchange.

Given the power wielded by traditional authorities over land, in particular unallocated land, it is difficult to see how this unallocated land could be referred to as communal. As stated above, it is this ambiguity and the power of traditional authorities that colonialists exploited. According to colonialists, the centre of authority in African societies was the traditional authority-in-council. The latter could take binding decisions on any matter without the need to consult the wider community, not even the general assembly of married men. This view was given legal muscle in the case of *Hermansberg Mission Society* v. *Commissioner of Native Affairs and Darius Mogale*, 1906. The court rejected the argument that "a chief may not alienate land without the direct consent of the community," and held that "an African chief, as trustee of the community's land, may alienate land with the consent of the chief's council and without the direct participation of the community."

The question that arises is, How did people deal with unpopular traditional authorities? Traditional authority was hereditary, not elected – representative government emerged with the development of capitalism in Europe and was unknown at the time of colonial intrusion – but rural people could decide to vote with their feet and move to areas of more popular leaders (Tapscott 1997, 277; Lambert 1995, 277). Alternatively, traditional authorities could be deposed or even killed. In theory, the next leader was supposed to be chosen from the next in line in the lineage. In reality, the transition was not smooth, given political competition between chiefs (Peires 1981, 29).

These options were, however, restricted by colonial conquest and land dispossession. The decision to depose a traditional authority was removed from the people and could only be taken by the state. Killing became an offence that was presided over by government officials. As land became limited and the procedure for moving from one area to the next became tighter, it was no longer easy for rural people to vote with their feet. This meant that rural people were left with virtually no option for dealing with unpopular traditional authorities.

Even when Africans started to organize themselves as political organizations, the relationship between traditional authorities and their people, including the options available for rural people in cases of unpopular traditional authorities, was not taken up as an issue. The ANC, from its establishment in 1912, wooed those traditional authorities who had been marginalized by colonialists, but without any clear strategy as to their role in a society based on the universal suffrage that the ANC was fighting for.

BEFORE THE UNION OF SOUTH AFRICA IN 1910

Before the Boer War (1899–1902) and the subsequent Union of South Africa in 1910, the country was divided into two British colonies (the Cape and Natal), and two Boer Republics (the South African Republic/Transvaal and the Orange Free State). This subsection will consider land tenure and local government under British and Boer rule during the nineteenth century leading up to the Union in 1910. It does not attempt to provide a detailed analysis of land tenure and local government issues in these areas, but rather it seeks to make the case that the Union of South Africa incorporated *colonies* and former *republics* that had their own specificities. Despite policy and legislative attempts to bring uniformity to the various Bantustans, there are still major differences among them. This makes it extremely dangerous to generalize on the basis of studying one Bantustan, and almost impossible to conduct an in-depth analysis of all, or even a few Bantustans.

BRITISH RULE

Whenever the British conquered and dispossessed Africans, they set aside land for African occupation (*reserves*). The British colonial answer to the question of how to administer Africans was indirect rule. The traditional structures based on the leadership of traditional authorities were adapted to suit the ends of colonialists. Rebellious chiefs were marginalized, dethroned and replaced with appointed chiefs and headmen. The appointed chiefs and headmen were directly accountable to colonial structures, particularly the magistrate. Lastly, they were paid a salary, which confirmed their new role as paid servants of the government.

The appointment of traditional authorities marked a departure from the then existing African tradition of hereditary leaders. Although, according to Beinart and Bundy, the appointees were often drawn from the ranks of relatives; for example, a brother or an uncle (Beinart and Bundy 1987), and in the case of Phondoland (Hendricks1990; Beinart 1982) chiefs were appointed, this still did not alter the fact that the appointees were not necessarily in the line of lineage.[8] Above all, the appointment of traditional authorities was made by the colonial power, and not by councillors and elders. As will be seen below, by being paid a salary, traditional authorities became accountable to the government. This further weakened the little power rural communities had to make traditional authorities accountable to them.

Colonial policy governing land reserved for African occupation in South Africa goes back to the early part of the nineteenth century. Land was owned by the state. However, there was fair protection for those who were in occupation of land. An 1829 proclamation issued by the governor of the Cape, Lt. Gen. William Butler, generally accepted that land belonged to the chief, but that allocated land belonged, for all practical purposes, to the occupying household (Hendricks 1990, 61).

When the British annexed the Transvaal from the Boers in 1877, they changed the regulations governing African occupation. Prior to this regulation, Africans in the Boer Republics were allowed to purchase land, although they could not register it in their own name, but in the name of missionaries. After the annexation of the Transvaal, land bought by Africans was registered in the name of the Secretary of Native Affairs, in trust for the people concerned. This phased out the missionaries.

With the establishment of the Transvaal Location Commission in 1881, the Location Commission held land in trust. From July 1918, after the union, the minister of Native Affairs (Mbenga 1998, 5) held land bought by Africans in trust. The Glen Grey Act of 1894, which was promulgated when Cecil John Rhodes was the governor of the Cape, and the same year that Phondoland was annexed, established a system of local government and land tenure that was to be influential in determining policy after the union of South Africa. There were three major elements to the Act: a change in the nature of land tenure; local District Councils in the African areas; and a labour tax. With regard to land tenure, its key tenets were:

- policy of *one-man-one-lot*

- division of the land into four or five morgen allotments

- restrictions on the alienation of land, and

- liability of forfeiture in the case of non-beneficial occupation (Hendricks 1990).

Commenting on this version of land tenure, Beinart has noted that "[c]ommunal tenure was to be replaced by a system of individual tenure under which title would be given to plots of land which could be neither alienated nor accumulated" (Beinart 1982, 43). The question that arises is how different this tenure system was from the one based on the 1829 proclamation, and to what extent it affected the powers of traditional authorities. The difference brought about by the Glen Grey Act was that title would be granted, but such title would have severe limitations; namely, it could not be alienated nor accumulated.

As regards local government, the 1894 act established a council system (*iBhunga*) made up of a mixture of elected and nominated members. The council system was initially[9] meant to undermine the power of traditional authorities who had led a series of frontier wars against the British (Mbeki 1984, 33). It operated at two levels; namely, a District Council in each magisterial area, and the United Transkeian Territories General Council (UTTGC). The District Councils consisted of six members. To ensure that the traditional authorities did not dominate the council, only two members were nominated by the paramount chief. Two were nominated by the Governor-General and the remaining two elected. In areas where there were no paramount chiefs, the government nominated two and the rest were popular representatives (Mbeki 1984, 35). The Bhunga dealt with a wide range of issues such as education, roads, agriculture, irrigation, customary law, and limitation of stock.

This might seem to be a radical plan to transform rural local government by introducing the notion of elected representation, albeit partial, thus undermining traditional authorities, hereditary and appointed. However, this partially elected representation was only at a district and territorial level, not at the grassroots village level where the real power of traditional authorities lay. At village level, traditional authorities were left largely intact. The only major difference was that headmen and compliant chiefs were appointed to replace recalcitrant traditional authorities. The former were given a semblance of power, and the colonial hope was that this would safeguard the allegiance and acquiescence of the reserve residents. A distinction was made between traditional authorities appointed by the GovernorGeneral, and those who would merely be recognized by the government. The former were given limited powers, while the role of the latter was not clarified. Traditional authorities were substantially removed from the direct rule they had enjoyed before colonial defeat, in favour of centrally appointed village headmen. Hammond-Tooke argues that this position of powerlessness allowed the chiefs to maintain much of their traditional prestige and popularity, for in this bureaucratic system the centrally appointed location headmen[10] "assumed the scapegoat role" (Stultz 1979, 51). In areas that were annexed, for example, Phondoland, the system of appointing headmen was largely unsuccessful and chiefs who were prepared to collaborate with the colonial power were not removed (Hendricks 1990; Beinart 1982), but had to operate under the magistrate who could remove them if they proved recalcitrant.

With regard to the powers of traditional authorities over land, the case of *Hermansberg Mission Society* v. *Commissioner of Native Affairs and Darius Mogale,* 1906, that has already been quoted, strengthened rather than diminished the power of traditional authorities at a local, village level. As noted, the court rejected the argument that "a chief may not alienate land without the direct consent of the community," and held that "an African chief, as trustee of the community's land, may alienate land with the consent of the chief's council and without the direct participation of the community."

THE BOER REPUBLICS

The situation in the Boer Republics was slightly different. In these Republics, no *reserves* were created. For the purposes of this study, we will consider the case of the BaFokeng people in the *Transvaal* (from 1994, the North West Province). The BaFokeng were initially invaded by the amaNdebele and later collaborated with the Voortrekkers who fought the amaNdebele and defeated them in 1837. Despite this, the Voortrekkers considered themselves the owners of the land and as having jurisdiction over the BaFokeng. Africans were, however, allowed to purchase land, but could not register it in their name. According to Mbenga:

> Africans acquired land they could call their own only as a "grant" or, much later, through purchase from the Boers. In the western Transvaal, the earliest cases of land "grants" to Africans by the Boer emigrants [sic] date back to 1837 when the commandants ... "rewarded" the Barolong chiefs ... with grants of land for having assisted the Voortrekkers in expelling Mzilikazi out of the Transvaal.... In fact, throughout the Transvaal, the Voortrekker commandants gave land to black groups "for services rendered" or loyalty. This was ratified by a Volksraad resolution of November 1853 which formerly authorised commandants to grant land for African occupation, but conditional "upon good behaviour and obedience," because ... the land was not for the Africans property but for their use only. (Mbenga 1998, 2–3)

Grants, therefore, were one way of gaining access to land but not to full title. Only much later, from the late 1860s, could Africans *buy* [their] land, but the land could still not be transferred to them. According to Mbenga:

> Africans ... could only buy land in the name of a missionary or through a 99-year lease from any white person. Regarding the first method, the land was paid for by an African group, but registered in the missionary's name in trust for them. Through the second method, the Africans paid for a 99-year lease and the white person then promised to transfer the land to the Africans concerned, "as soon as the laws of the country permitted Natives to hold land in their own names." ... This type of lease, because it was not registered, was a major disadvantage for the African purchasers who frequently lost their properties through deceit by the white lessors. (Mbenga 1998, 4)

As previously discussed, when the British annexed the Transvaal in 1877, the regulations governing African landownership changed. Land bought by Africans was registered in the name of the Secretary of Native Affairs, in trust for the people concerned. This phased out the missionaries. When the Transvaal Location Commission was established in 1881, land was held in trust by the Location Commission. From July 1918, land bought by Africans was held in trust by the minister of Native Affairs (Mbenga 1998, 5). This was well after the 1910 union of South Africa which brought the British colonies and Boer Republics together.

The BaFokeng, once again, offer an example.[11] One question that arises is how the BaFokeng purchased the land. In the first place, land was not bought by individuals, but by the BaFokeng as a group under their traditional authorities. According to Mbenga, traditional authorities "collected the purchase price from the people, mainly in cattle, and the missionary arranged the transaction. The Bafokeng also paid for farms in cash even as early as that time," by sending young men to the mines to earn money for the group to buy farms (Mbenga 1998, 4). Although land was bought with funds contributed by the group, traditional authorities continued to play a key role in land allocation.

In short, the British and Boers left structures at the local, village level largely intact. The attempt to democratize local government in the Cape did not affect this local level of government. Elected representation was not extended to the grassroots village level. The villages were under the rule of collaborating hereditary and appointed traditional authorities. These remained the main link between the colonialists and the rural people, and continued to play a vital role in the allocation of land.

AFTER UNION IN 1910

After the union of 1910, the Cape system of local government was endorsed. The Transkei became the testing ground. By the early 1930s, district councils had been established in the twenty-six districts of the Transkei.

The first major legislative attempt to bring uniformity to rural local government was the promulgation of the Native Affairs Act. The Transkei experience was used as an example. According to Mbeki:

> Africans in reserves elsewhere in the country were brought to
> the Transkei by the government to see how good the Bhunga
> system was. The Ciskei General Council was formed after the
> Transkei model, and attempts were made to bring Zululand and
> the Transvaal reserves into line by the Native Affairs Act of 1920.
> (Mbeki 1984, 34)

From the establishment of the Union of South Africa, which excluded the so-called non-whites of the country, a tension existed between British and Boers. The Cape, and to a limited extent Natal, allowed Africans a qualified franchise. The African hope was that this franchise would be extended to other provinces. The Cape, as we have noted, introduced the Bhunga, which had elected candidates. Afrikaners were not entirely happy with developments in the former British colonies. The Pact Government of the 1920s gradually moved towards a policy of segregation. In this project, "chieftaincy in a modified form came to be seen by segregationist ideologues as a means to defuse agrarian and industrial class conflict in the 1920s" (Beinart 1982, 6). In 1927, the Native Administration Act was passed. Its intention was 'to shore up the remains of the chieftaincy in a countrywide policy of indirect-rule, which would allow for the segregation of the administration of justice" (Ntsebeza and Hendricks 1998, 5). The segregationist project culminated with the notorious 1936 Natives Acts.

One of these acts, the 1936 Natives Land Act, was promulgated to purchase additional land, called *released areas* for consolidation of the Reserves.[12] In terms of this act, rural people applying for land would be granted a *permit to occupy* (PTO), as proof that the piece of land had been allocated to the holder of the document. Section 4 of Proclamation No. 26, 1936 as amended, empowered the magistrate to grant permission

> to any person domiciled in the district, who has been duly authorised thereto by the tribal authority, to occupy in a residential area for domestic purposes or in an arable area for agricultural purposes, a homestead allotment or an arable allotment, as the case may be.

The allocation of land according to the Act was, inter alia, subject to the following condition:

> [N]ot more than one homestead allotment and one arable allotment shall be allotted ... to any Native [*sic*], provided that if such Native [*sic*] is living in customary union with more than one woman, one homestead and one arable allotment may be allotted for the purpose of each household.[13]

The pervasive influence of the Glen Grey Act can be seen here.

In terms of the *permission to occupy* system, the holder of the site was entitled to remain in occupation until his death and to elect the person to whom he would like the site to be allocated on his death. In theory, the holder's rights could be forfeited for the following reasons:

- failing to take occupation or to fence within a year of allocation, and

- non-beneficial use for two years.

In practice, the above conditions were often not adhered to.[14] At the same time, while the PTO guaranteed its holder permanent occupation, the holder thereof was vulnerable. For example, PTO holders could be forcibly removed without being consulted if the government, the nominal owner of land, deemed fit. This was the case when the government introduced its Betterment Plan,[15] or when development schemes, such as irrigation schemes, tea factories, nature reserves, and so on, were introduced.[16] Some PTO holders were victims of banishments, in which case their houses would be demolished, often without compensation and recourse to law. Finally, PTOs were not recognized by financial institutions as collateral. It is this latter limitation of the PTO that seems to dominate current discussions around the security of tenure derived from PTOs. It is precisely because financial institutions do not recognize PTOs that they are seen as limiting investment opportunities, more productive use of land, and prospects of getting housing subsidies.

The question that may arise is how communal or individual this system of tenure was. This study argues that the system was neither communal, in the sense that the community(ies) concerned had full ownership and control of land, nor individual; that is, freehold. Hence the conclusion by some commentators that the system was a distorted version of communal tenure (Hendricks 1990). We have seen that the 1829 proclamation, the Glen Grey Act of 1894, and the 1936 Native Land Act adopted, by and large, a similar position regarding the rights of those who had been allotted land. Once land has been allotted to a family, it becomes virtually individualized:

> As far as possible, land is kept in the family of the previous holder
> unless it has been lost by forfeiture. The theory is that the land is a
> joint possession of the family, administered by the head thereof –
> his right is not a purely personal one and on his ceasing to hold the
> office of head of the family, the new head becomes the managing
> director, as it were. (Hendricks 1990, 64)

Commenting on the difficulty of categorizing communal tenure under colonization, and questioning the very notion *communal* in African societies, it has been argued that:

> under the system of quit-rent all arable land is individually registered
> at the magistrate's court in the name of the family head, who then
> accepts liability for the annual rent. All such land is vested in and
> revertible to the state. By this token, are not all peasant cultivators
> in the reserves, far from being owners of land, tenants of the State
> in the strict sense? ... but registered plots are heritable according
> to African customary law.... In practice, it means that particular

descent groups are able to hold the original plots in perpetuity. What is communal about that? (Hendricks 1990, 64)

What the above suggests is that it is not accurate to refer to rural areas that are controlled by traditional authorities as *communal* areas. What could be referred to as *communal* land is, in fact, land that has not been allotted for residential and/or arable purposes; for example, grazing land, forests, and so on. It is this category of land that will be dominating debates about ownership rights in the countryside in post-apartheid South Africa.

THE NATIONAL PARTY RULE

After the Second World War, the Bhunga became more and more radical, and started to make demands for individual franchise for all Africans in South Africa. Outside South Africa, colonialism was also under pressure. Against this background, the National Party came to power in 1948 on the ticket of apartheid. One of their prime objectives was to resolve the question of *native administration*. Three years after coming to power, they introduced the Bantu Administration Act. This act put traditional authorities at the helm of things. It abolished the Native Representative Council that was set up in terms of one of the 1936 Natives Acts. Bantu authorities were organized at three levels; namely, tribal, regional, and territorial authorities. At all three levels, traditional authorities were dominant. It is this dominance of traditional authorities at all levels that marked a major shift from the Bhunga system, the aim of which was to undermine the power of traditional authorities, save those at the local, grassroots level. This dominance caused Mbeki to remark:

> It is clear from the composition of these bodies that they represent merely the messengers of government will; the elected element is so small and so remote from the voters that it can hardly be held even to contribute to popular participation. The thesis of government policy is clear – Africans are still in the tribal stage, chiefs are the natural rulers, and the people neither want nor should have elected representatives. (Mbeki 1984, 40)

In restoring the powers of traditional authorities, the act represented one of the building blocks of apartheid policy by consolidating *reserves*, which were later to become *self-governing*, and for some, *independent*. Although traditional authorities were placed firmly in charge of local administration, during the period up to the introduction of self-government in the early 1960s they were directly linked to the central government through the Department of Native Affairs.[17] The minister of Native Affairs had ultimate control. In terms of the 1956 proclamation which gave effect to the Bantu Authorities Act, the minister had the power to: depose any chief, cancel the appointment of any councillor, appoint any officer with whatever powers he deemed necessary, control the treasury and budgetary spending, and authorize taxation. As was the case during the preceding colonial period, new loyal traditional authorities were appointed, and new lineages were recognized and created. When Bantustans became *self-governing* and (some) *independent*, the responsibilities of the Department of Native Affairs fell into the hands of the Bantustan governments, with support from the apartheid regime.

During the 1950s, traditional authorities were used by the apartheid government to implement the draconian and hated conservation measures, called *betterment schemes*. The catalogue of their abuse of power during this period is well documented. Mbeki has written that the government turned to chiefs "offering to those whose areas will accept rehabilitation measures appropriate incentives: increased special stipends, increased land allotments, words of praise, and places of honour, and, behind all, the right to continue as government appointed chiefs." On their harshness and the undemocratic methods they applied, Mbeki continues:

> With these fruits of office dangling before them, the chiefs often commit peasants to acceptance of the rehabilitation scheme without consulting them. Then, when preparations are made for the implementation of the scheme ... the peasants question with surprise the cause of all this activity.... And now the Chief hits back at them mercilessly. The instigators of the discontent are brought to the Bush Court (Chief's Court) with the greatest haste and the least formality. (Mbeki 1984, 97–98)

There was resistance to the introduction of the Bantu Authorities Act and the implementation of the *betterment scheme* in the 1950s and early 1960s.

Corruption and repression were features of traditional authority during *self-government* and *independence*; the period after the 1951 Bantu Authorities Act up to the demise of apartheid in the late 1980s. One of the instruments traditional authorities had at their disposal was control of land allocation. Their power in this regard, was largely enhanced, as Tapscott (1997, 295) has noted, by the fact that Africans' access to land was restricted to the Bantustans, the latter being "the only place where the majority of Africans could legitimately lay claim to a piece of land

and a home ... for an individual's family and a future place of retirement." Although not the owners of land, traditional authorities had enormous power in the allocation thereof. This is despite the fact that it is the magistrate that finally granted the PTO. Traditional authorities derived their power in the sense that no application could be considered without the signature of the head of the tribal authority, some councillors, and the secretary of the tribal authority. Traditional authorities abused this power by charging unauthorized fees (*iimfanelo zakomkhulu*) to applicants. These fees ranged from alcohol, poultry, sheep, to even an ox. This practice reached its zenith in the early 1990s when some cottage sites were illegally allocated to some *whites* along the Wild Coast. These sites were dubbed *brandy* sites, as it was imperative that applications be accompanied by a bottle of brandy.

The *independence* of some Bantustans between 1976 and 1981 did not alter land tenure and power relations in rural areas. If anything, the power of traditional authorities, from sub-headman to paramount chief, was strengthened. The two Bantustans in the Eastern Cape, Transkei and Ciskei, continued to issue PTOs in terms of the 1936 Land Act.[18]

The other areas in which traditional authorities abused their power were state pensions, tribal courts, and applications for migrant labour. The situation in rural areas was such that a vast number of rural people could not even get the benefits that they were entitled to without the approval of traditional authorities, who had to witness applications for these benefits. In the absence of alternatives, rural people were forced to recognize these authorities. In this regard, traditional authorities derived their authority, not from popular support, but from the fact that they were feared and that rural people did not have any alternative ways of accessing their benefits. A large proportion of rural people were affected by this, especially the elderly (for pensions) and migrant workers (to renew their contracts).

The role of traditional authorities in infrastructural development and service delivery, mainly roads and water, education, and development (to the extent to which such existed), was marginal. They acted largely as representatives of the relevant government departments. The secretaries of tribal authorities administered the budget for these services.[19] This meant that traditional authorities were not empowered to deal with development issues.

Part of the reason for this was that traditional authorities are a highly differentiated lot. As with most Africans, some took advantage of Western formal education initially offered by missionaries. Those who live permanently in the rural areas are often illiterate or semi-literate, and poor. They thus could/cannot cope with the demands of development planning.

It is worth noting that traditional authorities responded differently to the pressures imposed by the Bantu Authorities Act. Hitherto, traditional authorities that were marginalized during the colonial and segregation periods ironically, as Hammond-Tooke noted, gained legitimacy among their people at a local level. Because they were excluded, they were not viewed as government stooges. However, as the apartheid regime tightened its grip of power, there was little room left for this variation. They were forced to comply. This even applied to traditional authorities such as Victor Poto of Western Phondoland and Sabata Dalindyebo of Tembuland, both of the Transkei. At the heart of this compromise was the fact that traditional authorities were paid a salary by the government. Hendricks quotes Victor Poto as having made the following pledge:

> I have pledged my loyalty and trust to Dr. Verwoerd's government which has brought so many benefits for the enjoyment of the Bantu people. (Hendricks 1990, 48)

Dalindyebo's case is somewhat different. According to Goven Mbeki, Paramount Chief Dalindyebo had "been in a state of continuous conflict with the government over Bantu Authorities." Despite this, though, when the Recess Committee of the Transkei Territorial Authorities, which included Dalindyebo, was required to endorse Bantu Authorities, "all twenty-seven members," including, according to Mbeki, "those who during the session were to oppose its major aspects," signed. Paramount Chief Dalindyebo was one of those who was to oppose. His reason for signing, as quoted in Mbeki, was given in the form of the following question: "Are you aware that when I was requested to sign I *had* to sign because I am a government man?" (Mbeki 1984, 58).

The above clearly demonstrates how difficult it became, even for the most progressive traditional authority, not to toe the apartheid line. Having said this, traditional authorities did not all relate in the same way to the apartheid system. There were those traditional authorities, such as K. D. Matanzima, who shamelessly collaborated with the apartheid regime. Others, such as Sabata Dalindyebo, were reluctant participants in the apartheid game. Dalindyebo was eventually stripped of his power as paramount chief, prosecuted, and finally hounded out of the country by K. D. Matanzima. He joined the ANC in exile, where he died. Others included Albert Luthuli and Nelson Mandela. With regard to the latter, though, it should be said that it is as leaders of political organizations, and not as traditional authorities, that they won their recognition.

In sum, land in the rural areas of the former Bantustans during the period from colonialism to apartheid was state land. Initially sidelined, especially by the Glen Grey Act, traditional authorities became central in the plans of the apartheid architects to establish Bantustans that would become *self-governing* and *independent*. During the apartheid period, traditional authorities dominated all three levels of power; namely, tribal, regional, and territorial. They became a highly differentiated group, some becoming politicians, business people, or lawyers, but the majority were illiterate or semi-literate and poor. Tribal authorities became the primary level of rural local government and played a key role in the administration of land, in particular, land allocation. They also had judicial and executive powers, thus fitting Mamdani's thesis of a clenched fist. During this period, most traditional authorities derived their power from their viciousness, protected by an equally vicious apartheid system, leaving rural people with few options but to comply. By the 1980s, the majority of traditional authorities had discredited themselves and were seen as an extended arm of the detested apartheid regime.

THE DEMISE OF APARTHEID AND TRANSITION TO THE 1994 DEMOCRATIC ELECTIONS

Given the above, it is surprising to note that traditional authorities have won recognition in the post-apartheid dispensation. Only in the late 1980s and early 1990s, mass mobilization, which was characteristic in most urban areas in South Africa during the 1970s and 1980s, had shifted to rural areas. Tribal authorities became the chief target. During this period, the Bantu (by this time Tribal) Authority system came under renewed attack. There were calls for the resignation of headmen – *pantsi ngozibonda* (down with the headmen) – and for the first time the system of tribal authorities was challenged in some areas, in favour of alternative, democratically elected civic structures. In vast areas of the Ciskei, the Tribal Authority system collapsed and the Civic Associations took over (Manona 1990; 1998). Tribal authorities in most parts of the Transkei region were also challenged,[20] but it was not always clear what was being challenged. In some case, civic organizations wanted to replace traditional authorities. In others, the corrupt practices of traditional authorities were questioned. Some drew a distinction between *genuine* traditional authorities, with which they were happy, and *illegitimate* traditional authorities. In KwaZulu-Natal, an intense and bloody war took place mainly between the supporters of the Inkatha Freedom Party (IFP) and the United Democratic Front, and later the ANC, after the latter was unbanned. The IFP's support base was the rural areas of Natal and they strenuously defended traditional authorities.

In order to understand the current recognition of traditional authorities, a number of factors need to be taken into account. First is the nature of rural society. As has been shown above, traditional authority structures were the only structures through which rural people could access a whole range of benefits; notably, land, renewal of contracts for migrant workers, and pensions. There were no alternative channels. Due to the migrant labour system, and the fact that young and educated rural people are inclined to seek work outside their home areas and in the urban areas, the majority of people who reside in these areas are children, married women, and retired elderly men. Most of these people are not entirely aware of their rights. They are thus not willing to challenge traditional authorities. Migrant workers who have been retrenched since the late 1980s and have returned to their rural homes, often do not regard themselves as permanent residents. They see themselves as job seekers. Consequently, they do not participate in rural activities and meetings. In the case study, retrenched migrant workers spend most of their time in rural areas in shebeens, or looking for work. This also applies to the youth and to students.

Linked to the above is that when the focus of resistance shifted to rural areas, the youth, students and retrenched migrant workers became the main leaders of these struggles. This intervention, by the youth in particular, received mixed reactions from rural people, especially from the less educated and from elderly men. As indicated, the latter were fearful of traditional authorities. The youth saw this as an endorsement of the rule of traditional authorities. The militant youth was often not tactful in dealing with the elderly and ended up alienating large sections of this category. Given generational considerations, these elderly men preferred traditional authorities to *boys*.

Secondly, the position of the ANC towards traditional authorities has always been ambivalent. To a large extent the historical division between *loyalists* and *rebels* has influenced this. It has been noted above that when the ANC was formed, some traditional authorities were among the founding members. As the ANC started becoming a radical organization from the 1940s onwards, with strong pressure from the Youth League and a growing alliance with the communists, two broad streams began to emerge; namely, those who supported traditional authorities who were critical of government policies, and those who, clearly under the influence of communists, argued that the institution belonged to a previous feudal era and needed to be replaced by democratic structures. Mbeki represents the latter in this often- quoted statement:

> If Africans have had chiefs, it was because all human societies have had them at one stage or another. But when a people have developed to a stage which discards chieftainship, when their social development contradicts the need for such an institution, then to force it on them is not liberation but enslavement. (Mbeki 1984, 47)

However, the ANC was inclined to continue its strategy to woo *progressive* traditional authorities, rather than to evolve a strategy to establish alternative democratic structures, which would replace traditional authorities in rural areas. In the same book, Mbeki argues that if traditional authorities failed "the peasants," the latter would "seek new ones" (Mbeki 1984, 46). Here he is not arguing that the peasants would create alternative structures in keeping with the ANC's demands for a universal suffrage, but that they would seek new traditional authorities.

The ANC strategy of broadening its support as widely as possible, which reached its height in the mass mobilization period of the 1980s, was exploited by the Congress of Traditional Leaders in South Africa (Contralesa). Contralesa proved to be critical in the recognition of traditional authorities. The organization was established in 1987 by a group of traditional authorities from KwaNdebele who were opposed to the declaration of apartheid-style independence. By this time, Bantustans had been discredited and there was no prospect that they would ever be recognized. At the same time, apartheid was in its decline, and the ANC was seen as a government in waiting. It had been fashionable for individuals and organizations to visit the ANC in exile. Contralesa was no exception. Keen to broaden its support base, the ANC was driven to woo traditional authorities. During the dying moments of apartheid, a large number of traditional authorities jumped on the bandwagon and joined Contralesa. By the mid-1990s, Contralesa was dominated by the formerly discredited traditional authorities.

The exception was those traditional authorities that were members of the IFP. The latter continued to challenge the UDF, and later the ANC, when it was unbanned in 1990.

When negotiation talks, initiated by the NP government and the ANC, resumed after the collapse of Codesa, traditional authorities, which were initially excluded, were invited. There were basically two reasons for this. First, the ANC did not want to harm relations with Contralesa before the envisaged elections. Second, both the ANC and the National Party wanted to ensure the participation of the Inkatha Freedom Party, led by Chief Buthelezi, in the negotiation process.

The third and final factor in the current recognition of traditional authorities is the collapse of land administration in most of the Bantustans during this period. As noted above, land administration in rural areas has always been a problem, precisely because colonial and apartheid regimes relied on traditional authorities to assist them, rather than establishing alternative structures of their own. What characterized the late 1980s and, in particular, the early 1990s was the degree of degeneration. In Mqanduli, for example, officials reported that they had not had applications for PTOs for some three years or so.[21] Along the Wild Coast in the Eastern Cape, traditional authorities in Phondoland and Tshezi were implicated in the illegal allocation of cottage sites to such an extent that the matter is being investigated by a unit appointed by Parliament, the Heath Special Investigation Unit. Traditional authorities do not have any jurisdiction over the zone extending one kilometre from the sea. However, due to the collapse in administration, especially during Transkei *independence*, numbers of traditional authorities exploited the situation and swelled their pockets through bribes. Traditional authorities in these areas were not seriously affected by the wave of resistance of the early 1990s. In the Tshezi area, no civic association was established. But this is not necessarily a sign that traditional authorities are considered legitimate; it could be that they are still feared, given their ruthlessness over almost four decades.

In white South Africa, some changes began to take place in the early 1990s. Under the leadership of its reformer, F. W. de Klerk, the National Party made radical proposals that would alter the role of the state as the nominal owner of communal land in favour transferring land to *tribes* and upgrading PTOs to full ownership, thus effectively repealing the 1913 and 1936 Natives Land Acts.[22] In 1991, a White Paper on Land Reform was launched. The objective of the *new land policy* is set out in the introduction in these terms:

> The new policy has the definite objective of ensuring that existing security and existing patterns of community order will be maintained. The primary objective is to offer equal opportunities for the acquisition, use and enjoyment of land to all the people within the social and economic realities of the country. The government firmly believes that this objective can best be achieved within the system of private enterprise and private ownership.

The White Paper was supported by five bills; namely, the Abolition of Racially-Based Land Measures Bill,[23] the Upgrading of Land Tenure Rights Bill,[24] The Residential

Environmental Bill, the Less Formal Township Establishment Bill, and the Rural Development Bill.

The White Paper and the bills were challenged by, inter alia, the National Land Committee (NLC), the Legal Resources Centre (LRC), and the Centre for Applied Legal Studies (CALS). One of the shortcomings pointed out was that the National Party proposals ignored critical realities on the ground; namely, the problem of issuing title where there could be overlapping land rights. Secondly, the World Bank argument that individual title, as opposed to communal or group title, provides tenure security and thus enhancement of productivity, was not supported by the findings of a study commissioned by the World Bank on the relationship between tenure security and agricultural production (Bruce and Migot-Adholla 1998).[25] Eventually, three of the bills were passed into legislation. This study will focus on the Upgrading of Land Tenure Act.

Two proposals were made. In terms of section 19 of the Upgrading of Land Tenure Act, 1991:

> Any tribe shall be capable of obtaining land in ownership and, subject to subsection 2 [which deals with limitations on land disposal], of selling, exchanging, donating, letting, hypothecating, or otherwise disposing of it.

Secondly, the act created conditions for upgrading the PTO to full freehold title. The essence of the argument for the upgrading of PTO land rights was the view that the right to title deeds had been denied blacks in the past, as manifested in trust-held land and the system of PTOs. In terms of National Party thinking, the alternative to communal land tenure was individual freehold title, and it is this possibility that the Upgrading Act provided for; the upgrading of PTOs to freehold title. It also provided for the transfer of communal land to tribes, but the policy preference was for upgrading PTOs.[26]

As can be seen, there was a great deal of fluidity during the early 1990s. Traditional authorities in most parts of South Africa, with perhaps the exception of KwaZulu-Natal, were uncertain about their future. Although they were no longer repressive under these uncertain conditions, there is evidence that corruption never abated. It is also during this period that they were recognized in the constitution without sufficient guidelines as to their role in land reform and local government. At the same time, the same constitution upheld democratic principles, including elected representation and democracy in local government and land. This spells out the context within which the ANC-led government attempted to formulate and implement its land and local government reform programs.

TENURE REFORM, TRADITIONAL AUTHORITY, AND LOCAL GOVERNMENT IN POST-APARTHEID SOUTH AFRICA

As noted in the introduction of this paper, post-apartheid South Africa's Constitution is attempting to separate land tenure and local government functions which were concentrated in traditional authorities during previous periods, giving a minimum role for traditional authorities. However, the role of traditional authorities is still upheld in the constitution. The central argument of this paper is that implementation of post-apartheid policies on land tenure and local government is hampered by the recognition of the institution of traditional authorities and government's reluctance to enforce its policies, in the face of rejection by traditional authorities. This is well demonstrated by the Tshezi communal area case study.

LAND TENURE POLICY – THE PROCESS

The Department of Land Affairs (DLA) is required by the constitution to ensure security of tenure for all South Africans, especially women. Government policy on the reform of land tenure is outlined in the constitution:

> A person or community whose tenure of land is legally insecure as
> a result of past racially discriminatory laws or practices is entitled,
> to the extent provided by an Act of Parliament, either to tenure
> which is legally secure or to comparable redress. (Sec. 25 (6))

A positive policy and legislation on land tenure reform in the rural areas of the Bantustans have been slower to emerge than the other components of the land reform program. A Tenure Research Core Group (TRCG) to guide the land tenure reform process was only established in 1996. Since then, the following pieces of legislation and policy affecting tenure reform in the Bantustans have been developed.

- Amendment of the 1991 Upgrading and Land Tenure Rights Act, 1996, to ensure that the opinions of rural people are sought before any major decisions are made about their land.

- Interim Protection of Informal Land Rights Act, 1996, to formalize the process by which decisions are taken. It lays down a rigorous procedure for major decisions affecting people with so-called informal rights, including people in rural areas.

- A document issued by the minister of Land Affairs in 1997, which declares that decisions pertaining to ownership rights in communally owned land are most appropriately made by the majority of the members of such communal systems

- Communal Property Associations Act, 1996, which established an accountable land-holding entity, the Communal Property Association (CPA), as a model for group ownership.

- White Paper on Land Policy, April 1997. The policy, among others, draws a distinction between *ownership* and *governance* of communal land. The state is no longer both owner and administrator. Ownership can be transferred from state to the communities and individuals on the land.

Most of the above is interim legislation that protects land rights of rural people against abuse (Claassens and Makopi 1999). At the beginning of 1998, DLA developed a set of principles to guide its legislative and implementation framework (Thomas, Sibanda, and Claassens 1998). The key features are:

- Landownership is separated from governance. This means that members of particular communities can co-own the land and decide how they want their land administered.

- A clear separation of powers as opposed to the fusion of authority characteristic of the past. Tribal authorities and local government will not be the owners of land, and will not have the right to allocate land, unless specifically asked by the landowners to do so.

This means that tribal authorities, whose function it was in the past to administer land under the guidance of magistrates, are no longer guaranteed this function. Neither are the newly elected local government structures. These structures can only administer land if elected by the landowners; namely, members of communities. As far as DLA is concerned:

> Systems of land administration, which are popular and functional, should continue to operate. They provide an important asset given the breakdown of land administration in many rural areas. The aim is not to destroy or harm viable and representative institutions. Popular and democratic tribal systems are not threatened by the proposed measures. (Thomas, Sibanda, and Claassens 1998)

This document, though, does not provide any evidence of "popular," "functional," and "democratic tribal systems" in existence after years of colonial and apartheid distortion of traditional systems.

LAND TENURE OPTIONS

Currently, there are two options for tenure security in the rural areas of the former Bantustans: individual freehold and group/communal ownership. Individual freehold is difficult to implement because:

- communal land in the former Bantustans is unregistered and unsurveyed

- individuals who want freehold would probably have to bear the cost of surveying and registering. Most occupants of land could not afford this, and

- a tribal resolution also needs to be passed by the majority of members of the particular group or community before freehold is granted.

As regards communal ownership: Communities applying as groups for transfer of land must constitute themselves as a legal landholding entity such as a CPA. Members are defined in terms of households and must agree to a set of rules and regulations for landownership.

During the course of 1998, a legislation drafting team was assembled to draft appropriate tenure legislation. The draft Land Rights Bill proposal argued:

- A new form of ownership, *commonhold*, which bypasses the requirements for establishing a legal entity. *Commonhold* would mean that the land vests in the members of a community as co-owners; decisions in respect of the land are made on a majority basis; and co-owners choose or elect the body to manage their land- related affairs on a day-to-day basis.

- The creation of statutory rights, which apply where transfer of land from the state has not been applied for; the state would remain the nominal owner of land but protects the rights of people on the land. These rights will have the status of property rights and cannot be removed except with consent or by expropriation. (Claassens and Makopi 1999, 10)

LAND ADMINISTRATION

In terms of land administration, the Land Rights Bill proposes various levels. At a District Council and magisterial district level, a Land Rights Board to be established by the minister is proposed. This will bring together different interest groups, including the proposed Land Rights Officer and elected rural councillors.

At a local level, it proposes a rights holders structure to be accredited by the Land Rights Board. It is further proposed that a Land Rights Officer be appointed by the directorgeneral to monitor compliance with the proposed Land Rights Act.

If this proposed bill were to become an act, it would go a long way towards protecting rural people from arbitrary decisions by the state and tribal authorities. It will have far reaching implications for traditional authorities, which for over four decades have not been accountable and democratic.

LOCAL GOVERNMENT POLICY

Policy on rural local government is guided by the constitutional requirement that the local sphere of government should consist of municipalities. Over and above the traditional service delivery and regulatory functions of municipalities, the constitution enhances the powers and functions of local government by placing greater prominence on the role of local government in supporting socio-economic upliftment. Section 153 (a) of the constitution stipulates that a municipality must

> structure and manage its administration and budgeting and planning processes to give priority to the basic needs of the community, and to promote the social and economic development of the community.

THE DISTRICT MODEL

Policy and legislation on local government is contained in the following documents: the constitution, the Transitional Local Government Act of 1993, the Development Facilitation Act, the White Paper on Local Government, and various research documentation on the White Paper process. More documentation will be generated by the White Paper on Traditional Affairs that has been drawn up to resolve the thorny question of the roles, functions, and powers of traditional authorities.

A feature of the negotiation process that began in earnest in the early 1990s was its urban bias. The 1993 Transitional Local Government Act was initially silent on the form that local government would take in rural areas. In the urban areas, transitional structures called Negotiation Forums were set up. Nothing of this kind was provided for rural areas. However, the ANC-led Government of National Unity recognized this deficiency, and in June 1995 passed amendments to the Local Government Transition Act of 1993. These amendments focused specifically on local government in rural areas. They provide for a district council model for rural areas. The district council model is a two-level structure which consists of Transitional Local Councils (TLCs) for urban areas, and Transitional Rural Councils (TRCs) or Transitional Representative Councils (TrepCs), established at a magisterial district level.

The TrepCs were seen as representatives and brokers who would evolve into effective and democratic local authorities. They were thus not accorded the powers of a fully-fledged local authority. The functions of a TrepC were envisaged as follows:

- to nominate from among its members a person or persons to represent the council on the district council in question

- to secure, through the said person or persons, the best services possible for the inhabitants of its area

- to serve as the representative body of its area in respect of any benefits resulting from the reconstruction and development program, and in the development of a democratic, effective, and affordable system of local government

- in general, to represent the inhabitants of its area in respect of any matter relating to rural local government.

During this transitional period, the district councils would undertake all service delivery in the rural areas.

In November 1996, further amendments were made regarding the powers and functions of the Transitional Representative Councils. This was to ensure that they were given powers to establish themselves as fully-fledged local government structures in rural areas. In terms of section 10(d)(2) of the Local Government Act, second amendment, 1996:

> A representative council shall within the area of jurisdiction have those powers and duties as the MEC may, in consultation with the minister and after consultation with:
>
> the representative council concerned, and the district council concerned, by notice in the Provincial Gazette, identify as a power or duty of the representative council concerned, whereupon such representative council shall be competent to exercise such power or perform such duty within the area of its jurisdiction....

This section further provides that the district council shall, with the approval of the local council, rural council, and representative councils concerned, formulate, and if so requested, implement an Integrated Development Plan (IDP) in respect of each local council, rural council, and representative council within the area of jurisdiction. If so requested, the district council will also ensure the proper functioning of and the provision of financial, technical, and administrative support services to all the local councils, rural councils, and representative councils within its area of jurisdiction.

With regard to the composition and election of TrepCs, the act stipulates that a Transitional Representative Council (TrepC) shall consist of:

- members elected in accordance with a system of proportional representation, and if the MEC considers it desirable,

- members nominated by interest groups recognized by the MEC.

Provided that:
- no single interest group shall nominate a number of members

which exceeds 10 per cent of the total number of members to be elected and nominated in respect of the relevant Transitional Representative Council;

- the total number of members nominated by interest groups shall not exceed 20 per cent of the total number of members to be elected and nominated in respect of the relevant Transitional Representative Council.

Interest groups are defined as:

- levy payers
- farm labourers
- women, and
- traditional leaders.

The election of councillors is, thus, by means of proportional representation only. In other words, in terms of these amendments, rural people voted for political parties only, and unlike their urban counterparts, were not given the opportunity to vote both on proportional representation and for candidates.

TRADITIONAL AUTHORITIES IN LOCAL GOVERNMENT

Traditional authorities were excluded from the initial negotiations around the Conference for a Democratic South Africa (CODESA) in 1991 and 1992. The talks temporarily collapsed in 1992. When negotiations resumed at the World Trade Centre, traditional authorities were invited. There were basically two reasons for this. First, the ANC did not want to harm relations with the Congress of Traditional Leaders of South Africa (Contralesa) before the envisaged elections. (See also Ntsebeza and Hendricks 1998.) Second, both the ANC and the National Party wanted to ensure the participation of the Inkatha Freedom Party, led by Chief Buthelezi, in the negotiations process. The upshot of these negotiations was a compromise that led to the recognition of the institution of traditional authorities. Consequently, on the eve of the 1994 elections,[27] a clause was included in the interim constitution recognizing the institution of traditional authorities. However, no guidelines were given as to the roles, functions, and powers of traditional authorities in a society that had opted for elected representation. Principle XIII of the interim constitution merely states that:

> The institution and role of traditional leadership, according to the indigenous law, shall be recognized and protected in the constitution. Indigenous law, like common law, shall be recognized and applied by the courts, subject to the fundamental rights contained in the constitution and to legislation dealing specifically therewith.

The final constitution of 1996 is also not helpful in resolving this tension between the recognition of the institution of traditional leadership, which is an unelected structure, and a commitment to a democracy based on elected representation. Furthermore, it is also vague about the roles, functions, and powers of traditional authorities. Chapter 12, one of the shortest (if not *the* shortest) chapter of the constitution provides that:

> The institution, status, and role of traditional leadership, according to customary law, are recognized, subject to the constitution.

On the role of the institution, ART. 212 has this to say:

(1) National legislation may provide for a role for traditional leadership as an institution at local level on matters affecting local communities.

(2) To deal with matters relating to traditional leadership, the role of traditional leaders, customary law, and the customs of communities observing a system of customary law:

    (a) national or provincial legislation may provide for the establishment of houses of traditional leaders; and

    (b) national legislation may establish a council of traditional leaders.

It should be noted that the constitution does not provide a specific role for traditional authorities in local government. Their role *may* be provided for by national legislation. Their recognition is extended to customs and traditions in "communities observing a system of customary law." However, whatever the concrete powers of traditional authorities, the constitution requires that such powers be performed "subject to the constitution."

Further, we have seen that the Transitional Local Government Act provides an extremely limited role for traditional authorities in local government, defining them as an *interest group* with no more than 10 per cent representation.[28] Their role in the Provincial Houses of Traditional Leaders and the National Council of Traditional Leaders as government advisors on customary law, traditions, and customs is, to say the least, dubious. What counts as customary law, tradition, and custom in a late-twentieth-century, rapidly urbanizing South Africa? As Maloka quite rightly argues, "African political and socio-economic structures were significantly transformed by the combined impact of merchant capital, missionaries, and colonialism" (T. A. Maloka 1996, 174; see also E. Maloka 1995). The exact meaning of this role in contemporary South Africa needs urgent explanation.

The much-awaited publication of the White Paper on Local Government in March 1998 did not resolve the issue of local government in rural areas, especially the roles of traditional authorities. The White Paper makes what appear to be broad and sweeping statements about the possible role which traditional authorities can play. On the vital issue of who will represent rural people at a local, village level, the White Paper remarks:

> It is proposed, in accordance with the constitution, that there will be elected local government in all the areas falling under traditional authorities. Traditional leadership should play a role closest to the people. Their role will include attending and participating in meetings of the Councils and advising Councils on the needs and interests of their communities. (South Africa 1998, 77)

On the issue of development, a task that has been added to local government by the constitution, the White Paper boldly asserts:

> There is no doubt that the important role that traditional leaders have played in the development of their communities should be continued. (South Africa 1998, 77)

The above statements do not seem to take into account the roles played by traditional authorities from the time of colonial conquest, but more specifically during the apartheid period. They generalize about traditional authorities and do not take into account the differentiated nature of traditional authorities as dealt with in the introduction to this study. It is not clear on what basis these statements are made, as they clearly are not borne out by the roles that traditional authorities played in South Africa from colonialism to apartheid. This paper has argued that traditional authorities were marginalized when it came to development issues, and, according to Hendricks, were a dismal failure. Above all, it is not clear from the above statements how unelected traditional authorities will coexist with democratically elected representatives (Ntsebeza and Hendricks 1998, 20–21).

The White Paper makes suggestive statements such as the above, but does not resolve the issue of rural local government, in particular the role of traditional authorities in this. Instead, it proposes a White Paper on Traditional Affairs to deal with the structure and role of traditional leadership and institutions:

- principles relating to remuneration

- a national audit of traditional leaders

- the role of women

- the role of traditional leaders in politics

the future role of the Houses and Council of Traditional Leaders:

- the rationalization of current legislation dealing with traditional leadership and institutions. (South Africa 1998, 76)

During the course of 1998, the Department of Constitutional Development announced a program for the process to be expanded in developing the White Paper on Traditional Affairs. In terms of this proposal, a Discussion Paper was supposed to be ready for comment by the end of 1999, to be followed by a Green Paper, that would ultimately lead to a White Paper by May 1999. In 1999 alone, the Department of Constitutional Development voted about R 32 million for salaries, including benefits, for traditional authorities. These salaries have been voted without regard to the role of traditional authorities. In practice, transferring some of their local government functions to elected rural councillors has diminished the functions of traditional authorities. Further, these salaries are paid ahead of the promised national audit on traditional authorities to determine who genuine traditional authorities are.

During 1997, the Eastern Cape Legislature passed the Regulation of Development in Rural Areas Act. This act transfers all development functions enjoyed by tribal authorities in terms of the Bantu Authorities Act of 1951, as amended, to elected councillors. This is in line with the development functions of local government as prescribed in the constitution. One of these functions relates to the role played by tribal authorities in making recommendations about the allocation of land. This aspect of the act has the potential to clash with the policy of the Department of Land Affairs, which clearly states that the question of who allocates land will be determined by the owners of land. We have seen above that, according to the Department of Land Affairs, rural people who have been living on land that they have regarded as their own for generations must be treated as the owners of land, even though existing legislation does not accord them legal ownership.

The passing of the Regulation of Development in Rural Areas Act highlights what this study regards as one of the fundamental stumbling blocks to delivery; namely, poor communication, co-ordination, and co-operation within and among departments.

PROBLEMS OF PRACTICE

Both departments are encountering serious problems in implementing the above. This study will highlight four; namely, structural/organizational constraints, budgetary constraints, lack of democratic structures at a local level, and tensions around traditional authorities.

INTER-DEPARTMENTAL COORDINATION CONSTRAINTS

Poor communication, coordination, and co-operation, both inter and intra departments is one of the major reasons why implementation of these policies has been unsatisfactory. A number of departments, at national, provincial, and local level, need to coordinate with each other in order to implement land tenure and local government reform. Some of the land policies developed by DLA, for example, policies on land allocation, will be difficult to implement if the Bantu Authorities Act, which falls under the Department of Constitutional Development, has not been repealed. However, there is poor coordination and co-operation among these departments.

As regards DLA, there are also problems of coordination and co-operation. For example, policy on land tenure reform is developed by DLA at national level, but a number of departments and structures are involved in its implementation. DLA has established offices at provincial level (PDLA) to implement its policy. At the same time, at provincial level in the Eastern Cape, there is a Department of Agriculture and Land Affairs (DALA) that is part of the Eastern Cape government. Eastern Cape DALA has regional (sometimes coinciding with District Council boundaries), and magisterial district offices. Often there is no communication and/or co-operation among these departments, especially between PDLA and DALA, although all are, in theory at least, accountable to DLA for implementing policies; for example, land allocation. It is not surprising, as the case study shows, that government officials in these departments are often not aware of DLA policies.

A similar situation exists in the Department of Constitutional Development. In the Eastern Cape, the provincial department that is supposed to implement national policies is Housing and Local Government. This department has regional offices as well as Local Government offices. The boundaries of the region and local government areas are not necessarily the same. In general, it is difficult to see whose jurisdiction begins and ends where. Here too there is a great deal of communication breakdown, confusion, and conflict. To compound matters, the Department of Trade and Industries is leading Spatial Development Initiatives (SDI) along the Wild Coast in the Eastern Cape, many of which are areas falling under tribal authorities. The Department of Economic Affairs, Finance, and Tourism in the Eastern Cape is implementing the SDI project. Finally, there is the House of Traditional Leaders and Contralesa, both representing traditional authorities.

BUDGETARY CONSTRAINTS

Closely linked with the above are budgetary constraints. In most cases, new staff have had to be employed, and the old staff had to adjust to new demands. New structures have had to be established. All this led to capacity problems. Financial resources become critical to develop effective and efficient human resources. Government, though, claim that they are encountering budgetary constraints and often have to put up with cuts. Ideally, functions such as service delivery are paid for through taxes generated from users. The rural areas of the former Bantustans are made up, for historical reasons, of a large number of poor people who cannot afford to pay for services. This is the dilemma of rural areas. Invariably, newly elected rural councillors are affected by this situation as they are seen as not delivering. This dilemma is vividly captured in the Green and White Papers of Local Government in South Africa.

> It is generally true that few powers and duties have been devolved to rural municipalities due to their lack of capacity.... Although TRCs have taxing powers, they have very limited potential to generate adequate tax and service charge revenue, and thus very little ability to sustain a level of fiscal autonomy. They are reliant on grants from and through the District Councils. This fiscal support is limited, and the basis for transfer is not entirely clear and so does not generate fiscal certainty. The limited powers and resources of rural municipalities, and their consequent inability to serve local communities, has lessened their credibility. This loss in credibility poses a threat to the future development of local government in these areas.

The White Paper on Local Government, which was launched in March 1998, resolved the above dilemma by recommending that the number of councillors be reduced. It further propagates an amalgamated model of urban and rural municipalities. By so doing, so the thinking goes, there will be some saving, and it is hoped (?) that a leaner administration will be more efficient.[29] What the White Paper does not address is the difficulty of administering and managing resources from a distance, especially in often inaccessible and remote rural areas.

LACK OF ACCOUNTABLE STRUCTURES
AT A LOCAL (VILLAGE) LEVEL

In the event the recommendation to reduce the number of elected councillors be implemented, rural areas that are in remote parts are most likely to be further marginalized, and it will be difficult to manage such areas as this will be too big a task for few officials. Already, there are complaints among rural people that they hardly see the existing elected rural councillors. These councillors are few and cover vast areas without infrastructure; for example, transport, to support them. Fewer councillors will certainly aggravate matters. The only structure that stands to gain from this proposal is the unelected tribal authority. This is the only structure that in the past has been, and still is, closer to the people. Previous regimes never attempted to replace this structure. Instead, they used it to achieve their ends. Post-apartheid South Africa has retained and recognized the institution in the constitution. As we have seen, the White Paper on Local Government unequivocally proposes unelected traditional authorities at local level.

This means that in so far as local government and tenure reform is extended to rural areas, democratically elected structures are removed from the people, and unelected ones left intact. This, it seems, is a recipe for failure on the part of elected structures and will, by comparison, make traditional authorities, despite their past record, look credible. Moreover, the White Paper does not take into account the differentiated nature of traditional authorities, the majority of whom may not carry out what is expected of them, while there may be some people who could carry the tasks. Traditional authorities on the other hand, have not demonstrated that they are ready to embrace democracy, and this is the fourth and final constraint that this study has identified.

TENSIONS AROUND TRADITIONAL AUTHORITIES

This chapter argues that it is mainly tensions around traditional authorities that have so far proved to be a major stumbling block in implementing policy. It is striking that traditional authorities, despite earlier divisions, mainly between traditional authorities in Contralesa and Inkatha, seem to be drawing closer and closer to one another. Their response to land tenure and local government reform provides a good example.

With regard to land tenure, DLA, in keeping with the declared policy of the ANC-led government to consult stakeholders, invited traditional authorities, through their structures, the Houses of Traditional Leaders, the Council for Traditional Leaders, and Contralesa, to respond to the DLA tenure reform policy in the former Bantustans. In their submission, the KwaZulu-Natal House of Traditional Authorities agreed that land should be returned and were unequivocal that land belongs to traditional authorities, and that the title deed should be in their name.

> We hope that central Government will not create obstacles to the
> transfer of title to Traditional Authorities which will sanction
> that our initiatives have set KwaZulu Natal several years ahead
> of the rest of the country in the process of returning land title to
> our people.

On the question of whether land should be transferred from the state, the House of Traditional Leaders in the Eastern Cape endorsed the government position, but, unlike their KwaZulu-Natal counterparts, were less clear on the question of landownership. The submission tended to dwell on the allegedly democratic nature of pre-colonial traditional authority rule and their betrayal by the ANC during the negotiation talks in the early 1990s. Their position has since become clearer; namely, that land should be transferred to tribal, some would say, traditional authorities. This position became clear in two meetings, one in July and the other in August 1998, that I attended in the House of Traditional Leaders in Bisho.[30] In the July meeting, traditional authorities were still equivocal. Whilst some agreed that land belongs to the people, others argued that land belongs to the chief or king. The latter were of the opinion that the title deed should be registered in the name of the chief or king of the area. Be that as it may, by the end of the meeting, there was an agreement that land belongs to the people, and not to an individual or representatives. What remained to be resolved, according to the agreement, was the *legal entity* that will hold land. The meeting resolved that officials from the national office of the Department of Land Affairs should be invited, and the understanding was that discussions would centre around the *legal entity*.

The follow-on meeting was held in August, and it was attended by a large delegation from the Department of Land of Affairs led by the chief director of the Land Tenure Directorate, Glen Thomas. At this meeting, traditional authorities changed the goalposts. Some went back to their earlier position that communal land belongs to the chief. According to chief Mgcotyelwa:

> Why bring CPAs (Communal Property Associations) to traditional land? Minister Hanekom knows very well that we want land to be transferred to traditional authorities. The House of Traditional Leaders is opposed to CPA.

Another traditional authority, Kakudi declared:

> There has always been a system that governed traditional systems, with administrative guidelines. CPA constitutes another system. That is the creation of conflict. This act was passed in 1996, and we were never consulted. Two years thereafter the DLA consults. Already under this government, there are elements to change the usual order.[31]

Although Chief Ngangomhlaba Matanzima confirmed the agreement of the previous meeting when reminded, Chief Gwadiso announced that traditional authorities were conducting discussions on these issues at the highest level involving Minister Hanekom and Deputy President Thabo Mbeki. He went on to declare their position that they want land to be transferred to traditional authorities. The meeting was also informed that Contralesa holds the same position. The meeting ended on that note.

As regards local government reform: traditional authorities reject the notion of municipalities in rural areas. They also regard the 10 per cent representation in local government, as an *interest group* as an insult. In the Eastern Cape, they do not send any representative to Transitional Representative Council. Here, too, they demand that tribal authorities should be the main structures for rural local government. In other words, traditional authorities want to cling to apartheid-style structures that were created to set them up as undemocratic, unaccountable structures, quite contrary to the spirit of the constitution.

Where civic organizations and elected TrepCs are active in rural areas, as is the case in Guba, there are often titanic struggles between traditional authorities and these structures. Traditional authorities in the Transkei did not participate in the local government elections as they were opposed to the notion of municipalities, elected rural councillors, and the fact that they were given a mere 10 per cent representation. Where they agree with the principle of elected councillors, it is only in so far that these councillors will be part of tribal authorities.

Traditional authorities in the Eastern Cape, through their bodies, the House of Traditional Leaders in Bisho and Contralesa, reject the Regulation of Development in Rural Areas Act of 1997. They claim, wrongly,[32] that they were at the forefront of development in rural areas, and have threatened to disrupt initiatives by elected rural councillors to effect development in *their* areas. In practice, as the case study will illustrate, the Regulation of Development in Rural Areas Act has not been implemented, largely because of capacity constraints on the part of rural councillors.

Government, as represented by the Departments of Land Affairs and Constitutional Development, had not taken any position regarding the rejection of policy by traditional authorities. This is despite clarity of policy on these matters. As indicated, the much-awaited White Paper on Local Government avoided a clear policy on the role of traditional authorities on local government.

How do we explain this convergence of ideas and actions on the part of traditional authorities in the Houses of Traditional Leaders? Part of the answer lies in the fact that when the demise of National Party apartheid rule was imminent in the early 1990s, a vast number of traditional authorities who collaborated with the apartheid regime abandoned the sinking ship and jumped on the bandwagon, Contralesa. As noted, the ANC, given its anti-apartheid broad front, and the need to get votes, did not discriminate. By 1994, the bulk of the membership of Contralesa was made up of the collaborating traditional authorities. It is the latter that also make up the majority of the members of the Eastern Cape House of Traditional Leaders. Most of them have concluded that the ANC is hostile towards traditional authorities and have begun to look to allies elsewhere. Some have joined the newly formed United Democratic Movement of Bantu Holomisa and Roelf Meyer, while it is widely rumoured that others are in the National Party. Some are impressed by what is perceived to be Chief Buthelezi's tough line towards the ANC, and the concessions Buthelezi seems to be getting. Any explanation should take this combination of factors into account.

CASE STUDY: TSHEZI COMMUNAL AREA

The case study of the Tshezi communal area in the Eastern Cape illustrates the complexities involved in implementing land tenure and local government reform.[33] The Tshezi case study identifies three major constraints to delivery. First is the difficulty of implementing policy, such as land tenure reform, that is based on democratic principles whilst at the same time recognizing traditional authorities. The issue is not simply the question of recognizing traditional authorities, it is that government, represented in this case by the DLA, has not demonstrated commitment to implementing its policies. Secondly, the case study illustrates the problem of relating detailed research to policy and implementation strategies. Lastly, the case study shows the lack of interdepartmental coordination that delays development projects which are crucial to the livelihoods of poor rural communities such as the Tshezi.

ESTABLISHING A CPA IN THE TSHEZI AREA

The Spatial Development Initiatives (SDI) led by the Department of Trade and Industry, and the identification of the two resorts of Coffee Bay and Hole-in-the-Wall, which fall under the Tshezi communal area, made the Tshezi area a test case for the implementability or otherwise of the policies and legislation of the DLA and the Department of Constitutional Development. The initial concept study of 1996, which led to the identification of the area for SDI purposes, identified land and local authority as posing major blockages to development in the area. Following this study, the DLA was invited onto the SDI team, specifically to help resolve the land-related issues.

One of the requirements of the SDI was the need to establish a legal entity for the Tshezi community to place the community in a position to be able to negotiate and contract with potential developers and to be able to receive and disburse funds for SDI-related development in the area. An SDI Committee was to facilitate this process, but did not know how to proceed. The DLA tenure process brought the landownership issue into stronger focus and resulted in several workshops with the SDI Committee to assess the pros and cons of different legal entities. Eventually, the Committee decided to opt for a CPA for the Tshezi area. From that point on, the focus was on assisting with the establishment of a CPA for the Tshezi area (referred to as the Tshezi Communal Property Association or TCPA), in particular, the development with the SDI Committee of a TCPA Constitution with rules, regulations, and procedures for land use.

Throughout this process, the chief of the area, Chief Dubulingqanga, and his son, Ngwenyathi, were kept informed about the process. Their initial response was supportive. They were excited at the prospect of getting *their land* back. The SDI Committee was chaired by one of the four headmen, Mr. Mbambazela, and he too was very supportive of the land transfer process. The idea of the legal entity also received the support of the *legal* cottage owners and the Ocean View Hotel.

By the middle of June 1998, public meetings (involving the department and the researchers) had been held on the CPA in all the four administrative areas. The CPA concept was well received at the meetings held in three administrative areas; Lower Nenga, Lower Mpako and Nzulweni, with the headmen for these three areas supporting the CPA. It was not possible to hold a meeting in the fourth, Mthonjana. A small, but vociferous group refused to be involved in meetings that had not been called by the chief. This is despite the fact that the group leader had earlier expressed a vote of no confidence in chiefs as leaders in development. This group also indicated that they rejected the CPA, without, it should be noted, any knowledge of what it really entailed. It is the selfsame leader who unilaterally withdrew his participation and that of the other representative of Mthonjana in the SDI committee. An interim Tshezi Communal Property Association (TCPA) was established. Chief Dubulingqanga's son, Ngwenyathi, was elected as chair.

By this time, Chief Dubulingqanga was prevaricating, expressing doubts about the CPA. In fact, these doubts were initially expressed at the tribal authority meeting in April 1998. At this meeting, Mr. Mbambazela, the chairperson of the SDI who, as earlier stated, is also a headman at Nzulwini, expressed concern that traditional authorities might lose their control if the CPA were established. He made an appeal to the meeting that "we should guard and protect chieftaincy." He was supported by the son of the chief, Ngwenyathi. The latter suggested that traditional authorities should be given more time to consult with other traditional authorities outside the Tshezi area, including the Eastern Cape branch of Contralesa. He suggested that they would ask Contralesa to draft a constitution for them, seemingly disregarding the draft constitution prepared with the SDI Committee and discussed with him and his father. Chief Dubulingqanga did not attend the April meeting.

It became apparent with the march of time that the chief's position was strongly influenced from outside by people like chiefs Nonkonyana, Patekile Holomisa, and Gwadiso who were arguing and advising him against the CPA in favour of the transfer of the land to the tribal authority. On one occasion, whilst the researchers were conducting fieldwork in the area, the chief, his son, and councillors announced that Chief Patekile Holomisa had paid an unexpected visit to Chief Dubulingqanga where the CPA process was discussed. Chief Holomisa advised Chief Dubulingqanga and his son to request a meeting of the DLA with the House of Traditional Leaders in Bishop to discuss the CPA in the Tshezi area.

Two meetings with the House of Traditional Leaders in Bishop resulted from this; one on 2 July 1998 attended by Lungisile Ntsebeza as DLA consultant. The next meeting was on 17 August 1998, and the DLA was powerfully represented by the chief director of the Land Tenure Reform Directorate in Pretoria, Glen Thomas. The position of the House of Traditional Leaders was that they accepted transfer of land, but rejected the DLA policy that land be transferred to land rights holders as co-owners. They declared that land must be transferred to tribal authorities. Further, they informed the DLA delegation that this matter was in the hands of the deputy president and the minister of Land Affairs.

When the outcome of the July 1998 meeting was reported to the SDI and interim TCPA committees in the Tshezi area, committee members, including headman Mbambazela and Chief Ngwenyathi, felt strongly that the establishment of the CPA should proceed. At that stage, the view held by committee members was that CPA opposition was not against the content of the legal entity (which accommodated the tribal authority), but the name, particularly the use of the word *Communal* in CPA. The proposal was that the name should be changed to *Tshezi Property Association* or *Tshezi Tribal Property Association*. However, it soon became apparent that nothing less than the transfer of land to the chief or the tribal authority itself would satisfy Chief Dubulingqanga. For example, in September, a delegation from the Tshezi area, led by the chief, held discussions with Chief Nonkonyana, an advocate, the vice-president of Contralesa, and the Chair of the House of Traditional Leaders in the Eastern Cape. The meeting resolved that:

- Tshezi land should be transferred into the name of the Tshezi tribal authority, and that the constitution prepared with the SDI and interim CPA committees should be adjusted accordingly.

- The Tshezi tribal authority should write to the minister of Land Affairs requesting him to appoint a lawyer to assist them to constitute and register the Tshezi tribal authority.

Attempts on the part of the TCPA to involve the *king* of the abaThembu, Paramount Chief Buyelekhaya Dalindyebo, who was also supportive of the CPA, were not successful. Chief Dubulingqanga, under the influence of key traditional authorities in Contralesa and the House of Traditional Leaders in the Eastern Cape, rejected the CPA outright, and began to mobilize opposition.

DLA avoided taking a clear-cut position on the rejection of the CPA by some traditional authorities and a tiny minority of individuals in Mthonjana. Instead, in March 1999, the chief director of the Tenure Directorate visited the Tshezi area, to inform the Tshezi tribal authority that the DLA had abandoned the establishment of the CPA in the Tshezi area. He further explained the procedure to be followed in the event that development projects requiring the consent of the minister were proposed. The chief directorate also addressed similar meetings with the interim TCPA committee, effectively telling them that they should disband.

RELATIONSHIP BETWEEN DLA AND RESEARCHERS

Over two years or so, the DLA commissioned research in the Tshezi area in order to facilitate SDI development, and to test its policies on land tenure reform. This section takes a critical look at the relationship between the DLA and the researchers, and the extent to which the detailed research has informed ongoing policy development and implementation.

Despite pleas from the researchers, no feedback on the research reports, which were regularly submitted, was forthcoming. The researchers reached such levels of frustration that they sent copies of their reports to whoever they considered to be keen to understand and comment on their work. It is the well-considered opinion of the researchers that some of the problems encountered in the Tshezi area could have been avoided had there been responses to the proposals and findings of the research.

The DLA decision to abandon the CPA in the Tshezi area was never discussed with the researchers, despite the fact that they were commissioned to help resolve landownership and governance issues in the area. It was abundantly clear that the recommendations made by the researchers had never been taken into account. In fact, representatives from the national office of the DLA who had been assigned to the Eastern Cape had not been properly briefed about the Tshezi case. They had not read the numerous reports and field notes that were prepared and regularly submitted to the

DLA. When the chief director visited the Tshezi area in March 1999, he had not read the progress report that had been compiled by the researchers.

LACK OF INTERDEPARTMENTAL COORDINATION

One of the SDI projects in the Tshezi area is infrastructural development in the resort area in the form of beach and parking facilities. This project was implemented in February 1999 as a Public Works program. However, the Public Works Department did not properly consult the following:

- DLA, as the nominal owner of land
- The Heath Special Investigation Unit, who issued a moratorium on development along the Wild Coast
- Department of Environmental Affairs for environmental impact studies
- The Tshezi people, including the TCPA and the tribal authority.

This led to legal action being taken by Chief Dubulingqanga and one of his head-men, and to interventions by DLA landowners and the Heath Special Investigation Unit. Ultimately, this development was delayed as a result of this confusion, caused by a lack of interdepartmental co-operation and coordination.

CONCLUSION

The central argument of this chapter is that current initiatives to implement policy and legislation on land tenure and local government are frustrated by a fundamental contradiction in the South African Constitution. On the one hand, the constitution enshrines a bill of rights based on elected representative government, while it also recognizes the unelected institution of traditional authorities which are hereditary and/or appointed by previous regimes. The chapter has looked at current attempts to mix elected representation and unelected traditional authorities[34] in land tenure and local government in the rural areas of the former Bantustans.

The chapter argues that the existing model of rural local government that is based on a District Council model is too remote from rural people to make elected representatives effective in delivery and accountable to their rural constituencies. The District Council is made up of urban Transitional Representative Councils (TLCs) and rural Transitional Representative Councils (TrepCs). The latter are elected at a magisterial district level, resulting in a few councillors elected for vast, scattered and often inaccessible areas. This makes it difficult for rural councillors to be visible and available when needed. The recommendation by the White Paper on Local Government that there should be fewer councillors will thus further discredit elected councillors. This, coupled with the proposal that traditional authorities "should play a role closest to the people," will enhance the position of traditional authorities, with negative consequences for democracy based on elected representation.

The chapter does take into account other factors that affect delivery, such as, problems of poor communication, coordination, and co-operation, within and among departments. Also taken into account in the study are budgetary constraints. While a case can be made that these various constraints impede delivery, this study argues that it is the fundamental contradiction of recognizing unelected institutions in an elected representative democracy that is at the heart of nondelivery. The Tshezi case study brings out this tension starkly.

The Tshezi case study illustrates the difficulties involved in implementing policies based on principles of democracy while recognizing unelected traditional authorities. We have seen how tenure reform in the area, in the form of transferring land to the Tshezi people through a Communal Property Association (CPA), or a similar entity, have constantly and consistently been frustrated by the chief of the area and a handful of self-serving individuals who are benefiting from the land administration vacuum. Despite the Department of Land Affairs' clear policy on the role of traditional authorities in land tenure reform, there is reluctance on the part of government to confront traditional authorities on their rejection of DLA policy. Instead, the department has been forced to reconsider its policy on land transfer by discouraging the *upfront* transfer of land, in favour of confirming land rights, with the state still holding ownership of land. Although land transfer has not been discarded, it is not seen as an immediate option. The absence of local, village level democratic structures, including NGOs and CBOs, in the area that could take advantage of favourable land and local government policies, aggravates the position.

The other lesson that can be learnt from the Tshezi case study is about poor communication, coordination, and co-operation. For example, the Department of Housing and Local Government and the Department of Land Affairs (DLA) are not co-operating on service delivery in the Tshezi area, especially the resort area. The decision by the Public Works Department to implement the infrastructural programs of the SDI, namely, beach facilities and parking facilities, without consulting DLA as the landowner, shows poor communication, coordination, and co-operation.

The same problem has also manifested itself in the Regulation of Development in Rural Areas Act of 1997 passed by the Eastern Cape Legislature. This act transfers all *development* functions that tribal authorities were given by the Bantu Authorities Act to elected rural councillors. One of the functions of tribal authorities was to make recommendations regarding land allocation. By October 1997, when the act was passed, the DLA had already launched its White Paper on Land Policy six months earlier. In terms of DLA policy, the decision as to who should allocate land in the rural areas of the former Bantustans must be taken by the affected rural people, who are regarded as the owners of land by the department, despite the existing legal position. The Eastern Cape law thus contradicts the policy of the DLA, which creates insecurity of tenure, and is a recipe for unnecessary tensions.

Another lesson to be drawn from the Tshezi case study, is about the role of commissioned research. In the Tshezi case, research was commissioned by the DLA. After two years of detailed research, mainly, but not exclusively, in the form of in-depth interviews and fieldwork, followed by recommendations and proposals, there was little evidence that the steps taken in the Tshezi area were in any way informed by the research, which was specifically commissioned to inform practice. Where it is used, it was used eclectically, and the researchers were not consulted when decisions were made, neither was there any response to their recommendations and proposals.

The major conclusion of the chapter is that if government is committed to extending democracy to land tenure and local government reform, traditional authorities cannot play a decisive role in decision-making. If they want to be involved in decision-making structures, they must put themselves up as candidates and be elected. Government should make this clear to traditional authorities. This is not to say that traditional authorities should be abolished. They may well have a role in other aspects of rural life.

The chapter draws its theoretical basis from Mamdani's thesis on "decentralized despotism." Mamdani argues that a feature of Native (tribal) Authorities was the fusion of administrative, judicial, and executive powers in one authority, the *native authority*. Dismantling the fused character of tribal authorities and making them accountable and subjected to elections is seen by Mamdani as a prerequisite to democratic transformation in the rural areas of Africa.

REFERENCES

Beinart, W. 1982. *The Political Economy of Phondoland 1860 to 1930*. Johannesburg: Ravan Press.

Beinart, W., and C. Bundy. 1987. *Hidden Struggles in Rural South Africa*. Johannesburg: Ravan Press.

Beinart, W. and D. Saul, eds. 1995. *Segregation and Apartheid in Twentiethcentury South Africa*. London: Routledge.

Bruce, J. W., and Migot-Adholla, eds. 1998. *Searching for Land Tenure Security in Africa*. Duduque: Kendall/Hunt.

Claassens, A., and S. Makopi. 1999. South African Proposals for Tenure Reform; the Draft Land Rights Bill: Key Principles and Changes in Thinking as the Bill Evolved. Paper presented to an international conference organized by the Department for International Development, U.K., on Land Tenure, Poverty and Sustainable Development in Sub-Saharan Africa, Sunningdale, Berkshire, U.K., 16–19 February.

Edge, W. A., and M. H. Lekowe, eds. 1998. *Botswana: Politics and Society*. Pretoria: J. L. van Schaik.

Hendricks, F. T. 1990. *The Pillars of Apartheid: Land Tenure, Rural Planning and the Chieftaincy*. Uppsala. Sweden: Acta Universitatis Upsaliensis.

Lambert, J. 1995. Chiefship in Early Colonial Natal, 1843–1879, *Journal of Southern African Studies* 21, no. 2.

Maloka, E. 1995. Traditional Leaders and the Current Transition, *African Communist*, 2nd Quarter.

Maloka, T. A. 1996. Populism and the Politics of Chieftaincy and Nation-Building in the New South Africa, *Journal of Contemporary African Studies* 14, no. 2.

Mamdani, M. 1996. *Citizen and Subject: Contemporary Africa and the Legacy of Late Colonialism*. Princeton: Princeton University Press.

Manona, C. 1990. The Big Lip of Sebe has Fallen, *Indicator South Africa*, Quarterly Report 8, no. 1.

Manona, C. 1998. The Collapse of the "Tribal Authority" System and the Rise of Civic Associations. In C. de Wet and M. Whisson, eds., *From Reserve to Region: Apartheid and Social Change in the Keikammahoek District of (former) Ciskei, 1950–1990*. Grahamstown: ISER.

Mbeki, G. 1984. *South Africa: The Peasants' Revolt*. London: International Defence and Aid Fund.

Mbenga, B. 1998. The Acquisition of Land by Africans in the Western Transvaal, South Africa: The Case of the BaFokeng of the Rustenburg District, 1902–1931. Paper presented to the African Studies Association of America (ASA) Conference, Chicago, 29 October to 1 November.

Ntsebeza, L., and F. Hendricks. 1998. Democracy and Despotism in Post-Apartheid South Africa – The Role of Chiefs/Traditional Authorities in Rural Local Government. Paper presented to an international conference on Comparative Experiences on Democratization between South Africa and Nigeria, Centre for African Studies, University of Cape Town, 30 May to 2 June.

Peires, J. B. 1981. *The House of Phalo*. Johannesburg: Ravan Press.

South Africa [Ministry for Provincial Affairs and Constitutional Development] 1998. *The White Paper on Local Government*. Pretoria: Department of Provincial Affairs and Constitutional Development.

Stultz, N. M. 1979. *Transkei's Half Loaf – Race Separation in South Africa*. New Haven: Yale University Press.

Tapscott, C. 1997. The Institutionalisation of Rural Local Government in Post-Apartheid South Africa. In W. Hofmeister and I. Scholz, eds., *Traditional and Contemporary Forms of Local Participation and Self-government in Africa*. Johannesburg: Konrad Adenhauer.

Thomas, G., S. Sibanda, and A. Claassens. 1998. Current Developments in South Africa's Land Tenure Policy. A memo issued by the DLA.

NOTES

1. This is a reworked version of a paper originally prepared for a Land and Agrarian Reform Conference held at the Alpha Training Centre, Broederstroom, 26–28 July 1999. The paper was, in turn, an overview of a research report titled "Land Tenure Reform, Traditional Authorities, and Rural Local Government in Post-Apartheid South Africa." I wish to acknowledge the financial support of the Swiss Agency for Development and Co-operation, which made this study possible, and the many individuals who helped me in various ways. I am, however, solely responsible for the analysis and interpretation of events. This work was partially carried out with the aid of a grant from the International Development Research Centre, Ottawa, Canada.

2. The term *traditional authority/ies* is used throughout as an all-encompassing term to refer to chiefs of various ranks. It is used in this paper to refer to people, and not to structures. Tribal Authorities were structures established by the Bantu Authorities Act of 1951 and are composed of traditional authorities (the chief and his headmen), appointed councillors, and a tribal secretary. The extent to which chiefs can be regarded as traditional, as will be seen in the section dealing with traditional authorities, is highly disputed. The use of the term is not intended as acknowledgment that chiefs are necessarily legitimate leaders in their areas.

3. Mamdani seems to suggest that the *Native Authority* was dominated by the chief. In the case of apartheid South Africa, the tribal authority was made up of the chief of the area, his headmen, councillors (some – the majority – appointed by the chief, the rest elected), and a tribal authority secretary. Some chiefs, though, were more autocratic than others.

4. One of the objectives of this research was to identify and research a "popular and democratic tribal system," as assumed by the DLA quote at the beginning of the chapter. The choice of the Tshezi communal area was partly influenced by that. As will be clear from the analysis of this case study, the *tribal system* in the area is certainly not democratic. Its popularity is questionable.

5. The terms *self-government* and *independence* have been put in italics to register my rejection of these areas to having been self-governing and independent. They were a creation of a system that excluded the vast majority of South Africans in decision-making processes.

6. The amaMphondo are situated in the Transkei region of the Eastern Cape, along the Wild Coast. They were victims of the *Mfecane*, "the massive upheaval and dispersion of African people throughout Southern Africa in the 1820s and 1830s, principally as a result of the rise and consolidation of the Zulu kingdom in Natal." (See Glossary in Beinart and Saul, 1995, 287.)

7. Peires compares pre-colonial chieftaincy to Western Europe in the Middle Ages, where the relationship was between *lord* and *serf*.

8. We have noted above, in the quote from Peires, that, due to "political competition between chiefs," it was not always smooth going to establish who the next *chief* in line was.

9. The system was later put forward as an alternative to African representation in Parliament. During the apartheid era, the council system was replaced by Bantu Authorities, which was a major step towards the establishment of *self-governing* territories in the Bantustans. Some of these were granted *independence*.

10. These headmen were appointed by the British in the Cape when they established magisterial districts. These districts were run by magistrates, and in each village, a headman would be appointed as the local representative of the magistrate.

11. This is merely an example, and no attempt is made to generalize.

12. This would increase land for African occupation to 13 per cent.

13. This means that for each additional wife, a new homestead site would be allotted. The allotment was traditionally for both residential and agricultural allotment, but with the enormous pressure on land in some areas, people are willing to accept a residential site only.

14. Conversations with committee members of the Spatial Development Initiatives (SDI) and the Interim Communal Property Association (CPA) in Mqanduli, Eastern Cape, December 1997 – June 1998.

15. This was a form of *villagization* that was introduced in the 1930s, but only implemented in the 1950s as a conservation measure against soil erosion.

16. The majority of land claims in the Transkei region of the Eastern Cape are based on such removals.

17. This section on the Bantu Authorities Act is drawn largely from Ntsebeza and Hendricks 1998, 5, and Tapscott 1997.

18. The position remained unchanged.

19. Interview with secretaries of tribal authorities in Mqanduli, 10 March 1999.

20. Annual reports of Calusa and Health Care Trust (1990–97), two NGOs operating in the Xhalanga magisterial district, Eastern Cape.

21. Interview with Mgweba, 18 August 1998.

22. As noted, the 1936 Act is still used in the Transkei to issue PTOs.

23. Which provides for the repeal of all laws regulating the acquisition of rights in land according to race, including the 1913 and 1936 Natives Land Acts, and for the rationalization of other laws that directly or indirectly restrict access to such rights.

24. For the rationalization of land registration systems and the upgrading of lower-order land tenure to full ownership.

25. John Bruce works for the Land Tenure Center, University of Wisconsin, Madison. From the early 1990s, the Land Tenure Center has offered courses and opportunities for NGOs and post-1994 government officials, some of whom were in NGOs before 1994.

26. National Party thinking here was undoubtedly influenced by World Bank thinking that linked tenure security with individual title deed.

27. It should be pointed out, though, that as early as 1993, the issue of entrenching the recognition of traditional authorities in the constitution was considered.

28. This does not mean that traditional authorities do not have a role to play in the lives of rural people. As has been mentioned, they could, depending on their acceptance and popularity, still play an important role in the maintenance of law and order, dispute resolution, and so on.

29. It may be difficult, though, to sustain this argument, given the approval of huge amounts, around R 32 million to remunerate traditional authorities, at a time when their roles and functions are far from clear.

30. This and the following sections draw substantially from reports and field notes by Erik Buiten and Lungisile Ntsebeza (author). Both of us were commissioned by the Department of Land Affairs to "resolve landownership and governance issues in the Tshezi Communal Area, Mqanduli, Eastern Cape." I am fully indebted to Erik Buiten, but accept full responsibility for the interpretation of events.

31. Presumably "the usual order" refers to tribal authorities established under colonial and apartheid rule.

32. It is argued that traditional authorities were never empowered and merely acted as local representatives for line departments.

33. For details of these two case studies, see my research report cited in endnote 1.

34. The term *traditional authority(ies)* was explained in the introduction to be used in this study as an all encompassing term to refer to *chiefs* of various ranks. It is used to refer to people, and not structures. *Tribal authorities* is used to refer to structures that were established by the Bantu Authorities Act of 1951 and are composed of traditional authorities.

"WE RULE THE MOUNTAINS AND THEY RULE THE PLAINS":
THE WEST AFRICAN BASIS OF TRADITIONAL AUTHORITY IN JAMAICA

CHAPTER 8

WERNER ZIPS

WERNER ZIPS studied law and anthropology at the University of Vienna. He is a professor in the Institute for Social and Cultural Anthropology (ethnology) at the University of Vienna. He has written numerous articles on legal anthropology, political anthropology, ethnohistory, and Caribbean and African studies. Some of his recent book publications are: *Theorie einer gerechten Praxis oder: Die Macht ist wie ein Ei* (Vienna: Wiener Universitätsverlag, 2002); *Ethnohistorie – Rekonstruktion und Kulturkritik. Eine Einführung,* with Karl R. Wernhart, 2d ed. (Vienna: Promedia, 2001); *Nation X. Schwarzer Nationalismus, Black Exodus* and *Hip Hop,* with Heinz Kämpfer (Vienna: Promedia, 2001); *Black Rebels. African-Caribbean Freedom Fighters in Jamaica* (Princeton and Kingston: Markus Wiener and Ian Randle Publ., 1999); and *Sovereignty, Legitimacy, and Power in West African Societies. Perspectives of Legal Anthropology*, co-edited with E.A.B. van Rouveroy van Nieuwaal (Hamburg: LIT, 1998). He has also directed numerous films on Jamaica, Cuba, and Ghana.

INTRODUCTION

The condition of slavery left no way to the enslaved Africans for a meaningful social reorganization but one: *marronage*. It meant to try the vague chance to escape the slave-masters and their agents by flight to the interiors of the various plantation states in the so-called New World. For most individuals who attempted to travel this only path to freedom, it ended in torture or death. But throughout the African diaspora some managed to survive the persecution by slave-hunters, bloodhounds, and the militia. Wherever they were sufficient in numbers, new social groupings developed in parallel to slave society, which Patterson (1973, 9) correctly termed: "a monstrous distortion of human society." In Jamaica, these groups of original Africans called Maroons were particularly successful.[1] Their resistance against the longest reigning colonial power in Jamaica started when the British occupied the island from the Spaniards in 1655. For a period of almost eighty-five years, Great Britain, the then superpower of the world, failed to defeat them although they tried at periods with great expenditure to eradicate the physical threat to their sovereignty.

Certainly the plantocracy and the colonialists considered it as a tremendous disgrace to conclude a peace treaty with the black rebels (as the Maroons were generally termed by the British) in 1738/39. It is in this light that the following colonial discourse on the Maroon political and legal organization should be seen. Most of the pejorative descriptions have their root in the intellectual and moral incapability of the white capturers of the African people as well as the American and Caribbean territories to accept an independent social entity which was forged out of individuals who were treated as things by law. But most of their members came from highly differentiated West African societies. They were cruelly stripped of everything material in the course of their capture, forceful transplantation, and later enslavement. But their knowledge, experiences, and incorporated ways to perceive, interpret, and act could not be wiped out so easily. Manifold cultural expressions of the African diaspora have their bases in this mental or cultural resistance against the totality of enslavement. This is not to say that the enslaved Africans and their newborn successors simply held fast to the old traditions whenever they could. Rather, the experiential habitus formations in the different African spheres of society lay at the heart of the culture building process in the dramatically new social environments beyond the Atlantic (cf. Zips 1999b, 115–218).

Compared to the majority of the enslaved peoples of African origins, Maroon societies of course had a much greater freedom to reshape their African experiences into new organizational forms. Still even these relatively unrestrained social groups were by no means *New World replicas* of African societies or *tribes*, as some authors seem to suggest.[2] In contrast to this view, Maroon societies should be considered in tendency as dynamic organizations who link their management of the future in the presence by a strong sense of the ancestral ways in the past; a practical composure which was adequately characterized by Price (1992, 64):

> The cultural uniqueness of ... maroon societies ... rests firmly on their fidelity to "African" cultural principles at these deeper levels – whether aesthetic, political, or domestic – rather than on the frequency of their isolated "retentions" of form. Maroon groups had a rare freedom to develop and transform African ideas from a variety of societies and to adapt them to changing circumstances. With their hard-earned freedom and resilient creativity they have built systems that are at once meaningfully African and among the most truly "alive" and culturally dynamic of African-American cultures.

COLONIAL TRIBES OR NEO-AFRICAN SOCIETIES?

Most of the colonial literature and administrative or military sources depict the Jamaican Maroons as semi-dependent villages inadequately governed by their headmen. Certainly the colonial agents had no interest to create an impression of existing quasi-African states within the state in Jamaica (nor elsewhere). But to read these colonial political interests of historical representation into the scientific analysis means to continue overlooking the deeper incorporated structures of Maroon authority and politics; i.e., the African habitus formation. It is true that Maroon decisions always had to include strategic planning and policy considerations in relation to the plantocracy and the state throughout the colonial history in Jamaica (until the 1962 independence declaration). Yet to reduce the Maroon policies to direct results of colonial policies loses sight of the structural African basis of their organizational achievements. The ethnohistorical description of Maroon political history by Kopytoff (1973: 347) gives an example of such a reductionist historical reading (even though she seems to acknowledge the limitations of such an interpretation):

It is noteworthy that while we are describing periods of Maroon political organization, the periods are bounded by acts of another government, that of the British in Jamaica. In part, this reflects our primary avenue of information into the Maroon societies, Jamaican Government records, but, more importantly, the Maroons were themselves what have been called "Colonial Tribes." ... Culturally similar to other Negroes of Jamaica, they came to constitute separate societies only because of their special relation to the Jamaican Government, first as fugitive bands, then, after the treaties, as allies and corporate land holders in the eyes of the Government, and finally, after 1842, as ex-corporate land holders who could not be disbanded.

Such a conclusion is logical only in the sense that it directly results from sheer ignorance of the African experiential and cognitive backgrounds of the individual actors who formed and transformed the original Maroon societies. The majority of Africans forcefully shipped to Jamaica originated from the former Gold Coast (today's Ghana). Named after the British Fort Kormantse on this stretch of the West African coastline, the so-called Coromantees preserved the common factor until today in their notion of Kromanti culture. Whereas the British used the ethnic misnomer as a brand name for all their human merchandise from the region, irrespective of their actual ethnic ties or port of embarkation,[3] the first freedom fighters viewed Kromanti as a cultural basin for their genuine (national) traditions and the symbolic landmark or social origin of their new commonality as Maroons. Therefore, they succeeded in changing a colonial denotation to a denominator for a jural corporateness forged out of the various Akan and other ethnic origins of the particular individuals. The physical place of the Fante village Kormantine turned into the metaphysical space Kromanti for the creation of a neo-African identity as Maroons (Zips 1999a, 43–67).

West Africa, and in particular the Akan regions of today's Ghana, is reflected in the symbolic landscape of meanings attached to landmarks such as the Kindah tree, just outside the Jamaican Maroon village of Accompong. Kindah, a large mango tree offering shade for the meeting of the dead ancestors and the living Maroons during the yearly festival on 6 January, points to the challenging process of political integration in the historical circumstances.[4] Even though the majority of individuals came from cultural backgrounds that shared many common features, the unification between, for instance, former Asante and Fante had to overcome earlier experiences of tension, imperialist menace, and even war on the African continent. The physical appearance of Kindah has the shape of a large umbrella (*kyinie*) with all the connotations of the overall symbol for kingship in the Akan context: the protection offered by the king or chief with its reasonable or *cooling* judicial solutions of heated disputes. This *kyinie* or great state umbrella (e.g.,) of the Asantehene, the king of kings of the Asante, is etymologically decoded by McCaskie (1995, 207) in the following analysis:

> The Asantehene, as the embodiment of culture, afforded a protective "coolness" at once physical and metaphorical. The motion of his great umbrellas signified this in a literal and symbolic way (supported, as they were, by the lesser umbrellas of ever diminishing degrees of size and costliness that belonged to descending ranks of office holders), as did the metaphor that likened him to *gyadua* (a large tree offering shade: i.e., (o) *gye*: receiving, acceptance, with the idea of protection + (e) *dua*: a tree). Synonyms encapsulated the idea that the Asantehene "protected" culture by offering a cooling "shade"; thus, for example, (o) *tew gyadua ahaban* ("he tears the leaves of the shade tree") intended the same meaning as, and could be used in euphemistic place of, *ohyira ohene* ("he curses the king's life").

Pacification and integration are as well the historical foundations of the importance of the Kindah tree in Jamaica. According to oral traditions in Accompong, its shade offered a "cool spot" for the strategic and later diplomatic consultations of Kojo's council of elders. A signpost attached to the tree trunk gives a definition of its symbolic meaning for the continued jural corporateness of Maroon society, from the earliest days of armed freedom struggle to the contemporary legal fight for constitutional recognition. It reads: "Kindah – we all are family."

With this deliberate and difficult unification of former members of Akan (Fante, Ahanta, Nzima, Wassaw, Akim, Akwapim, Sefwi, Brong, Kwahu, Denkyira, and Asante), Ewe, Ga-Adangme, and other African societies (especially a smaller group from the Congo region, which may have been successors of Africans brought already by the Spaniards) new dynamic traditions of authority were created.[5] They were predominantly rooted in West African forms of kingship (or chieftaincy). As in the West African contexts, the colonial state in Jamaica tried to dismantle the sovereignty and legitimacy of these traditional authorities who were *traditional* in the strict dynamic sense of *traditio*, basing their political formations on ideas, incorporated understandings, and cognitive models of their African forefathers. Only such symbols and practices survived in very similar expressions, which fitted into the new social and ecological environment. Whereas the umbrella of chiefs and queenmothers (*kyinie*) might have reappeared in its basic form of the large shade tree Kindah in the biggest Maroon community of Jamaica (Accompong), the sacred horn of the Akan (*Abentia*) which enables communication with the dead and among the living especially in times of war, took the almost identical shape of the *Abeng* among all Jamaican Maroon communities (Zips 1999b, 186–205; McCaskie 1995, 295ff.; Wilks 1975, 324ff., 667).

Within this neo-African system of chieftaincy, a potentially lifelong appointed chief controlled the jural corporateness of the community together with a council of elders. This principal structure was kept alive from the seventeenth century until the fundamental change to voting in the middle of the twentieth century in Accompong. Other Maroon communities in Jamaica, such as Moore Town, Scott's Hall, and Charles Town, appear to have stuck to hereditary procedures of selecting a chief until fairly recently (though not without internal conflicts over the adequacy of such a practice in modern times). However, the root of today's legal pluralism in Jamaica lies in the parallel development of a neo-African type of chieftaincy in the Maroon communities and the introduction of the Westminster model of parliamentarism by the British.

There is a long history of the existence of two legal traditions in this Caribbean island: a plantocratic distortion of a European – namely British – colonial state model "in which the legal system was quite deliberately a travesty of anything that could be called justice" (Patterson 1973, 9), and a new creation of a group of transplanted Africans with different languages and cultural experiences who had never before existed as a unified corporate entity. The latter obviously drew on various incorporated African structures. These differing though not altogether different traditions had to be negotiated between all the members who had decided to submit themselves to the jural corporateness as Maroons. If one bears in mind the necessary efforts to integrate new members, at least until the time when the peace treaty with the British closed the ranks of the Maroons for new runaways (in 1738/39), such policies can only be analyzed as active and not merely *re*active to the colonial policies. The empirical reconstruction of continual communicative processes of integration and decision-making in the fields of politics and law seem to defeat the discourse of the *colonial tribes* created by successful attempts to indirect rule (Zips 1999b, 273ff.).[6]

MAROON SOVEREIGNTY AS A COUNTERTRADITION TO PLANTOCRACY

Historically, the causes for and actual development of legal pluralism in Jamaica (and other parts of the African diaspora) nevertheless stand in sharp contrast to West African contexts. In the case of the Maroons, their disputed sovereignty and legitimacy of self-governance was shaped by the so-called *First-Time people*, the founding ancestors of Maroon nationality and ethnicity.[7] These original Maroons created the *tradition* of self-determination out of the incorporated African political legacies. Therefore, the particular *Maroon system* had never existed before and emerged as a distinct countertradition to the systematic injustice of enslavement and denigration of all rights as human beings. In some sense, Maroons were rather *anti-colonial tribes* for that reason. This aspect of initial resistance makes contemporary legal pluralism in Jamaica quite distinct from West African examples.

In these (African) contexts, as for instance in the comparative case of Ghana, the early European traders and later colonialists encountered sovereign states with strong legitimate authorities, like among the Asante with their elaborate system of kingship. At the same time, (in the eighteenth and nineteenth century) when the transplanted Akan and other African nationals fought their successful independence war in Jamaica and struggled to maintain their territorial claims and political freedom on the strange Caribbean islands, their brothers and sisters in the motherland sought to defend their political sovereignty against the increasing pressure of the European powers. As late as 1874, the British desire for sovereign rule in West Africa materialized with a British Order of Council that decreed the colonial state Gold Coast (Ray 1998, 49).[8]

But, seen from today's perspective on the factual coexistence of parallel institutions of the post-colonial Ghanaian state as the heir to the colonial foundations and the so-called traditional authorities with much older pre-colonial bases of legitimacy and a claim to partial sovereignty, the colonial attempts to undisputed legal centralism and overall political control appear to have ultimately failed. For times they may have come quite close to dismantle the earlier sovereignty of kingdoms and their legitimate representatives. But the sheer weight of military oppression proved insufficient to eradicate the symbolic and communicative basis of authority; a sharp reminder of the theoretical distinction between power and authority at the heart of legitimacy:

> Authority is a government's legitimate use of power. Legitimacy
> means that those subject to a government's authority consent to
> it. Power is thus different from authority. When pro-democracy

demonstrations in China broke out and the government responded
by imprisonment and killing the demonstrators, it was an exercise
of power, but also an indication of the government's loss of
authority. (Giddens 1997, 339)

Western assumptions of the sovereign state, with legitimate authority exclusively
shared between state institutions, is no more than an ideal type of a specific conception
of sovereignty; a sovereignty conceived as a centralized system of legal and political
control (Ray 1998, 53). But it does not even take the controversial interests of a post-
colonial condition to reveal the idealist contention of sovereignty as an exclusive
prerogative of but one actor:

[T]he legal reality of the modern state is not at all that of the tidy,
consistent organized ideal so nicely captured in the common
identification of "law" and "legal system," but that legal reality
is rather an unsystematic collage of inconsistent and overlapping
parts, lending itself to no easy legal interpretation, morally and
aesthetically offensive to the eye of the liberal idealist, and almost
incomprehensible in its complexity to the would-be empirical
student. (Griffiths 1986, 4)

In the case of post-colonial states such as Ghana where pre-colonial institutions
survived (in certainly altered ways with new meanings and functions) into the colonial
era, these actors even gained momentum in the transition period from the colonial to
the post-colonial state. With the proclaimed (re-)Africanization of governance, the
traditional authorities or chiefs entered the arena of active politics within the state
context. As aspirants to political power based on the symbolic means of their claimed
pre-colonial base of legitimate authority, they were therefore immediately conceived
as contestants over sovereignty by early civil leaders such as Kwame Nkrumah in
Ghana. Ghana's national liberation hero and first president continued the colonial
policy of necessary state recognition in the process to determine the *legitimacy* of a
chief (Ray 1998: 59f.).

This attitude of centralist control did not work well to attain political stability
according to the ideal Western model of the unified sovereign state.[9] Rather, the
civil authorities of the First Republic of Ghana (which lasted from 1 July 1959
until 23 February 1966), with its one-party state (parliament), had to share aspects
of sovereignty and legitimacy in practice with the older actors of the chieftaincy
institution(s), although, in theory, they contained the idea of a *pure*, undisputed

political rule of the nation state over the territorial area *inherited* from the colonial predecessor:

> The colonial and post-colonial states share a common heritage of legislative and constitutional instruments. It is argued that by contrast, there was a fundamental break between the pre-colonial states and other entities and that of the colonial state in terms of legislative and constitutional instruments. The colonial state stripped many aspects of sovereignty from the pre-colonial states, turning them into chieftaincies. "Chiefs," however, retained certain aspects of sovereignty as well as their own source of legitimacy: thus sovereignty and legitimacy have been divided in the colonial and post-colonial states. (Ray 1998, 48ff.)

Thus, the colonial and post-colonial governments shared quite similar visions of undisputed state hegemony or supremacy of authority over the transformed institutions from pre-colonial times. Both historical actors conceptualized their overall authority somewhat counterfactually, not in coherence with the actual recognition of chiefs by large sectors of society which invested them with legitimacy independently of state acts of recognition. Seen from the perspective of (a praxeologically-oriented) legal anthropology on actual social practices, Ray's analysis of "divided sovereignty and legitimacy" in the Ghanaian case deserves consent.

In concurrence to the sketched division of sovereignty and legitimacy in the Ghanaian case, the Jamaican Maroons struggled (from an entirely different historical experience) to maintain the countertradition of sovereign rule over themselves laid down in the peace treaties of 1738/39. Without any doubt, the British wanted to gain hegemony over the successors of the very first freedom fighters who had awaited them on the side of the Spaniards and kept on fighting long after the Spaniards were defeated and driven to neighbouring Cuba. Against the backdrop of the myriad of written sources, legal statements, and speeches from the comfortable distance of the London parliamentary chambers, a praxeological structural history of the interactions between the colonialists and the Maroons after the treaties, clearly demonstrates the futility of all discursive means in attaining colonial hegemony over the forced, negotiated, and agreed self-determination and territorial independence of the Maroon communities. (Zips 1999b, 274–314, 549–98.)

All attempts to assert some sort of *indirect rule* failed on the practical insistence of succeeding Maroon generations to be governed by their own authorities (colonels, captains, and councils) as decreed by Art. 15 of the peace treaty.[10] Even more importantly, article three of the same treaty was read as an everlasting guarantee of territorial rights (now termed *sovereignty* by contemporary political representatives of the Maroons): "for the born and the unborn."[11]

Until the very present, Maroons argue that the *everlasting* validity of the treaty is founded on the exchange of blood between the British representatives of the Crown and the Maroon leaders. The connotation of the living, being controlled by the *dead* in their management of the resources left to them in order to enjoy future posterity,, are coherent with the Akan ethic of the bond between the dead, the living, and the unborn: "The *odekuro* and the lineage heads were thus *nhwesofo* or *caretakers* of the land for the ancestors and on behalf of the unborn" (Wilks 1975, 666). It might be inferred that the formulation "for themselves and posterity forever" in ART. 3 of the agreement had been fostered by the insistence of the Maroons to protect all future generations against a renewed colonial challenge to Maroon land rights. Its full text reads:

> ART. 3: That they shall enjoy and possess, for themselves and
> posterity for ever, all the lands situate and lying between Trelawney
> Town and the Cockpits, to the amount of fifteen hundred acres,
> bearing northwest from the said Trelawney Town.

The land to maintain the growing communities and to foster the economic autonomy was also the backbone for their political self-determination. What the former deputy colonel of Accompong, Melvin Currie, has to say on the historical division of territorial sovereignty, as at least implicitly laid down by ART. 3 of the treaty, applies not merely to the colonial times. It seeks to oblige the successor of the British colony in the very present, namely the Commonwealth member of the Jamaican national state which still has a *foreign* queen as its formal head:

> As Kojo said: we rule the mountains and they rule the plains.
> You have to respect another man's right to live; and if you are
> democratic then be democratic. There would be no strife between
> you and us, cause you have left us with our mountains and we
> have given you your plains which you have chosen. Now it is for
> us to live in peace and unity, cause you want the things from the
> mountains and we want the things from the plains; so let us trade
> as people. I protect my sections, you protect yours. (Melvin Currie,
> in an interview on 1.8.1990).

Part of the evolving countertradition of governance linked to African ideas of the rule of law and justice is the concept of jural corporateness (cf. Hagan 1980; McCaskie 1995). Until recently, Maroons practiced their procedures of dispute resolution linked historically to African ideas of reasoning, discursive conviction, and pacification. It is in this respect that the Maroon law ways contradict the arbitrary legal and judicial processes encountered by Black people in Jamaica during the colonial period. Legal pluralism in Jamaica reflected the divided sovereignty and legitimacy between the two ruling actors: the British on the plains and the Maroons in the mountains. Accordingly, it took the form of a radical pluralism where the colonial law system was viewed by the majority as an alien means of minority control. As a law conceived as contingent from the perspective of the ruled, it was in practice contrasted by Maroon law. Yet, the relative isolation of the Maroon communities from the majority of the Jamaican population offered only a vague idea of the existence of a neo-African law backed by traditional authorities for most outsiders.

Of course, these aspects of actual *sovereignty* or *statehood* (in much later developed terminology) were part of the living experience for those living in the Maroon communities. The First-Time freedom song "Law hold ohh, law hold already ohh," still known and sung by even the youngest members of society today, reveals and commemorates the *rule of law*, indigenous law that is, in the mountain enclaves of the Jamaican interior. It is indissolubly linked to the corporate existence of a group of people who endured the whole period of slavery and colonialism and see little reason to bring their history of self-determination to an end, just because other people of (mostly) African descent (their *fellow Jamaicans*) accepted a constitution formed by the British House of Commons in London (in 1962). Seen in more theoretical terms, the ideological structuring of their community (*jural corporateness*) can be interpreted as an accumulated history – a living past which remained in the ear (characterized with the Twi saying *tete ka asum*) – renewed, reproduced, and transformed by the work of following generations (Zips 1999b, 315–509; 639–58).

Kromanti, as a notion for the core aspects of Maroon culture in the African diaspora, is still alive today among a people whose independence dates back into a period predating the independence war of the Asante against the Denkyira, around 1700, in the African motherland. The *legitimacy* of Kromanti – understood as a corporate identity or rather *jural corporateness* protected by *traditional* authorities – became definite by a so-called *blood treaty* in 1738/39. Jamaica's conception of a unified *centralized nation state* conflicts with the pluralist historical experiences of the Maroon freedom struggle which led to a divided sovereignty in actual practice. State strategies to overcome these divisions are quite reasonable even for most Maroons who vote not only in elections of their own authorities, but as *Jamaican Maroons* also in the state general elections. However, the forceful dismantling of the Maroon jural coporateness seems to lead to more tensions and therefore divisions, judging from my empirical research in Accompong. I will therefore ask in the next section, if a transition from a factual, yet constitutionally denied *divided sovereignty* to a legally recognized complementary form of sovereignty does not hold the *better* options for both actors, the national state and the Maroon (quasi-)states.

FROM DIVIDED SOVEREIGNTY TO COMPLEMENTARY SOVEREIGNTY?

After the independence declaration of 1962, the pressure on the Maroon authorities to integrate into the national state within the post-colonial framework of nationbuilding continued and even increased. This reflects a common post-independence tendency in many African situations where an *integral state* sought to achieve a perfected hegemony with unrestricted domination over civil society. Referring to the so-called "Jamaica Independence Bill," decided on 31 May 1962 by the House of Commons in London, Young's (1994, 283–85) generalizing observations on the *integral state* in a considerable number of post-colonial conditions in Africa appear also quite applicable in relation to the *Jamaican* Constitution of 1962:

> A genetic code for the new states of Africa was already imprinted on its embryo within the womb of the African colonial state.... The metaphor of the embryo did not suggest itself at the moment of independence. Rather, the common imagery perceived a triumphant nationalism storming the citadels of colonialism, erecting from its rubble an entirely new political order.... The African constitutions imported from London, Paris, or Washington became inverted versions of those after which they were modelled.

Certainly, the British colonialists in Jamaica never stopped to undo the disgrace experienced by the need to treat with the *Black rebels* of the seventeenth and eighteenth century. They promulgated laws to make it appear as if the recognized sovereignty of the Maroons could be unilaterally removed. But they never ventured to inform the Maroon officials in proper cause about such acts. Furthermore, they followed a policy of deceitful and unlawful sale of Maroon lands and tried everything to shift the border lines to the disadvantage of the autonomous Black communities. Still, the Maroon threat with an outbreak of violence and occasional demonstrations of their readiness for physical resistance sufficed to convince the colonial land departments to keep their "creeping in on Maroon lands" – as it is called by Maroons today – to a very limited extent. *Cum grano salis,* the colonial offices followed a course of disturbance but stopped short to enforce their claim to undivided sovereignty in practice. That cannot be said equally of the post-colonial state which attitudes parallel African developments of the *integral state* model at the same time:

> Soon after independence, reaching its zenith in the 1970s, a new vision of state began to emerge, what we might term, borrowing from Coulon and Copans, the "integral state." The state, with enlarged ambitions of transforming society according to its blueprint, sought an enhanced hegemony, to render it more capable of acting directly on civil society. (Young 1994, 287)

There can be little doubt that the Jamaican state suffered a deep crisis with political violence and loss of control over many sectors of society by attempting to use the institutions inherited of the colonial state to enforce the proclaimed idea(l)s of nationalism. One might draw another parallel to the state of crisis in many African states during the period of the 1980s. With the possible distinction that in parts of Africa (e.g., in Ghana) there is more than just a ray of hope on the horizon for new attempts of a more democratic renaissance, a process that seeks to draw on pre-colonial structures of discourse or consensual democracy including, in varying degrees, all sectors of civil society:

> Stripped to its essentials, the heart of the African state crisis of the 1980s lies in the lethal combination of the colonial state heritage, the failed vision of the integral state, and the prebendal realities of political management. The remarkable surge of self-assertion by civil society up and down the continent in the swelling demand for democratization in the early 1990s, can be best understood not as a mimetic response to global trends or melodramatic developments in Eastern Europe – although these had their impact – but rather as a cathartic reaction to an alienating state. (Young 1994, 292)

Jamaica had similar experiences with large sectors of civil society that resisted state institutions in myriad ways of daily practices and countertraditions to dominant (post-colonial) culture. The latter is no more identical with the former colonial dominant culture; in fact it developed against its grain. Nevertheless, its defining structures of irrational party alliances, nepotism and favourism – what the great

Jamaican sociologist Carl Stone (1994, 136) had adequately termed "garrison politics" – owed most of its features to the ideal of multi-party factions prescribed by the former colonial ruler. Its authoritarian prescription depended on a Eurocentric notion of democracy, which generally defines its core meaning in dualistic terms as governance of a ruling party (or coalition of parties) checked by an opposition (party or parties). Other (indigenous) forms of checks and balances were often overlooked, misrepresented or ignored. Against such biased conceptions of African traditions of governance, the hidden discursive institutionalized procedures inscribed in the traditional political system should be argued by African historical studies and political anthropology. Institutions such as the Asafo in Akan and in other societies of this West African region, or in particular the Nkwankwaa of the Asante reveal that criticism and opposition were well developed features of the original African political process. These aspects can therefore be ascribed to the traditional system of government where they have been omitted by European observers:

> A good example of this jaundiced perception of aspects of our culture on which modern authoritarianism feeds is the claim that there is not a word in any African or Ghanaian language for the English word "opposition." ... There was in the Akan political system an institution which was very similar to an "opposition" in a modern-liberal-democratic political systen. This was the institution of Nkwankwaa among the Asante.... Essentially the Nkwankwaa comprised the free citizens who were neither members of the chief's council nor "elders." ... In essence, the position of the Nkwankwaa was that of the opposition in a modern liberal-democratic system. It stood outside the chief's government and had the right to criticize it. Indeed it is significant that whereas an elder ran the danger of being suspected of disloyalty or even treason if he criticized the chief, the Nkwankwaahene (i.e., the Nkwankwaa chief) faced no such danger for discharging this function.... The political parties thus face no cultural barrier in developing the habits of responsible opposition and of acceptance of criticism. (Folson 1993, 18ff.)

On the contrary, one might argue that political parties in post-colonial states could have recourse to habitualized forms of traditional rational discourse over the validity of particular political programs and changes. Such discursive resources of democratic governance are suspected to have suffered a certain curtailment with petrified partisan partialism in many European systems and its exports into the former colonies. It is not easy to detect (communicative) reason in the historical exchange of the two leading parties (JLP and PNP) in Jamaica. A decade after independence, the oppositional structure developed from constant political strife and occasional outburst into something close to civil war. In this regard the question asked by Young (1994, 292) in the final summary and outlook on the "afterlife of the African colonial state" might as well be asked in connection to the afterlife of the African diaspora colonial state Jamaica:

> Can a new state be invented that sheds the debilitating traditions of the past? ... History tells us that the patterns of the past remain embedded in the present. Can they be rewoven to permit the emergence of a new kind of polity, one that employs the discourse of democracy but connects itself to the deeper African heritage?

Since the early 1990s there is a growing concern for decolonization or, in more positive terms, for a *Jamaicanization* of the British Constitution for Jamaica (and consequently the whole state). Led by the intellectuals of the University of the West Indies, and fuelled by the constant critique of pro-African agents, such as the symbolically strong Rastafari movement with the powerful medium of reggae music, politicians seem to follow the cry for a Jamaicanization; meaning in true fact an *Africanization*. Therefore, the answer given by Young (1994) to his own (above quoted) question on a necessary recourse to African heritage would be indeed used by a great number of Jamaicans too:

> In the longer run an affirmative response to this momentous question is indispensable to designing, to claiming, to seizing a future beyond crisis and decline. (292)

Ghana with its at least partial reconciliation of the state with traditional authorities (see, e.g., Ray 1996; van Rouveroy van Nieuwaal and van Dijk 1999), provides an example for attempts to Jamaicanize the constitution. Over the past years, contacts at the highest political level as well as in the field of cultural exchange have increased tremendously.[12] It remains to be seen if the Ghanaian experience to accept the complementarity of state and traditional authorities – as it is expressed by the presidential staffer for Chieftaincy Affairs, Nana Akuoko Sarpong (in an interview on 29 January 1998 in Accra) – will appear as a feasible option to the Jamaican state which indeed lacks legitimacy since its constitutional creation by the former colonial power:

> You see the mistake that people make is that democracy can only come from the ballot polls. But democracy has different shades of

colour. The important thing is the participation of the people in the political process. That is what democracy is all about. It does not have to take the form of election, because you get a dictatorship of the majority. But in the African concept of democracy it is all inclusive. It has internal arrangements. The people meet at the palace to decide on matters affecting their welfare. When you come to the palace it is the linguist who speaks. But when the linguist has spoken and the majority of the elders has spoken, they throw the matter open to the public and each can make a contribution and we agree on matters to be done on a consensual basis. If democracy should have any meaning, consensual democracy is the best form of democracy. Because when it becomes too competitive, people are pulling into different directions.

Until the time of writing, the proposed constitutional reforms started in the early 1990s by the introduction of various constitutional committees have not gone through because of the persistence of the *garrison politics mentality*. In Jamaica, the first Black freedom fighters are the only groups to claim historical legal and political independence backed by procedures of African origins reformulated in the new environment. A possible *Jamaicanization* of the constitution would allow considering the option of *complementary sovereignty* with a highly symbolic recognition to the African history on the Caribbean island.

JAMAICANIZING THE CONSTITUTION: A CONCLUSION

After a thorough and lengthy examination (dating back to 1991) by high profile committees nominated by Parliament, alongside numerous public discussions and media analyses of the possibilities and advantages of the proposed decolonization process, a final report summarized the findings as a necessary development to Jamaicanization (Joint Select Committee of the Houses of Parliament on Constitutional and Electoral Reform, Sec. F; 1995, 13):

> 52. The Constitutional Commission reported a strong feeling that the Jamaican Constitution should be "Jamaicanized."

In this regard, the Commission felt that it was inappropriate that a new Jamaican Constitution should remain a schedule to a United Kingdom Order in Council under a United Kingdom Act of Parliament.

53. The Joint Select Committee agreed with the Commission that the Jamaica (Constitution) Order in Council, 1962, should be revoked to:

- show that our new constitution is the product of the Jamaican people, and

- rid our basic law of its present colonial form.

The programmatic statement makes the search for an increase to state legitimacy easily detectable. Yet the final report, in its further proposals, also reveals a pending insecurity as to whereabouts other than colonial forms of law might be traced. At various occasions the report suggests "more democracy" in the form of a greater means for civil society to participate. It almost conjures a system of checks and balances (cf. Zips 1999b, 660–67) totally absent from the foundations of plantation society. But only in the more symbolic chapters of a proposed preamble for the true Jamaican Constitution, is the African ancestors' heritage explicitly mentioned, although without reference to the Maroons: "the recognition that for three centuries it was their black ancestors and not the European rulers, who preserved the passion for freedom and justice" (Sherlock in final report 1995, 46).[13]

Sir Philip Sherlock, O.J., highlighted in his blueprint of the preamble (1995, 46) the African heritage denied, veiled, and belittled by the valid constitutional set up of the Jamaican state:

Whereas Jamaica is the second black country in the hemisphere to achieve independence, and by reason of its history is closely and indissolubly linked with the West African people, and with the Afro-American people whose origins lie in the African diaspora, and ... whereas European domination was rooted in the doctrine of African inferiority, the denigration of Africa and the inculcation of self-contempt in people of African origin, it therefore becomes necessary to set forth certain principles enshrined therein, these being:

1. the affirmation that Jamaica is predominantly a black nation, that the great majority of its people are of African origin,

and that their history dictates that national consciousness also means racial consciousness;

2. the claiming likewise of a European heritage.

Public statements in relation to the future project of state reform circumscribed programmatically as the "Jamaicanization of the constitution" use very similar phrases of democratization in their overtones. In Jamaica, that means to promote participation and respect for the masses of Black people of African descent. Their perplexity to put such ideas into practice derives, in my view, on the one hand: from an inherited disrespect for the achievements of the only free Black communities before the abolition of slavery (in 1838), namely the Maroons, who look back exclusively on a history of self-governance backed by their experiences of West African structures; on the other hand: from the lacking ideas to reconcile the African and the European heritage of democracy. I will therefore conclude my consideration of the complementary option in a realization of a pluralist basis of sovereignty with a quote from the Ghanaian (Asante) paramount chief in the rank equivalent of a state senior minister, Nana Akuoko Sarpong (in an interview on 29 January 1998 in Accra). It links this successful West African experience of a reformed democratic process with the idea of complementarity, including the communicative tradition of reasonable discussion in the context of chieftaincy:

The mistake people make, is to assume that democracy can only come from the ballot polls. Democracy has different shades of colours. The important thing is the participation of the people in the political process. That is what democracy is all about. It does not have to take the form of election because you can get a dictatorship of the majority. So both of us (state and traditional authorities) have our status from the people and if you see the way the paramount chief and the traditional councils are structured, the paramount chief can not take a decision alone without reference to the representatives of the various lineages at the traditional council. So that is also democratic in content and in nature.

REFERENCES

Bastide, Roger. 1979. The Other Quilombos. In Richard Price, ed., *Maroon Societies: Rebel Slave Communities in the Americas*. Baltimore, Md., and London: Johns Hopkins University Press, 191–201.

Dantzig, Albert van. 1980. *Forts and Castles of Ghana*. Accra: Sedco.

Folson, Kweku G. 1993. Political Parties and the Machinery of Democratic Government. In Kwame A. Ninsin and F. K. Drah, eds. *Political Parties and Democracy in Ghana's Fourth Republic*. Proceedings of a Seminar Organized by the Department of Political Science, University of Ghana, Legon on 2nd and 3rd July, 1992. Accra: Woeli Publishing Services.

Giddens, Anthony. 1997. *Sociology*. Cambridge: Polity Press.

Griffiths, John. 1986. What is Legal Pluralism? *Journal of Legal Pluralism and Unofficial Law* 24: 1–56.

Hagan, George P. 1980. The Rule of Law in Asante, A Traditional Akan State. In *Presence Africaine* (University of Ghana), No. 113: 194–208.

Kopytoff, Barbara. 1973. *The Maroons of Jamaica: An Ethnohistorical Study of Incomplete Polities, 1655–1905*. PhD dissertation, Univ. of Pennsylvania.

McCaskie, Tom C. 1995. *State and Society in Pre-colonial Asante*. New York: Cambridge University Press.

Patterson, Orlando. 1973. *The Sociology of Slavery. An Analysis of the Origins, Development and Structure of Negro Slave Society in Jamaica*. Kingston, Jamaica: Sangster's Book Stores [1st ed. 1967].

Price, Richard. 1992. Maroons: Rebel Slaves in the Americas. In Smithsonian Institution, ed., *Festival of American Folklife*. Washington D.C.: Smithsonian Institution: 62–64.

Ray, Donald I. 1996. Divided Sovereignty: Traditional Authority and the State in Ghana, *Journal of Legal Pluralism and Unofficial Law* 37/38: 181–202.

———. 1998. Chief-State Relations in Ghana – Divided Sovereignty and Legitimacy. In E. Adriaan B. van Rouveroy van Nieuwaal and Werner Zips, eds. *Sovereignty, Legitimacy, and Power in West African Societies. Perspectives from Legal Anthropology*. Hamburg: LIT: 48–69.

Rouveroy van Nieuwaal van, E. Adriaan B., and Rijk van Dijk, eds. 1999. *African Chieftaincy in a New Socio-Political Landscape*. Hamburg: LIT.

Sherlock, Philip, O.J. 1995. Preamble Submitted by Philip Sherlock. In *Final Report of the Joint Select Committee of the Houses of Parliament on Constitutional and Electoral Reform* 45–46 (Appendix 1) Kingston, Jamaica.

Stone, Carl. 1994. The Jamaican Party System and Political Culture. In the Planning Institute of Jamaica, ed., *Preparing for the Twenty-first Century*. Kingston, Jamaica: Ian Randle: 132–47.

Wilks, Ivor. 1975. *Asante in the Nineteenth Century. The Structure and Evolution of a Political Order*. London: Cambridge University Press.

Young, Crawford. 1994. *The African Colonial State in Comparative Perspective*. New Haven and London: Yale University Press.

Zips, Werner. 1998. We are Landowners. Territorial autonomy and land tenure in the Jamaican Maroon community of Accompong, *Journal of Legal Pluralism and Unofficial Law* 40: 89–121.

———. 1999a. *Black Rebels. African Caribbean Freedom Fighters in Jamaica*. Princeton: Markus Wiener; and Kingston, Jamaica: Ian Randle.

———. 1999b. Gleiche Rechte und Gerechtigkeit. Eine ethnohistorische und rechtsanthropologische Rekonstruktion des Maroon-Rechtes in Jamaica im Kontext der afrikanischen Diaspora unter besonderer Berücksichtigung politischer Strukturen in Akan-Gesellschaften Ghanas. (Unpubl. Habilitationsschrift an der Grund- und Integrativwiss. Fakultät der Univ. Wien).

———. 1999c. One Route to the Roots. Das Panafest in Ghana als Wegbereiter der afrikanischen Wiedervereinigung – Ein Essay. In Karl R. Wernhart, ed., *Afrika und seine Diaspora*. Hamburg: LIT.

———. 1999d. Africa is Beautiful. Ghana als Fokus der transatlantischen Repatriierung. *Mitteilungen der Anthropologischen Gesellschaft in Wien* (*MAGW*) 129: 215–26.

CITED INTERVIEWS

Currie, Melvin. Morning of 1.8.1990 in Accompong Sarpong, Nana Akuoko (Presidential Staffer for Chieftaincy Affairs und Omanhene von Agogo, Asante) am 29.1.1998 in Accra, Ghana.

CITED FILMS

Puskas, Barbara, and Werner Zips. 1998. "Panafrican Festival. Ghana: Land der Hoffnung" (20 min.). Vienna: Lotus Film (Treffpunkt Kultur, ORF 2, 9.3.1998).
———. 1999. "Die Macht ist wie ein Ei. Ghana – Land der Könige" (50 min.). Vienna: Lotus Film.

REPORTS

Final Report of the Joint Select Committee of the Houses of Parliament on Constitutional and Electoral Reform," 31 May 1995, Kingston, Jamaica [Copy in private archive of the author].

NOTES

1. The notion *Maroon* is derived from the Spanish word *cimarrón*, which was first applied to runaway animals. Its meaning is wild, untamed, free (cf. Zips 1999a, 3).

2. Compare, e.g., Bastide (1979, 195) who treats such Brazilian Quilombos like Palmares as "tribal regressions" – "… a kind of return to Africa."

3. Interestingly enough, the notion *Coromantees* survived the early loss of Fort Kromantse to the Netherlands in 1655, who renamed it Fort Amsterdam. In the context of world history the gain of Fort Amsterdam might be seen as revenge for the later loss of New Amsterdam on the Hudson River to the British. At the time, the two locations might have appeared quite equivalent to the European contestors: a clear strategic miscalculation on the side of the Netherlands, if one compares the ruins of the recently half-renovated Fort Amsterdam in the vicinity of Cape Coast to the later history of New Amsterdam which became the very centre of the Western world: New York (van Dantzig 1980, 3–22; Zips 1999b, 4ff.).

4. This feast said to commemorate the signing of the peace treaty, and at the same time to celebrate Kojo's birthday, allows for comparisons with the Odwira and other Akan yam festivals, such as the Fante Fetu Afahye, in the theoretical framework of a (praxeological) structural history (see Zips 1999b, 200–19).

5. See in more detail Zips (1999a, 55ff.).

6. See also my extensive discussion (based on empirical research in Jamaica between 1984 and 1998) on the formation of the *Maroon states*, their defence against all endeavours to destroy or, at least, belittle their independence granted by the peace treaty of 1738/39, and their internal political organization and legal system in historical perspective (Zips 1999b, 273–584).

7. It remained disputed in times of peace against the negotiated agreements by the unilateral acts of the colonialists.

8. Only in 1901 did Asante lose its sovereignty *legally* and become unwillingly included in the Gold Coast Colony.

9. In more general terms, Griffiths (1986, 6) observed categorically: "Legal pluralism in this sense has been a fixture of the colonial experience. Furthermore, it has generally persisted beyond the moment of formal 'independence,' proving one of the most enduring legacies of European expansion and characterizing at the present day the larger part of all of the world's national legal systems."

10. The full article reads: "That captain Cudjoe shall, during his life, be chief commander in Trelawney Town, after his decease, the command to devolve on his brother Accompong, and, in case of his decease, on his next brother captain Johnny; and, failing him, captain Cuffee shall succeed; who is to be succeeded by captain Quaco; and, after all their demises, the governor, or commander in chief for the time being, shall appoint, from time to time, whom he thinks fit for the command." It is important to note that the last mentioned provision of a presumably British right to recognition, was continually interpreted by the Maroons as referring to their own commander in chief. However, the British never succeeded in gaining the hegemonic control of recognition of the Maroon authorities (Kopytoff 1973, 112, 338; Zips 1999b, 460).

11. The essential implications of this very phrase attributed to the cultural hero of independence, Captain (or *Generalissimo*) Kojo, are analyzed elsewhere (cf. Zips 1998).

12. The large and prominent delegation of Jamaicans to the Panafest 1997 in Cape Coast is but one sign in this direction (cf. Zips 1999c,d; see also the films, "Panafrican Festival" and "Power is Like an Egg": Puskas and Zips 1998, 1999).

13. Five proposals for a preamble were drafted by highly recognized members of society and can be found in Appendix 1 of the "Final Report" (1995, 41–46).

TRADITIONAL LEADERSHIP AND RURAL LOCAL GOVERNMENT IN BOTSWANA

CHAPTER 9

KESHAV C. SHARMA

KESHAV SHARMA, MA (Raj), MPA (The Hague), PhD (Amsterdam) is a professor in the Department of Political and Administrative Studies at the University of Botswana. He has lectured at several universities in Africa, Europe, and Asia, has published extensively, and has undertaken consultancies for international organizations. He is Vice-chairman of the Research Committee of International Political Science Association of Bureaucracies in Developing Societies. He is leader of the Botswana team engaged in the IDRC-funded research project on Traditional Leadership in Africa.

Cattle kraal behind the *kgotla*. This cattle kraal was used by chiefs to impound stray cattle. Chiefs would be buried below this ground. In this unusual case, a number of above ground grave markers can be seen in the kraal. The *kgotla* is the gathering place for all the adult citizens of the chieftaincy. It is a direct democracy local government structure (2002, photo by D. Ray).

TRADITIONAL LEADERSHIP AND INSTITUTION OF CHIEFTAINSHIP DURING PRE-COLONIAL AND COLONIAL PERIODS

Chieftainship is one of the oldest institutions of traditional leadership in Africa. It has enjoyed the glory, powers, and prestige of pre-colonial times, has survived through the vicissitudes of colonial times, and has reconciled to the new political system of the post-independence period in which the status, powers, and functions of traditional leaders have been gradually reduced. The traditional leaders (chiefs) during the pre-colonial period enjoyed unlimited and undefined powers over their tribe. Each tribe owned a given piece of land which was controlled by its chief. The chief was the custodian of tribal land and allocated it to tribesmen for ploughing or residential purposes. The villages were divided into several wards, each headed by a headman. The chief settled disputes, pronounced on tribal customs and traditions, and ruled on matters concerning the tribe in consultation with its members.

During the early period of colonial rule, the colonial government exercised minimal control over local administration at tribal level. The chiefs were allowed maximum independence in their tribal rule and in maintaining law and order. The Order-in-Council of 1891 authorized the British High Commissioner (stationed in Cape Town at that time) to appoint administrative and judicial staff in the Bechuanaland protectorate. A proclamation was issued during that year providing for appointment of a Resident Commissioner and Assistant Commissioners in districts. These were given jurisdiction as Resident Magistrates but the jurisdiction of their courts was limited to exclude all cases in which Africans were concerned, unless such cases were in the interest of good order or the prevention of violence.

In 1899, when the Hut Tax was introduced, the chiefs were appointed as local tax collecting officers and they received up to 10 per cent of the proceeds. In 1920, the Native Council (renamed the African Advisory Council in 1940) was constituted by an administrative order to serve as an advisory body on African interests to the Resident Commissioner. The Native Fund (abolished and replaced by Tribal Treasuries in 1938) was officially constituted by a proclamation in 1919. An annual levy of three shillings (after 1925, five shillings) per tax payer was paid into this fund which was to be used for development of African education, medical care, eradication of cattle diseases, the fencing of tribal areas, etc. In 1934, the Native Administration Proclamation was issued which formally recognized the tribal chiefs and their authority. The proclamation did not materially alter the traditional institution but simply formalized it. The chiefs opposed it, as an attempt to codify their authority was perceived by them as a limitation of their erstwhile sovereignty and unlimited authority. The Native Tribunal Proclamation of 1934 regulated the judicial powers of chiefs and subordinate headmen and formalized the tribal court system and jurisdiction. This was also met with opposition from the chiefs. In 1938, the Treasury Proclamation established the tribal treasuries into which local taxes and levies were to be paid. The chiefs were now to be paid a fixed stipend, and a percentage of tax collected was to be paid into the treasuries. These tribal treasuries were to be administered by the chiefs in consultation with their tribal councils and were to provide for the financing of education and agricultural activities in tribal areas. Two new proclamations were issued in 1943, which replaced the above mentioned proclamations of 1934. The *kgotla* (village assembly) was acknowledged as the advisory council of the chief without the formal composition by the Native Administration Proclamation of 1943. This proclamation broadened the local government functions of native authorities by granting them powers to make rules on matters relating to preservation of law and order and provision of local services, as well as the levying of fees for such services. The Native Courts Proclamation of 1943 restructured the tribal courts system in accordance with tribal law and custom.

In 1956, the Tribal Councils and District Councils were introduced. The chiefs headed these councils and the membership consisted of some members nominated by the chairmen and some elected by *kgotla*. These councils undertook limited local government functions during that period (1956–66). As pointed out by Vosloo et al., local government in the rural (tribal) areas of the then Bechuanaland Protectorate under British rule can be divided into three phases. The first phase could be termed parallel rule. It showed the maximum regard for the customary authority of the chiefs, and it restricted intervention to such measures as were necessary to satisfy the more simple requirements of local rule such as the collection of tax or the preservation of order. The second phase (i.e., between 1934 and 1957) could be called indirect rule as chiefs retained a powerful position as sole native authorities of their respective tribal areas. The implementation of the system of local councils from 1957 represents the third phase. This phase, which lasted until 1966, was a continuation of the indirect rule system of rural local government, but displayed some elements of democratization as the rule was of the chief-in-council. During all these phases, the traditional tribal authorities were utilized as rural local government. After independence in 1966 a new system of representative local government was introduced.

TRADITIONAL INSTITUTION OF CHIEFTAINSHIP IN POST-INDEPENDENCE PUBLIC ADMINISTRATION

The chieftainship was retained in Botswana after independence, and the chieftainship law provided the legal cornerstone for the recognition and functioning of the office of chieftainship at different levels of tribal rule. The President of the Republic was given the authority for the recognition, appointment, deposition, and suspension of chiefs (the authority was later vested in the minister). A chief exercises traditional authority, after consultation with the tribe, to determine the question of tribal membership. Identification of membership was significant when one had to get some rights or privileges belonging to the tribe, such as allocation of land. The chief arranges tribal ceremonies, assists in checking crime, promotes the welfare of his tribe, convenes and presides over *kgotla* meetings. It is significant to note that in Botswana the law requires every chief to carry out instructions given to him by the minister. Any chief who fails to comply with any direction given to him by the minister is liable to be suspended or deposed. The chiefs are paid salaries as fixed by the minister by order published in the Gazette. Different rates may be fixed in respect of different chiefs. The minister is also authorized to make regulations for the better carrying out of the provisions of the Chieftainship Act, including general conditions of service and the procedure for taking disciplinary action. Provisions of the Chieftainship Act, which give enormous authority to the minister, establish complete supremacy of the central government over these traditional leaders in Botswana. As compared to the colonial period, their subordination to the central government clearly increased after independence and their status was considerably humbled further when the Chieftainship Act Amendment of 1987 authorized the minister of Local Government instead of the president to deal with matters related to the chiefs.

The relationship between the traditional leaders and the central government has been a mixture of cordiality and conflict in Botswana. On the one hand Botswana's ruling party, the Botswana Democratic Party of Sir Seretse Khama has relied on the support of traditional leaders during the colonial and post-independence period. (Seretse Khama was himself a chief of one of the biggest tribes who relinquished his chieftainship and became a leader of the independence movement). On the other hand, due to the gradual reduction of their authority, the dissatisfaction of some chiefs has manifested itself in conflicts of different kinds with the ruling party and the central government. One of the prominent chiefs, Gaseitsiwe of the Bangwaketse tribe resigned his chieftainship after independence, joined an opposition party (Botswana

National Front) got elected to the Parliament on the ticket of that opposition party, and became a significant political leader of opposition in his own right. In order to ensure that they are not driven into the opposition, the ruling party in the government has apparently handled the traditional institution of chieftainship in such a way that the chiefs are formally retained, but do not possess significant powers. The central government has by and large been able to pursue this policy successfully over a period of time. In some cases, however, conflicts have erupted, particularly when the egos of a chief and the minister responsible have clashed. Conflicts have also arisen when a chief has not been co-operative, or the minister responsible has not been able to handle his relationship with a chief with due respect and consideration for the tribal custom. The case of suspension of a chief (Seepapitso of the Bangwaketse) in 1994 by the former minister of Local Government, Lands and Housing illustrates the type of conflict that has soured the relationship between the traditional and modern political leadership. The minister suspended the chief on grounds of lack of co-operation, deriving his authority from the act. The chief and his tribe complained, however, on the grounds that the minister's action was not in keeping with the traditions and there was no consultation with the tribe before the minister took the action for suspension of the chief. The chief challenged the minister's decision in the High Court for suspending him and appointing his son as acting paramount chief. The High Court upheld the minister's decision for suspension of the chief, but held that the appointment of his son (Leema Gaseitsiwe) as the acting paramount chief of Bangwaketse was unlawful since the statute did not authorize it. (Justice Julian Nganunu held that the appointment of a person to the position of acting paramount chief could not be made before the prior designation of the tribe.)

Although the government in Botswana retained the institution of chieftainship after independence, it was transformed considerably. There was a steep decline in the authority of the traditional leaders after independence when the new institutions like District Councils and Land Boards were given many of the powers and functions earlier exercised by the chiefs. The exclusive and prestigious authority for allocation of tribal land was given to the newly constituted Land Boards. Chiefs enjoyed a central position in the councils of the pre-independence period, but after independence the District Councils were to be controlled by councillors elected every five years on the principle of universal adult franchise. The District Councils were given the authority to handle *matimela* (stray cattle), which was earlier the responsibility of Tribal Administration. The District Commissioner's office assumed a dominant position after independence with regard to the operation of tribal administration, in so far as he was made responsible for reviewing the cases tried in the customary courts. The dependence of chiefs on the District Administration increased further as the tribal administration's financial administration was handled by the District Commissioner's office. Not only did the tribal administration not have a vote; the District Administration was made responsible for controlling transport and even stationary needs by tribal administration.

Taking note of these developments in this institution of chieftainship should not mean that the government of Botswana has been against this institution. On the positive side, one should take note of a number of positive steps taken by the government for strengthening this institution. For instance, the government has, in principle, accepted to review the conditions of service of Tribal Administration; the cadre is going to be integrated in to the Local Government Service Management; the number of customary courts has increased over a period of time; and the ministry has undertaken a needs assessment of Tribal Administration staff. The creation of a House of Chiefs by the constitution was a significant recognition and mark of respect for chieftainship, although the house does not have any significant powers. The chiefs have felt that the government does not take this house seriously, as follow-up action on its resolutions remains outstanding. While the members of the House of Chiefs might be correct to a certain extent, they also need to have a clearer understanding of the constitutional position, purpose, powers, and functions of this house. The chiefs have to understand that this house is different from a second house of parliament, like the House of Lords in Great Britain or the Senate in the United States. The House of Chiefs was established primarily for giving the chiefs a forum where they could articulate their views relating to this traditional institution's operation. A minister could consult the house for its opinion. The house is also entitled to discuss any matter it considers to be in interest of the tribe and tribal organizations. It needs to be noted that the National Assembly is not obliged to accept the recommendations or opinion of the House of Chiefs. The National Assembly might like to take note of the views of this house if it considers it is politically expedient to do so, or if it considers these to be in keeping with the national interest.

Botswana countryside: gamepark protected area outside Garbarone (photo by D. Ray).

TRADITIONAL LEADERSHIP AND RURAL LOCAL GOVERNMENT

The institution of chieftainship manned by traditional leaders is one of the four main organizations considered to be pillars of public administration machinery at local (district) level in Botswana. All the four organizations: District Administration, District Council, Land Board, and Tribal Administration have their significance, roles, jurisdiction, authority, responsibilities, and limitations. Rural local government in Botswana operates with close co-operation, communication, and coordination among these organizations.

TRADITIONAL LEADERS AND POPULARLY ELECTED RURAL LOCAL GOVERNMENT

Representative local government in African countries such as Botswana, as we understand it today, comprising of democratically elected councillors on the principle of universal adult franchise, was introduced only after independence. Local government here has evolved out of tribal administration, which performed limited local government functions before independence. The local government in Botswana grew under tribal administration during the colonial period with the introduction, in 1956, of tribal councils under the chairmanship of the chiefs of major tribes. These Tribal Councils included members nominated by the chiefs, members elected by *kgotla* (Village Assembly), and the chairmen and other nominated members of the lower level district councils within the tribal area. The District Councils within the tribal area constituted the second and lower tier of local government and were subordinate to Tribal Councils. These District Councils were composed of subordinate tribal authorities as chairmen; some nominated members, and some elected at the *kgotla*. This pattern of local government continued up to the time of independence, when the government decided to introduce the present pattern of District and Town Councils controlled by elected representatives of the people with a view to strengthen democracy.

District Councils have been given responsibilities mainly for administration of primary education, primary health services, construction and maintenance of rural roads, water supply, community development, and social welfare. Although the administrative capacities of councils for the performance of these functions have improved gradually, these remain considerably limited. Besides other measures for developing administrative capacities, the local authorities need to develop harmonious and co-operative relationships with other district and local level institutions, including the traditional institution of chieftainship. As the traditional leaders lost so much of their authority to these modern institutions of local government, their resentment during the first few years of independence was understandable. The present relationship between the traditional leaders and the District Councils does not display serious conflicts but it has to be based on a positive, forward looking, and co-operative team spirit for rural development administration in the future.

TRADITIONAL LEADERS AND LAND BOARDS

Land Boards, which were established as statutory bodies in Botswana in 1970 through the Tribal Land Act, took away the exclusive authority of chiefs for allocation of tribal land. These newly created bodies in Botswana, once created, held the tribal land in trust and started allocating it for residential, commercial, agricultural, industrial, or general development purposes. In the initial period of their establishment, these Land Boards included the chiefs as members along with some members elected by *kgotla*, some nominated by the minister of Local Government Lands and Housing, and some ex officio members of government ministries. During this period, the chiefs had to share their traditional authority of land allocation with the other Land Board members. After some years of their operation, the chiefs were removed from the membership of Land Boards.

Land is an important resource in rural development administration hence its allocation assumes significance. Land Boards have a significant role to play in the process of land allocation and district level development planning. As land becomes scarce in the future, Land Boards will assume greater importance for handling the exercise with foresight, rationality, and integrity. Co-operation of traditional leaders who have undertaken this task in the past could facilitate the smooth functioning of Land Boards. The Land Boards in the initial years of their creation were faced with the problem of lack of co-operation of traditional leaders as many of these were frustrated at the loss of their authority. Chiefs in some cases continued to allocate land without reference to Land Boards. Due to the absence of written records, the newly created Land Boards had to rely on the information only the traditional leaders possessed. They were handicapped when that information was not readily made available. The newly created Land Boards had limited staff and facilities. Defiance of Land Board decisions, unauthorized allocation, or extension was not uncommon. During the last few years the situation in these respects has improved considerably. The Land Boards now have better facilities, and the public is better informed about their authority and new procedures for land allocation. The Land Boards are still faced with some problems like lack of authority for enforcing their decisions, control and supervision of subordinate Land Boards, and harmonious relations with various government organizations. Relationship of Land Boards with the traditional leaders does not display serious conflicts now, although in some cases the relationship has not been very cordial. The traditional leaders have by and large reconciled to the changed situation. The Land Boards will, however, continue to need the co-operation of chiefs and village headmen. Treatment of chiefs with respect and dignity could help in getting their co-operation.

TRADITIONAL LEADERS AND DISTRICT COMMISSIONERS

The District Commissioner's office was established during the colonial period. The powers and the status of colonial district commissioners were firmly established in the system of public administration. During that period, the district commissioners enjoyed enormous prestige and considerable delegated authority as representatives of colonial government. After independence, the role and responsibilities of district commissioners changed drastically. During the colonial period, the district commissioner was primarily concerned with the maintenance of law and order and performance of magisterial functions, whereas after independence rural development became one of his primary responsibilities. The District Commissioner's office plays a central role in district level development planning and coordination of rural development. The District Development Committee (DDC), which is one of the significant organizations at the district level for coordination of rural development activities and district level development plans, is headed by the District Commissioner. The DDC is a forum for communication for all the district level organizations involved in rural development. Chiefs participate in this forum as equal partners along with the district administration, district council, and district level officers of different ministries. District level rural development requires active participation and co-operation of traditional leaders, who can help in articulating the felt needs of local population and get their co-operation in the implementation of development programs.

The District Commissioner has to give leadership to and develop team spirit among all the actors in rural development. Co-operation and mutual understanding between the chiefs and the district commissioner assumes significance in this respect.

The actual contribution of chiefs in these respects leaves much to be desired. The relationship between the district commissioner and the chiefs has not always been cordial. Conflicts have surfaced from time to time. Some chiefs have often complained for not being treated with proper respect and dignity by the district commissioners. In many cases personality factor has influenced the relationship between the district commissioner and traditional leaders. Different individuals with different personalities, approach, style, and attitude have developed different kinds of relationships. If chiefs are treated with dignity and respect by public servants, their relationship could be cordial and the morale of chiefs could be raised for getting their effective participation in the combined teamwork for rural and national development. In the development of team spirit, the district commissioner who has been given responsibility for coordination of district level rural development activities has a special role. He has to be gentle, respectful, considerate, and co-operative with the chiefs. Both have to be responsible, responsive, and sensitive to public aspirations and expectations. Both have to try to develop partnership between the people and the government. Both have to be sensitive to the political environment, cultural values, and social norms. Both the organizations have to try to encourage people's participation in the formulation and implementation of district level development plans, which have so far remained a *top-down* exercise undertaken by bureaucrats. District Commissioners have undergone considerable change since independence and development administration has become their primary function, but in the future the district commissioners will be expected to display increased commitment to the task of rural development and greater sensitivity to the plight of the poor masses. They will need greater support from the traditional leaders in their task.

CONCLUSION

Although the powers, functions, and status of traditional leaders have declined over a period of time, chieftainship remains a significant institution in its public administration and the set-up of its local government administration in Botswana.

Tribal Administration is recognized in Botswana as one of the four pillars of rural local government and administration, the other three being District Councils, Land Boards, and District Administration. The tribesmen in the rural areas have considerable respect for their traditional leaders. The chiefs could use this respect for facilitating the work of central and local government organizations, particularly in educating, guiding, informing, and advising the people in their areas on matters contributing to tribal welfare and development. The chiefs serve their community by maintaining the best customs and traditions, arranging tribal ceremonies, serving as spokesmen of their tribes on issues of customary nature, presiding over *kgotla* meetings, (where matters of interest to the community are discussed), helping in the prevention of offences within their tribal boundaries, and encouraging rural development by co-operating with other governmental and non-governmental organizations. Traditional leaders and forums like *kgotla* could be used more effectively for facilitating the consultation process in formulation and implementation of public policies, district level development plans, and programs and projects for rural development. Chiefs could give leadership in mobilizing public opinion in various development activities and in encouraging people's participation in development programs undertaken by different government organizations. They could be instrumental in initiating social change by striking a healthy balance between tradition and modernity. By remaining informed, they could disseminate information about activities of organizations like District Development Committees. Grassroots organizations like Village Development Committees need their support in self-help activities. In countries like Botswana, the significance of chiefs in imparting justice on customary lines is evident from the fact that they handle approximately 80 per cent of all criminal and civil cases in the country. The customary courts are popular with the people in rural areas, as they are easily accessible, cheap, fast, and comprehensible. The contribution of chiefs in this regard could continue to remain significant. The central government needs to display greater sensitivity to the expectations of traditional leaders. The facilities need to be backed by vigorous training in the form of workshops and seminars for different categories of chiefs from highest to the lowest levels in the field of law (particularly customary law), public administration, public relations, development policies, and development administration. Democratic and representative rural local government in Botswana will be strengthened with the co-operation and partnership of traditional leaders.

ACKNOWLEDGMENT

This work was partially carried out with the aid of a grant from the International Development Research Centre, Ottawa, Canada.

REFERENCE

Vosloo, J. B., D. A. Kotze, and W. J. O. Jeppe. 1974. *Local Government in Southern Africa.* Pretoria: Academia. (Heavy reliance on this for information related to the growth of traditional institution of chieftainship in Botswana during the colonial period is gratefully acknowledged.)

RURAL LOCAL GOVERNMENT AND DEVELOPMENT:
A CASE STUDY OF KWAZULU-NATAL: QUO VADIS?

CHAPTER 10

P. S. REDDY AND B. B. BIYELA

Purshottama Sivanarian (P.S.) Reddy is a local government specialist and professor in the Public Administration Programme in the School of Governance at the University of Durban–Westville in South Africa. He has a BAdmin, BAdmin (Hons.), M Admin, and a D Admin in Public Administration degrees from the University of Durban–Westville. Since 1998, he has been the Project Director of the Working Group on Local Governance and Development of the International Association of Schools and Institutes of Administration (IASIA), headquartered in Brussels. He is an alternate member of the Board of the Commonwealth Local Government Forum (headquartered in London). Professor Reddy is the editor/co-editor of four books focusing on local government management and development in the Southern African Region, namely: *Perspectives on Local Government Management and Development in Africa*; *Readings in Local Government Management and Development: A Southern African Perspective*; *Local Government Democratisation and Decentralisation: A Review of the Southern African Experience and Local Government Financing, Financial Management*; and *Development in Southern Africa and Metropolitan Government and Development: Present and Future Challenges*. Professor Reddy is a founder member of the Centre for Development Management, which is the training arm of the School of Governance of the university.

B. B. BIYELA is a BA (Hons.) graduate and is currently registered for his master's degree in public administration. He has considerable public sector experience having worked in the public service and local government. He is currently the municipal manager for Uthungulu District Council in Kwazulu-Natal. He is also the president of the Institute for Local Government Management of South Africa, which is the professional body for municipal managers in South Africa. He is also a community development and local government consultant.

INTRODUCTION

The establishment and development of rural local government structures in the province of KwaZulu-Natal in South Africa has indeed been a watershed given the historical and political legacy of the province. Seven Regional Councils that were initially established to manage the rural areas in the province, have since been transformed to ten District Councils following the demarcation process and local government elections.

Given the reduction in the number of municipalities nationally, the increase in the number of rural local authorities from seven to ten has emphasized the fact that the government is placing considerable emphasis on service delivery. District Councils are faced with tremendous challenges; namely, funding, capacity development, provision of basic infrastructure, and the increasing politicization of its activities. Critical to its success in the province is the blending of local democracy and traditional leadership. It is imperative that a complementary relationship should develop between elected local leadership and traditional structures in the rural areas. It is an undeniable fact that there is general acceptance and strong support for traditional leadership in the rural areas. Consequently, traditional structures should become an integral part of the local governance process and, furthermore, development issues. In addition, strong linkages should be developed with the local community, traditional structures and elected councillors. This will facilitate rural development while at the same time securing community participation and ensuring legitimacy for the process. It is quite apparent that the government is placing considerable emphasis on municipal service delivery in the rural areas. It is incumbent on the different stakeholders in the rural areas to form partnerships to develop the capacity of the newly established municipalities and also the local economy. The demarcation process created a major conflict between the traditional leaders and the government and had the effect of almost delaying the local government elections which took place on 5 December 2000. However, the government has given the assurance that the relationship between traditional and democratic leadership would be clarified after the elections.

Local government has undergone a process of fundamental political, economic, and social restructuring in South Africa in the past five years. The government has introduced a series of policy/legislative measures to restructure and transform local government, thereby ensuring that it is empowered to carry out its constitutional mandate. It is imperative that the political, financial, social, and institutional framework is conducive to facilitate meaningful governance at the local level, more particularly in rural areas. The lack of adequate human, financial, and technical resources in the rural areas in South Africa, and more particularly KwaZulu-Natal, constitutes a major challenge for effective local governance and rural development. Given the historical and political context, the establishment and development of appropriate rural institutional structures has been problematic for obvious reasons; namely, the blending of democratically elected local government with traditional leadership structures. This chapter reviews the legislative and administrative framework for District Councils (formerly Regional Councils) and highlights present and future challenges that have to be addressed relative to service delivery and local governance. In addition, it will also focus on the issue of traditional leadership in the context of local democracy, development, and of late the demarcation process.

LEGISLATIVE AND ADMINISTRATIVE FRAMEWORK FOR DISTRICT COUNCILS IN KWAZULU-NATAL

ESTABLISHMENT AND COMPOSITION

It should be noted that the district council option developed out of policy proposals put forward by rural non-governmental organizations. It argued for a strong two-tier system of local government in non-metropolitan areas comprising district and local councils/local authorities. The first tier would comprise large district council areas, notably commercial centres commercial farmland as well as former homeland areas (currently under traditional authority areas). This is aimed at maximizing local revenue sources and ensuring that a variety of different settlements have access to such revenue. Furthermore, it also seeks to maximize economies of scale relative to service delivery.

The Demarcation Act, 1998, and the Municipal Structures, 1998, was key to the demarcation of districts. Given the diversity of districts, there was very little guidance relative to the demarcation process. Some of the principles taken cognisance of in the demarcation of districts included, inter alia, functional linkages showing a coherent social and economic base; manageability of size, population, and spatial aspects; character of the area; applying the principles and indicators (Municipal Demarcation Board, 1999).

The following district councils were established in Kwazulu-Natal and became operational after the local government elections (Kwazulu-Natal 2000, 555):

District Council	Councillors per District Council
DC 21: Ugu District Council	34
DC 22: Indlovu District Council	41
DC 23: Uthukela District Council	30
DC 24: Umzinyathi South District Council	23
DC 25: Umzinyathi North District Council	25
DC 26: Zululand District Council	34
DC 27: Umkhanyakudu District Council	27
DC 28: Uthungulu District Council	37
DC 29: Ilembe District Council	30
CBDC5: Cross Border District Council (without Eastern Cape)	13
Total	**294**

The demarcation process has resulted in an increase in the number of rural local government structures from seven to ten; i.e., there were seven regional councils prior to the demarcation process. It would appear that the government is placing considerable emphasis on municipal service delivery in the rural areas given the increased number of district councils in the province. Given the historical legacy particularly in relation to traditional leadership and local political dynamics, the establishment of district councils has indeed been a watershed in the province.

POWERS AND FUNCTIONS

The development of strong and effective local government in the rural areas and the rendering of services is a complex and sensitive issue, which requires the co-operation of the *Amakhosi* (chiefs), headmen, political parties and local communities. The Municipal Structures Act, 1998 (Act 117 of 1998) provides for the division of functions and powers between district and local municipalities. The powers of the district municipality as detailed in section 84(1), includes, inter alia, integrated development planning; bulk supply of water; bulk supply of electricity; bulk sewage purification works and main sewage disposal; solid waste disposal sites; municipal roads; regulation of passenger transport services; municipal airports; municipal health services; fire-fighting services; fresh produce markets; cemeteries and crematoria; local tourism; municipal public works; grants and the imposition and collection of taxes, levies and duties related to the above. Given that district municipalities cover a much larger geographical area and consequently have a larger population, they have a pivotal role to play in the holistic development of the area. In addition they will have to be proactiveproactive in terms of building the capacity of local municipalities and promoting the equitable redistribution of resources. They are seen as being critical to addressing the historical backlogs and facilitating much needed rural development.

CHALLENGES OF SERVICE PROVISION

It is generally accepted that District Councils have a critical role to play in providing basic municipal services and improving the quality of life of the local citizenry in the rural areas in KwaZulu-Natal. In this context, the following factors are seen as being critical to the successful delivery of municipal services in the rural areas; namely (Institute for Federal Democracy 1998, 23 [adapted]):

- Institutional capacity: a key consideration in the provision of basic services is often lacking.

- People-centred development: the local community should be able to identify and prioritize needs and work in collaboration with the council in addressing the needs.

- Co-operative governance and intergovernmental relations: there should be legislation to ensure that minimum standards are laid down for the provision of municipal services. Furthermore, there should also be equitable distribution of resources to the District Councils.

- Accountability and transparency: all public institutions should be accountable to the local communities they serve. Consequently, there should also be clear roles, channels of communication, and responsibilities between the different stakeholders relative to service delivery. The local citizenry should be informed of the councils' sources of revenue and, furthermore, how the money has been spent. The local community should also evaluate the quality of services, thereby ensuring value for money.

- Affordability levels: the delivery system has to take cognisance of what the local community can afford. Expensive delivery methods have to be avoided in the provision of basic services. Consequently, active community participation should be an integral part of local governance, thereby ensuring that this objective is reached.

- Sustainability: projects initiated and developed by the councils should be financially and politically viable.

The rural area of KwaZulu-Natal, which was neglected during the apartheid era, has to be developed as a matter of urgency. A major challenge for the District Councils presently and in the future is the provision of basic municipal services, thereby improving the quality of life of the local citizenry. The success of District Councils presently and in the future will to a large extent be measured by the capacity to provide basic services in the rural areas and in the same time facilitate rural development. In the absence of this, the establishment, development, and general legitimacy of District Councils will be questioned and in the final analysis will become meaningless to the communities living in the rural areas.

TRADITIONAL LEADERSHIP AND STRUCTURES

At present the Province of Kwazulu-Natal has one king, and 277 chieftaincies, comprising 195 officially appointed chiefs (*Amakhosi*), forty-four officially appointed acting chiefs, and thirty-eight vacancies. The four elected chiefs who are heads of their community authorities have all been officially appointed. In addition to the eight deputy chiefs who have been officially appointed by the government, there are also other deputy chiefs who have been officially appointed by the traditional leader concerned. It should be noted that none of the ten thousand headman have been officially appointed or even recognized (Republic of South Africa 2000, 15).

There are approximately 277 traditional authorities, consisting of the chief (as chairperson) and elected councilors. The Regional Authorities, each of which combine a number of Tribal Authorities, currently numbering twenty-three, are constituted of all the traditional authorities in a given magisterial district. At present, the traditional authorities outside the Kwazulu-Natal homeland are not represented on the Regional Authorities. There are four community authorities, each headed by an elected chief (Republic of South Africa 2000, 15).

The province has the largest number of traditional leaders and structures in the country. Consequently, traditional leadership and structures should be an integral part of formal local government given their grassroots support and legitimacy in the rural areas.

RECENT POLICY DEVELOPMENTS –
WHITE PAPER ON INTEGRATED RURAL DEVELOPMENT

A White Paper on Integrated Rural Development was introduced in June 1998. It sets out a vision for rural development; i.e., rural communities should have fair access to development resources and opportunities; different systems of power, namely traditional authorities and elected local government councillors have to work in harmony; governmental policies (national, provincial, and local) should complement each other; rural communities should take decisions on how development should affect them; and poverty alleviation (McIntosh, Xaba, and Associates 1998, 11). The White Paper highlights the essential concepts and approaches for Integrated Rural Development in the Province and is divided into three parts; namely, (v–vii):

PART 1 deals with the context for Integrated Rural Development Policy, demographics, poverty, human development needs, and AIDS; international trends and the national and provincial framework for rural development are highlighted, and key factors in the development processes are identified.

PART 2 sets out the main thrust of an integrated approach to rural development. The benefits of rural development are dependent on effective management and certain key principles; i.e., the building of local capacity and the accommodation of customary systems of power. Key considerations include, *inter alia*, an effective and targeted land reform program; an agricultural support function which has a broad livelihoods orientation; the development of tourism to create jobs and add value to land reform; effective support for small businesses; and improved access to financial services in the context of a rationalized and decentralized delivery system.

PART 3 focuses on implementation; namely, strategies to facilitate economic development and to alleviate poverty, and the re-orientation within national and provincial line departments, which is imperative for local control of the development processes. Programs and projects creating an enabling legal and policy context for rural development are highlighted. Finally, the issue of funding and institutional arrangements for rural development are addressed.

It would appear that the White Paper is a relatively unknown policy document among rural local government functionaries in the province. There has not been much reference to it in rural local government circles. It is generally believed that unless the barrier with the community is broken, development will not get off the ground. Given the above, the implementation of developmental policies in the absence of active community participation and ownership would be meaningless. In this regard, considerable groundwork will have to be done to encourage participation within the context of a formal institutional framework.

MUNICIPAL DEMARCATION PROCESS AND LOCAL GOVERNMENT ELECTIONS

The Demarcation Board has played a pivotal role in the delimitation of municipal boundaries, nationally and provincially. One of the important criteria used by the board was to try to integrate various communities into some form of single tax base in terms of economic linkages and otherwise.

The success of such integration would require the change of the mindset of traditional communities as well as the farming communities. The positive role, which needs to be played by both A and B category municipalities cannot be overemphasized, as it will improve the service delivery to the rural communities.

There was some resistance to the demarcation process from the Inkatha Freedom Party-aligned *Amakhosi*. Many *Amakhosi* in the province were opposed to the new boundaries as they felt that it would interfere with their authority (*Daily News*, 10 January 2000). Some of the criticism levelled at the demarcation process was that the authorities wanted to impose a uniform municipal government system on the entire country in total disregard to its suitability to the rural and traditional areas. Furthermore, the perceived lack of consultation has been cited as a problem. In this regard, a meeting of more than two hundred leaders took place on 15 January 2000 to discuss, *inter alia*, the demarcation process. The meeting was attended by the provincial premier, Mr. Lionel Mtshali and King Goodwill Zwelithini who both expressed concern about the demarcation process, notably the lack of consultation. At that stage it was envisaged that a meeting would be set up with President Thabo Mbeki to discuss the process in the province (*Daily News*, 14 January 2000; *Sunday Tribune*, 16 January 2000).

In his state of the nation address, President Mbeki assured traditional leaders that their powers and functions would not be diminished. Meetings would be held with them to dispel misconceptions on the demarcation process and the constitutionally guaranteed role of traditional leaders in institutions of governance (*Daily News*, 7 February 2000). However, in April the IFP-aligned *Amakhosi* once again called on the Demarcation Board to reconsider its proposals for municipal boundaries for the province. The call was consistent with the proposal by traditional leaders who were firmly of the view that this would render them powerless (*Daily News*, 19 April 2000).

Responding to questions in Parliament, President Mbeki stated that traditional leaders should not fear democratic local government. He also assured traditional leaders that the government would ensure that the demarcation of municipal boundaries did not infringe on their right to play their leadership roles and stressed the need for proper delegations to ease tensions. He indicated that he would be shortly meeting with traditional leaders in KwaZulu-Natal to discuss these concerns (*Daily News*, 11 May 2000).

Two delegations of traditional leaders representing the National House of Traditional Leaders, their provincial counterparts and members of Congress of Traditional Leaders of South Africa (Contralesa), and the other representing traditional leaders from Kwazulu-Natal, respectively. Both groups indicated that they support the demarcation process. In addition, they were also prepared to join the government in the process of defining more clearly the role of traditional leaders and structures. In this regard, they would be making submissions and responding to the White Paper on Traditional Leadership and Institutions released by the Department of Provincial and Local Government (*Independent on Saturday*, 20 May 2000).

Traditional leaders representing the National House of Traditional Leaders and the Kwazulu-Natal leadership represented by *Inkosi* M. Buthelezi made a submission to the state president. The document highlighted, *inter alia*, their status and more importantly the question of land belonging to the tribal authorities. They have maintained their stance on demarcation and believed that the process should not have taken place in tribal-controlled areas. Other aspects that needed to be addressed included, *inter alia,* the remuneration of traditional leaders and the issue of mineral rights (*Daily News*, 29 June 2000).

The conflict between traditional leaders and the Government had almost delayed the local government elections, which took place on 5 December. The announcement of the election date was initially delayed to create conditions that would be conducive to free and fair elections. The Municipal Structures Second Amendment Bill was published on 3 November to address the concerns of traditional leaders. It proposed that municipalities be authorized to delegate some of their functions to traditional leaders subject to the constitution. The bill lists seventeen functions including, *inter alia*, the collection of fees and fines related to the exercise of customary law, convening meetings of community members, providing direction and leadership in cultural activities, coordinating the clearing of fields to ensure good harvests, and officiating at the opening and closing ceremonies of municipal councils. Traditional leaders are also required to carry out all orders given to them by competent authorities and must inform their communities about any new legislation. The voting powers and participation of traditional leaders has remained unchanged; i.e., they do not have voting rights on elected councils, but must be consulted about decisions which affect traditional areas. They may participate in elected municipal council proceedings, provided they do not exceed 20 per cent of the council (*Sunday Tribune*, 5 November 2000). Although the amendment fell short of the demands of traditional leaders; i.e., powers equal to those of elected municipal councillors, it was an interim measure. Traditional leaders believed that the amendments did not address their concerns. In addition, they indicated that the proposed amendments were tabled in Parliament without their being consulted (*Daily News*, 29 November 2000). An improved version of the bill recognized the right of traditional leaders to administer communal land. Furthermore, the provincial ministers of Local Government no longer have any powers to regulate the participation of traditional leaders in communities (*Daily News*, 17 November 2000). However, a range of stakeholders, including the Congress of South African Trade Unions (COSATU), South African Local Government Association (SALGA), and the Commission on Gender Equality raised procedural and substantial concerns on the constitutionality of the bill (*Daily News*, 17 November 2000). Consequently, it was decided to postpone the bill. The president indicated that after the elections, the government would start immediately reviewing fifteen hundred pieces of legislation pertaining to traditional leaders. This should clarify the relationship between traditional and democratic leadership (*Daily News*, 20 November 2000).

It would appear that the government would continue with the process of formulating the White Paper on the role, powers, and functions of the institution of traditional leadership. This will lead to the enactment of national framework legislation in July 2001.

IMPACT OF THE DEMARCATION PROCESS

The demarcation process in Kwazulu-Natal has created ten new district councils. This is an important development given the fact that were seven Regional Councils in the province and the ultimate objective of the demarcation process was rationalization. This development highlights the fact that the government has placed a high priority on local democracy and development in the rural areas.

It is generally accepted that rural areas have been marginalized and under-resourced in the past. The increased number of district councils will ensure that municipal service delivery will take place in all the former neglected tribal authority areas. In this regard, the demarcation process has given rise to the additional rural government structures as well as preserving the unity of Durban. Seventy-five municipalities have been reduced to fifty-two, including the ten district municipalities and the unified City of Durban. The number of urban municipalities have decreased whilst the rural structures have increased and the resultant impact is that service delivery will now take place at a rapid speed since the institutional mechanism to do this has been achieved. It remains for the government and the private sector to form partnerships in order to build the required capacity of the newly established municipalities.

The major challenge that has to be addressed in the transformation process, particularly in rural areas, is defining the role of traditional leaders and the mayor, given that there are now local government structures an all parts of the country. Furthermore, the demarcation process will not solve economic problems per se in the rural areas. It is incumbent on the different stakeholders in rural areas to develop the local economy.

DISCUSSION DOCUMENT: WHITE PAPER ON TRADITIONAL LEADERSHIP AND INSTITUTIONS

Traditional leadership in South Africa has been constitutionalized. However, the role and general functioning of this institution of governance has yet to be clarified. Given the policy vacuum, it was decided to develop a White Paper on Traditional Leadership.

It will consist of three phases; namely, Phase 1 focusing on the national audit; Phase 2 where the emphasis will be on the launch and culminating with the production of a White Paper, and finally, Phase 3 focusing on implementation (Republic of South Africa 2000, 5).

It would appear form the above-mentioned developments that the government has acknowledged the importance of traditional leadership and institutions and are endeavouring to develop a policy framework to facilitate governance in this regard.

The Department of Provincial and Local Government hosted a two-day workshop on the role and functions of traditional leadership on the 17 and 18 August 2000. It would influence the formulation and development of a policy on traditional leadership in a democratic South Africa, which would culminate in the enactment of legislation at the end of the year (*Natal Mercury*, 16 August 2000). More specifically, the issues that needed to be addressed included, *inter alia*, the powers and functions of traditional leaders, the relationship between traditional leadership and other structures of government, the role of the Houses of Traditional Leadership, participation in elected local government structures, the co-operative model contained in the Municipal Structures Act, and issues around the demarcation of municipal boundaries and the objections of traditional leaders in this regard (Department of Provincial and Local Government, 2000). However, the Congress of Traditional Leaders of South Africa and the House of Traditional Leaders withdrew its participation at the workshop for political reasons (*Daily News*, 18 August 2000).

Delivering his state-of-the-province address, Kwazulu-Natal Premier Lionel Mtshali warned that there a serious possibility that the clash between the municipalities and traditional authorities would give rise to profound social instability. He noted in terms of the constitution that municipalities had the power to do what traditional authorities were doing. Municipalities delegating their powers and functions in rural areas to traditional authorities, together with the required human, financial, and logistical resources (*Daily News*, 27 February 2001), could address this overlap. The government was urged in the national Parliament to speed up legislation to formalize the status of traditional leaders in the new local government dispensation (*Business Day*, 21 February 2001).

The government has received invaluable feedback from people who participated in the workshops, which took place in different parts of the country on the Discussion Document. The relevant Portfolio and Select Committees conducted public hearings, which generated a lot of useful insights. The government is proceeding with the development of the White Paper on the role, power, and functions of the institution of traditional leadership. It is believed that this will lead to the enactment of national framework legislation.

GOVERNANCE ISSUES: PRESENT AND FUTURE CHALLENGES

Local governance in the rural areas is a major challenge in the South African context, given the historical backlogs in service delivery and the institution of traditional leadership.

The lack of basic infrastructure (notably roads, water, and electricity) is a major hindrance to service delivery in the rural areas. Housing, clinics, halls, and sports fields cannot be provided and would be unacceptable in the absence of basic infrastructure. Consequently, priority would have to be accorded to providing basic infrastructure in improving the quality of life of rural communities. Education is currently not a local government responsibility. However, the community regards the provision of schools as a priority; at present the District Councils are constructing new classrooms and schools, using funds earmarked for other development projects. There is no financial compensation from the Provincial Department of Education for the costs incurred in this regard.

The sources of funding for some of the District Councils have been a matter of concern. District Councils do not have a revenue base. A major source of revenue is the levies collected from the Local Councils in their respective areas of jurisdiction. In addition, they are supposed to receive an equitable share of their revenue in the form of grants from the national government. There is a view that, since all the District Councils in KwaZulu-Natal are controlled by the Inkatha Freedom Party, the national government is far from generous. Attention, by way of example, is invited to the fact that one council that was supposed to have received R 13 million, only received R 3 million in that year. However, this has to be seen against the general financial constraints being faced by the national government and the ongoing requests for additional funding. The issue of intergovernmental grants is also problematic. If funding could be made available at the beginning of the financial year it would certainly facilitate financial arrangements for the year. Furthermore, there should be one pool to draw from as opposed to dealing with a number of departments.

There is a major problem relative to capacity in the rural areas, and this ultimately impacts on sustainability. The local community lacks the capacity to drive a project when it is brought to it; furthermore, they do not take ownership of it and in some cases are quite apathetic. The project is quite often politicized by creating the impression that it is brought to the area by a particular councillor belonging to a certain political party. Given the political connotations attached to the project, the local community quite often withdraws from the project and, consequently, there is minimal support for it. Community participation is critical to the success of the project and, consequently, the local communities should be brought on board right from the inception. Project committees should be established and they should be democratically elected, thereby ensuring that they are apologetic. Councillors should also be encouraged to be apolitical in discharging their functions as members of the District Council. Training and development programs should be introduced as a matter of priority to develop the skills, knowledge base, and expertise of councillors, thereby ensuring that they work in the interests of the local community.

The political situation currently prevalent in the rural areas in the province is not conducive to development and is in fact a stumbling block to service delivery. There is, at present, a tendency by the local community to associate provincial departments headed by ministers belonging to a political party with that particular party. The perception is that if one belongs to an opposition party, one would be immediately disadvantaged. If ministers visit certain areas to open or review the progress on certain projects, this is also construed in a negative light by the local citizenry. There is also a view that ministers tend to take development to their political strongholds in the province, thereby promoting party interests. If there is a proposal from the local community, it has to be channelled through the *Induna* (headman), thereby ensuring that it has his support. However, the *Induna* and the elected councillor are quite often at loggerheads, as the latter is democratically elected and the former is from the tribal structure. In addition, the councillor receives an allowance as opposed to the *Induna* who does not receive any remuneration for any additional work carried out.

The Tribal Authority Offices in the rural areas that are controlled by the *Amakhosi*, do not have the required basic infrastructure (water, lights, toilets, staff, and computers) for general use by the community. These offices have been built by the Department of Traditional Affairs and Local Government of the province and are not being used to full capacity. They should, for all intents and purposes, be a hive of activity for development in the area; instead they are only used on Saturdays and Sundays for court cases and meetings. An added factor is that the local citizenry have also boycotted these facilities, since they are managed by the local Inkosi (chief). The local community sees themselves as being urbanized and, consequently, does not want to be associated with anything that has tribal connotations. In this regard, serious consideration should be given to the provision of basic infrastructure in these Tribal Offices, thereby encouraging its use as a local Development Office.

The *Amakhosi* are custodians of the major part of the land in rural areas in the province. Consequently, it is imperative that the *Inkosi* should be involved in every development project for the area from inception to completion. There is a view that quite often councillors from particularly the African National Congress tend to disregard the *Inkosi* because they feel that they have been democratically elected while the latter is a traditional leader. On the other hand, the African National Congress, as a political party, believes that it is disadvantaged in the rural areas because permission to hold meetings is generally not granted by the *Amakhosi* to hold meetings. In some cases, there is not much feedback from meetings of the District Council to the *Inkosi* and the resultant effect is that there is a breakdown in communication, which in turn impacts negatively on development in the area.

There is a perception among stakeholders in the rural areas that the municipal demarcation that recently took place in South Africa was questionable. It is believed that the process itself was a subtle attack on the Inkatha Freedom Party strongholds and the *Amakhosi* structures. There is the belief that as one becomes more urbanized, one starts to show more allegiance to the ruling African National Congress. Consequently, the power base of the Inkatha Freedom Party in the rural areas is believed to be eroded. However, it should be noted that no provision has been made for political representation on the demarcation board. The board is apolitical and consists of officials representing the different provinces.

District Councils are obliged in terms of legislation to draw up an Integrated Development Plan. However, despite much time and financial resources being spent on developing such a plan, not much reference was made to it. The demarcation of the boundaries will result in a reduction in the number of municipalities. The question that arises is that if there is amalgamation of municipalities, whose Integrated Development Plans would be implemented and, furthermore, by whom.

TOWARDS VIABLE RURAL LOCAL GOVERNMENT STRUCTURES IN KWAZULU-NATAL

There are certain basic principles guiding the establishment and development of viable local government structures in the rural areas. They include, *inter alia*, funding of local government, landownership and the clear roles that will be played by various stakeholders who constitute rural communities; i.e., traditional communities and owners of farmlands.

FINANCING OF RURAL LOCAL GOVERNMENT

An important basic principle is that local government must be able to generate its own revenue, which will enable it to be self-sustainable. In most cases urban structures which have been established over a number of years are not financially viable. The majority of rural communities who are resident in such areas under the control of the traditional leaders are unemployed, which makes it difficult to expect them to pay for the services rendered to them. The farming communities who appear to be financially well off are not used to the payment of land tax and this has a major impact on the development of rural local government in South Africa.

LAND TAX

In urban areas worldwide the main sources of income of local government is land tax, which is paid in the form of rates. At present, properties in rural areas are not rateable. In traditional authority areas it will take some time for communities to accept the principle of the payment of land tax. When this principle is accepted, local government will have to be innovative in its thinking and find new ways for creating job opportunities to enable rural communities to be able to pay property tax. It will also be very important for the farming community to change their attitude as far as the payment of land tax is concerned.

SALE OF SERVICES

The sale of services such as water, electricity, refuse removal, sewerage disposal, etc., to the local community is a major source of municipal income. At present, due to the fact that the majority of rural communities are unemployed it makes it very difficult to provide such services, even if capital contribution is funded from other sources. The government has funded several water schemes in rural areas and the sustainability of such projects hangs in the balance, as communities are unable to pay for the services.

SALE OF LAND

Land is an important factor for production. The comparison between the urban structures and rural areas will show that viable local government is able to make a substantial income from the sale of land, whilst in areas under the jurisdiction of traditional leaders, land is communally owned. The land in the farming communities is privately owned which makes it difficult for local government to utilize such land for the benefit of the majority of the poor communities.

LOCAL ECONOMIC DEVELOPMENT

It is very important for the government to devote substantial amounts of money for economic development in rural areas. Local economic development will stimulate the economy and provide job opportunities for the majority of the unemployed rural communities. It is also important to note that the maximum utilization of land through agriculture, more especially in areas under the jurisdiction of traditional authorities, may contribute to the provision of job opportunities. Traditional communities are also important custodians of rich culture which, when passed on, could contribute substantially to tourism development in the rural areas, could attract tourists to rural areas, and thus create job opportunities.

LAND TENURE

Land tenure is an important issue for developmental local government in the rural areas; a comparison with urban areas will indicate that urban areas are able to alienate land to individuals or groups by a private deal or public auction. There are several forms of landownership, which has to be highlighted particularly in the KwaZulu-Natal context.

TITLE DEEDS AND SECTIONAL TITLE DEEDS

A landowner who has a title deed to the land has considerable benefits in the sense that financial institutions may lend to him or her the money required to start up a business, and if such a venture fails the financial institution will then hold onto the title deed as security to the investment made on such a venture.

Landownership, in terms of the Title Deed and Sectional Title Deed, is the best instrument for raising capital for development by individuals or groups.

DEED OF GRANT

This form of landownership was previously offered to the residents of the former R293 towns (ie. the former apartheid-era African townships) as a ninety-nine year lease. This form of landownership is now no different from the above as it is also convertible to a title deed ownership and, at present, has the same benefits as the title deed.

PERMISSION TO OCCUPY

Permission to Occupy is a common landownership scheme found in rural areas more especially in KwaZulu-Natal. In terms of this form of landownership, an applicant applies for land to a Tribal Authority and a recommendation is made to the Department of Local Government and Traditional Affairs which then grants the permission to occupy, and most financial institutions do not accept this form of landownership as a security for the money invested in rural areas. Currently it is the parastatal Ithala KwaZulu-Natal Finance Corporation that has invested large sums of money in rural areas on the strength of the PTO. It is important to note that for developmental, local government landownership must be reformed to a stage whereby capital investments for the creation of infrastructure for development are not going to be restricted by landownership. It would appear that both the province and the board were seeking a way forward in order to streamline the PTO application process, thereby allowing councils their development plans access into the Tribal Areas to develop these impoverished zones.

INGONYAMA BOARD

The Ingonyama Board is a body that is going to play a major role in reforming landownership in rural areas in KwaZulu-Natal. The board came into existence due to the fact that the land issues in terms of the 1996 constitution are a national competency responsibility. Furthermore, in KwaZulu-Natal the former KwaZulu government, in terms of the Ingonyama Trust Act, Act No., 3 of 1994, had transferred land belonging to various tribal authorities to the Ingonyama Trust for various reasons. An agreement between the central government and the provincial government of KwaZulu-Natal was reached whereby a board constituted by the representatives from the national, provincial governments, House of Traditional Leaders, and His Majesty the King was formed. This board is playing a major role in terms of land allocation in tribal authority areas.

INSTITUTIONAL ARRANGEMENTS

It is important that a hierarchy of institutional arrangements be formalized in order to expedite service delivery in the rural areas in KwaZulu-Natal. Tribal Authorities could be appointed as service providers, as will be illustrated hereunder.

TRIBAL AUTHORITIES

The institutional arrangements in rural areas in KwaZulu-Natal as it stands at the moment is that there are communities who live in wards or *izigodi*. The wards (*Izigodi*) constitute a Tribal Authority. At this level the District Council could contract the Tribal Authority as a service provider; for example, if it is responsible for the bulk supply of water, then the Tribal Authority could be entrusted with the responsibility to do the distribution.

REGIONAL AUTHORITIES

A number of Tribal Authorities are then grouped together to form the Regional Authority. Currently there are twenty-six Regional Authorities and they play a coordinating role as far as rural development is concerned. The Regional Authority also makes sure that the resolutions taken by various Tribal Authorities are not in conflict with both the national and provincial law.

ROYAL CONTACT

The Regional Authorities come together and form what is known as the Kingdom of KwaZulu with His Majesty the King acting as the head of the kingdom. If there are matters of concern from various Regional Authorities in respect of the institution known as "*Ubukhosi*" (royalty) they are taken up with His Majesty the King.

HOUSE OF TRADITIONAL LEADERS

When the new Government came into being in 1994, it was decided that in each of the nine provinces there could be a House of Traditional Leaders. The Provincial Houses of Traditional Leaders collectively constitute the National House of Traditional Leaders in South Africa. The main function of the House of Traditional Leaders is to look after the interest of traditional communities. It is, however, very important to note that the role of traditional leaders has not been spelled out clearly in the constitution and some of the traditional leaders are of the view that the government is about to do away with their institution. This has recently become evident by the rejection by some traditional leaders of the recommendations of the Municipal Demarcation Board, to transfer some of their tribal land to the municipalities.

It is generally believed that traditional leaders have a critical role to play in strengthening rural local government structures and developing them to carry out local government constitutional mandates. Any attempt to marginalize them or their structures, or even failure to develop them as local governance entities, will certainly hamper development and create social instability in the rural areas. However, it is generally felt that traditional leaders should not be involved directly in several areas of local governance; namely, voting, political debates, and financial issues. In this regard considerable emphasis has been placed on the dignity of the office directly. (Butler, 1999: 75.)

DISTRICT COUNCILS AND ORGANIZED LOCAL GOVERNMENT

District Councils currently participate in organized local government nationally and regionally in both an informal and formal manner.

ASSOCIATION OF REGIONAL COUNCILS IN KWAZULU-NATAL

There were seven Regional Councils in KwaZulu-Natal: ie. Ugu, uThukela, Indlovu, uMzinyathi, Ilembe, Zululand, and uThungulu. The seven Regional Councils formed an informal voluntary organization known as the Association of Regional Councils. The important function of the association was to discuss matters of common interest, which were unique to the Regional Councils only. The association also provided a forum whereby experiences on both political and administrative levels were shared.

KWAZULU-NATAL LOCAL GOVERNMENT ASSOCIATION (KWANALOGA)

Kwanaloga is an organized local government body in the province of KwaZulu-Natal. All local authorities in the province are affiliated to this body. It is the political forum of local government in the province. Each District Council is affiliated to this provincial association. Issues, which have been deliberated on by the association, are then forwarded to Kwanaloga for finalization, or for referral to the provincial government. Kwanaloga is a formal association of local government recognized by the provincial government and the South African Local Government Association known as Salga.

SOUTH AFRICAN LOCAL GOVERNMENT ASSOCIATION (SALGA)

Salga is an association representing all the municipalities in South Africa. There are nine provincial local government associations, which constitutes Salga at a national level. Salga is a political forum for all local authorities in the country. Local government issues are discussed at the informal meeting of the association and then referred to Kwanaloga. If Kwanaloga cannot finalize the matter in consultation with the provincial government, such an issue is referred to Salga who will then take up the matter with the Department of Provincial and Local Government affairs for finalization.

CONCLUSION

From the above exposition, it is evident that there is a considerable amount of groundwork that needs to be done in order to establish viable rural local government in the province. It is also very important for communities who reside in such areas to co-operate with the authorities in order to find solutions to problems which lie ahead. The institution of *Ubukhosi* (or Zulu royal or traditional leaders), as well as the role of the traditional leaders in local government, needs to be managed with a great deal of sensitivity. The establishment and development of rural local government structures in the province is a significant development given the historical and political legacy of the province. It is an undeniable fact that the rural areas were neglected during the apartheid era. Regional Councils have made and now District Councils are making concerted efforts to improve the quality of life of the local communities in the rural areas. However, there are some serious challenges that will have to be addressed in relation to governance, financing, and sustainability.

Given the popular support and acceptance of the *Amakhosi* in the rural areas, the institution of traditional leadership should be strengthened. Traditional structures should become an integral part of local governance and development issues. In this regard the role of the *Amakhosi* has to be clearly defined in terms of the constitution and, more importantly, by the National Government. The financing of District Councils and rural development in KwaZulu-Natal should become a priority. The capacitation of District Councils politically, managerially, and financially should be high on the agenda of the Provincial Government. In the final analysis, the strengthening and capacitation of District Councils would empower the local citizenry, and ultimately improve their quality of life in the rural areas.

The demarcation process has resulted in the creation of ten District Councils in the province. In some instances, the basic infrastructure for the new District Councils is already in place, whereas in other instances completely new structures would have to be set up. The demarcation process also created a major conflict between the traditional leaders and the national government and also had the effect of delaying the local government elections. However, the elections took place as scheduled after the Government gave the assurance that legislative and administrative considerations relative to the issue of traditional leadership would be addressed as a matter of urgency. It is believed that the white paper process will lead to the enactment of national framework legislation.

REFERENCES

Butler, M. 1999. Participative Democracy and Rural Local Government in KwaZulu-Natal. *Indicator*.

The Constitution of the Republic of South Africa, 1996 (Act 108 of 1996).

Department of Provincial and Local Government. 2000. List of Submissions on the Draft Discussion Document towards a White Paper on Traditional Leadership and Institutions, Pretoria, 8 August.

Ilembe Regional Council. 1999. Agenda for Council Meeting, dated 22 August 1999, Durban.

Institute for Federal Democracy. 1998. Towards a Better Understanding of Rural Local Government, KwaZulu-Natal Act of 1994 on the House of Traditional Leaders, Durban: Institute for Federal Democracy.

Interviews with high ranking officials/politicians:
Ilembe Regional Council
Umzinyathi Regional Council
Ugu Regional Council
Zululand Regional Council

Kwazulu-Natal. 2000. *Provincial Gazette* 125 (4 May).

McIntosh, Xaba, and Associates. 1998. An Integrated Rural Development White Paper for KwaZulu-Natal, Durban, January.

Municipal Demarcation Board. 1999. Framework for the Determination of Metropolitan and District Council Boundaries: Draft Boundaries, Pretoria.

National House of Traditional Leaders Act, 1998 (Act 10 of 1998).

Province of KwaZulu-Natal. 1996. Proclamation 100 of 1996 by the Minister of Local Government and Housing dated 19 November 1996.

———. 1998. Rural Development: Putting the Pieces Together: Your Guide to Understanding the White Paper on Integrated Rural Development in KwaZulu-Natal, Publication of Inter-Departmental Task Team on Integrated Rural Development and Cabinet of KwaZulu-Natal, Pietermaritzburg, June.

Republic of South Africa. 2000. A Draft Discussion Document: Towards a White Paper on Traditional Leadership and Institutions, Department of Provincial and Local Government, Pretoria.

WHAT ROLE FOR TRADITIONAL LEADERSHIP IN THE "PLURALISTIC STATE" IN AFRICA?[1]

CHAPTER 11

CARL WRIGHT

CARL WRIGHT is the first Director of the Commonwealth Local Government Forum, CLGF, established in 1995 with the endorsement of Commonwealth heads of government. He has served on several UN and international commissions and expert groups, and as Commonwealth election observer in Ghana, Nigeria, and Pakistan. He was previously assistant director at the Commonwealth Secretariat (1988–95), where he had responsibility for special programs on Mozambique, Namibia, and South Africa and was secretary to the Commonwealth Expert Group on Human Resource Development for Post Apartheid South Africa. He was founding director of the Commonwealth Trade Union Council (1980–87), secretary of the Economic Committee of the International Confederation of Free Trade Union (1974–80) and member of the Private Office of the Right Honourable George Thomson at the European Commission (1973–74). He was educated at the University College London (BSc Hon) and Reading University (MA Weidenfeld scholar).

Forested hills and grassy valley of the Akyem Abuakwa kingdom near Kyebi, Eastern Region, Ghana. The image of the forest is central to the kingdom and is part of the motivation for the environmental campaigns of the king, Osagefuo *Offori Atta (2002) (*traditional leader title) (photo by D. Ray).

INTRODUCTION

In September 1997, the Commonwealth Local Government Forum convened a symposium in Gaborone, Botswana to discuss traditional leadership and local government.[2] The symposium was in many ways the first of its kind, bringing together some fifty traditional leaders, mayors, and senior local and central government officials from twelve African countries. Equally striking were some of the conclusions, which emphasized the concept of partnership in local government by all stakeholders and foresaw an active role for traditional leadership in development and service delivery, social change and transformation, and governance, as well as with regard to its more well-known functions in areas of land and customary judicial functions.

Held against the background of growing interest throughout Africa in the role traditional leaders could play in the modern, pluralistic state, the symposium addressed questions of how the two could fit together productively. Discussions benefited from an earlier Commonwealth Local Government Forum (CLGF) research report on the subject, as well as a number of key background papers. Emphasis throughout the discussions was on practical policies and identification of best practices, with a view to seeing what tangible lessons could be learnt by all the stakeholders present; chiefs, councillors, and government officials. The symposium conclusions accordingly provide a valuable set of practical recommendations for follow-up action at local government level.

This chapter outlines what leaders – traditional and from democratic local government – agreed *should* be done. We do not seek to describe what currently obtains on the ground.

SCOPE OF THE ISSUE

Discussion at the symposium focused on the role of traditional leaders in Africa and the identification of appropriate good practice policy. Participants were able to visit the Botswana House of Chiefs, where they were hosted by Kgosi Seepapitso IV, who discussed the role and operations of the house, and to visit the *kgotla* (traditional meeting place) at Ramotswa where the Bamalete paramount chief explained certain aspects of traditional local governance. The participants were thus able to benefit from these aspects of the Botswana experience.

The giant umbrella is the symbol of the paramount chief's legitimacy in Ghana and some other parts of Africa. The size of the umbrella reflects the importance of the chief or king. In this case, the paramount chief is Odenho* Oduru Numapau who was also the President of Ghana's National House of Chiefs (Photo by Werner Zips, 1994) (*traditional leader title).

It was observed that generally the people still recognize traditional leaders as their head and it would be in the interest of the people and the country to incorporate the traditional leaders into all forms of government. The point was made that while the peoples of the world were recognizing the status of traditional leaders, some African politicians were critical of the system of traditional leadership. Governments were requested to encourage those traditional leaders who were developmentally oriented to play a part in the development of society.

Divergent views were expressed on the status of traditional leaders in local or national councils. While there are Houses of Chiefs in some countries, it was suggested that there is the need for comparative studies of their roles and functions so that a best practice policy could be developed. It was further suggested that there is the need to constantly compare systems in Africa with those of the United Kingdom, Canada, and other developed countries.

On the whole, the discussions revealed a general consensus of the role of traditional leaders. It was stressed that traditional leaders and local and central governments need to develop respect and appreciation for each other, and look into the ways and means for promoting co-operation in the contemporary system of government.

However, traditional leadership has been an important topic not only in Commonwealth Africa, but in other member countries ranging from Canada to Australia. Thus, this symposium with its examination of local government and traditional leadership has significance in many parts of the world. Furthermore, the overall work of the CLGF was enhanced by the call of then President Rawlings of Ghana for the October 1997 Commonwealth Heads of Government meeting in Edinburgh to add the topic of democratic, decentralized local government good practice to their list of topics.

SYMPOSIUM CONCLUSIONS AND RECOMMENDATIONS

The symposium considered that the role of traditional leadership should be recognized and, where appropriate, incorporated into the constitutional framework of each state. Furthermore, it confirmed that traditional leaders and local government should be active partners in development initiatives.

This sign is part of a local environmental campaign by the traditional leader of the Okyeman, i.e., the Akyem Abuakwa kingdom (photo by D. Ray).

In essence the traditional leaders and local government representatives expressed the importance of each enabling the initiatives of one another.

DEVELOPMENT AND SERVICE DELIVERY

The participants agreed that development should be pursued through a bottom-up approach involving all stakeholders at each stage of decision-making, planning, and implementation. Each stage should also take place in appropriate open and accountable forums. In this regard, participants wished to draw attention to the need to harness knowledge indigenous to the communities to be served, so as to preserve and develop that knowledge and to apply it actively in ensuring ecological conservation and environmental equilibrium.

Making use of their different networks, the leaders decided that raising public awareness of these matters, and the promotion of civic and community education in ways accessible to all members of the community, was the responsibility of all local and community leaders.

The success of development initiatives was seen as resting on two critical factors: a keen sense of community ownership, and an adequate resource base. In light of this, the symposium recommended the promotion of fiscal decentralization, with accountability and transparency within the framework of national fiscal policies.

Participants agreed that co-operation between traditional leaders and local development agencies would enhance the potential for the effective delivery of development services to local communities. It was further agreed that to achieve the above, in those areas where people accept traditional leadership, the political legitimacy of traditional leaders should be added to those of local government.[3]

PARTNERSHIP FOR SOCIAL CHANGE AND TRANSFORMATION

The symposium recognized the need that traditional leadership structures require capacity-building support – both in terms of training and infrastructural assistance – in order to be able to work constructively with local governments towards facilitating change and social transformation at the local level. The value of traditional leadership is contained in its contribution as a unifying force and as a base for strengthening national identity and culture which, allowing for the rich diversity of our communities, should be harnessed for the education and welfare of present and future generations. It was agreed that the collaboration between traditional leaders and local governments should enhance social and cultural stability, actively promote the welfare of women and children within the community, and works towards the elimination of all practices which are abhorrent and detrimental to the health and welfare of any member of the community.

PARTICIPATION IN GOVERNANCE

The value of traditional leaders in participating in local governance was held to be the legitimacy and continuity it can offer in its ability to mobilize the population behind development initiatives where it is effective. The symposium concurred that in order to promote just and honest government, principles of transparency and accountability must be pursued by traditional leaders and local government administrations alike. It was agreed that serving traditional leaders should be discouraged from involvement in partisan politics at any level, and recommended that there should be a time-bar between abdication and participation in partisan politics.

It was suggested that the representation of traditional leaders in local government structures should be achieved either by statutory provision or in an open and transparent way, through the appropriate and relevant houses or groupings of traditional leaders in the community involved. Alternatively, their representation might be best served through an advisory and consultative capacity on an ex officio basis.

It was agreed that at all levels of a state's administration – local, provincial/regional, and national – there should be an open-door relationship between government structures and institutions of traditional leadership, as well as regular exchanges between associations of local government and traditional leaders' organizations.

LAND AND JUDICIAL FUNCTIONS

The symposium recognized the diversity of land tenure structures in Commonwealth Africa, and agreed that there was a critical need to establish transparent and accountable systems of land management that allow for the sustainable use of land as a local and national resource, and which safeguard the rights of the communities which live and invest in any given area.

In many instances, the exercise of customary judicial functions by traditional leaders offered easy access to arbitration in a timely manner (as do other formal and informal systems of arbitration within our communities), but recognized that the extent of their jurisdiction, with rights of appeal to the regular court system at the appropriate level, should be clearly defined, and that these judicial functions must take place within the framework of national and international provisions for the protection of civil, human, and people's rights.

FOLLOW-UP ACTION

The symposium agreed that each participant should carry the conclusions/recommendations of this symposium back to their member states, disseminate them within the appropriate institutions, monitor progress towards their implementation, and continue the exchange and dialogue begun at this symposium.

The Board of the CLGF was requested to consider the agreed conclusions of the symposium and bring them to the attention of the Edinburgh Commonwealth Heads of Government Meeting, and that the Commonwealth Secretariat and CLGF take note of the symposium's conclusions in the development of capacity-building programs for the promotion of good local governance in Commonwealth Africa.

The symposium supported the creation of a traditional leaders applied research network – the TAARN proposed by Prof. Donald Ray – as a resource to facilitate the exchange of experience and build sub-regional, African, and other Commonwealth links of association between traditional leaders and other local government practitioners, and furthermore, that this should relate closely to the planned CLGF Local Government Information Centre in Harare. In this regard, it considered that there should be further examination of the mechanisms and institutions by which traditional leaders and states' government can interact.

COMMONWEALTH EXPERIENCE IN DECENTRALIZED GOVERNANCE

The paper by Dr. Victor Ayeni (MTSD, Commonwealth Secretariat) focused on the decentralized governance experiences of Commonwealth African countries. There are lessons that can be drawn for present and future decentralization as a process of redistribution of power from the centre to the periphery. Four types of decentralization can be identified; namely, political, economic, administrative, and fiscal.

The focus in this presentation was on political decentralization. When African countries became independent they introduced very centralized systems of government, in some cases in concert with military rule. By the 1980s, there was a shift in the role of the state as the type of governance was reviewed. In addition, there were several push factors that contributed towards a shift between decentralization and good governance which were beyond the Commonwealth African network; namely, international trends and developments and globalization. However, the Harare Declaration, the work of the Commonwealth Secretariat, and the establishment of CLGF assisted most Commonwealth African countries in this regard.

After discussing the main features of this trend, which included the reduction of the state sector, decentralization of government, increased citizen participation, the demise of apartheid, and the beginning of a reappraisal of traditional leaders, a variety of strategies for implementing political decentralization, including traditional leaders, were considered.

CONCLUSION

Traditional leaders and traditional institutions vary in nature within countries and from country to country. Developing and responding to the social, economic, and legal/constitutional environment in which they exist, each seeks to have impact on their community and, where possible, in national politics.

The point at which democratic local government and traditional leadership meet is best tailored by the development needs of local community. It is unlikely that democratic local leaders and traditional leaders could each rally strong popular support for opposing propositions, and *both* claim they have a legitimate majority.

The conflict is much more likely to arise where a development plan serving an area larger than the immediate locality is being imposed from above, and local leaders are seeking to implement it without sufficient consultation.

Local communities and local governments need to work closely with one another in order to forge a strong working relationship. Traditional leaders, in many communities throughout Commonwealth Africa, voice the concerns of a significant proportion of the citizenry. As such, consultation with them, and where appropriate the formal incorporation of traditional leadership into the structures of government, is worthy of greater consideration and discussion.

NOTES

1. Special thanks are due to the Botswana Association of Local Authorities, Gaborone City Council and Mayor Bagwasi, the Ministry of Local Government, Lands and Housing, and to the House of Chiefs, especially Kgosi Seepapitso IV, for hosting the symposium upon which this article draws heavily. Also the CLGF would like to thank the sponsors – the Commonwealth Secretariat, the Municipal Development Programme and the Federation of Canadian Municipalities – for enabling it to take place. Warm appreciation is also recorded for the able work of the key resource persons, Professor Don Ray, who edited the report in collaboration with Professor K. Sharma, and Mr. I. May-Parker.

2. Report edited by Donald. I. Ray, in collaboration with K. Sharma and I. I. May-Parker, *Symposium on Traditional Leadership and Local Government*, London: CLGF, 1997.

3. See the 1995 Harare Commonwealth Roundtable on Democratisation and Decentralisation for Senior Policy Makers in Local Government, co-organized by the CLGF, IULA–AS and the FCM, as well as the 1997 Ray paper contained in the *Symposium on Traditional Leadership and Local Government* report.

INDEX